McGRAW - HILL
SPELLING

AUTHORS

Dr. Gillian E. Cook

Dr. Marisa Farnum

Terry R. Gabrielson

Dr. Charles Temple

CONSULTANT

Dr. Judy Wallis

McGraw-Hill
School Division
New York   Farmington

McGraw-Hill School Division

A Division of The **McGraw·Hill** *Companies*

Alphabet font used with permission of Zaner-Bloser.

McGraw-Hill School Division
1221 Avenue of the Americas
New York, New York 10020

Printed in the United States of America
ISBN 0-02-2442294 / 4
  4 5 6 7 8 9 VHJ 02 01 00 99 98

To the Student,

Spelling is part of everything you do in school. It helps you in your writing, in your reading, and in your other subjects. Spelling is also important outside of school. Knowing how to spell helps you share information with friends, family, and other people you need to communicate with.

This book will help you learn to spell the words in each lesson. It will also give you important tools, hints, and tips that you can use with any words at any time.

☞ The **Spelling Bee** points out spelling words that have unusual spellings of a sound. Pay special attention to these words so that you will remember how to spell them.

In the back of the book, you will find resources to help you as a speller and a writer. Take a look at the contents on page 158 to see what's there.

You can help yourself by creating your own **Spelling Journal**. All you need is a lined notebook. Start by making different sections. Here are some ideas.

■ **A Personal Dictionary** Label each right hand page with a letter of the alphabet. If you fill the page, use the back of the page. Add words throughout the year that are important for you to remember how to spell and to use in your writing.

■ **Difficult Words** Keep track of words that give you trouble. Write the word and circle the part that is hard for you. Refer to this section as you write.

■ **Related Words** List words that are related in meaning and spelling. For example, the long vowel sound you hear in *please* can help you to remember how to spell *pleasure*. Add to this section whenever you come across words that will help you to spell other words.

■ **Memory Helpers** Collect sayings that you make up that help you remember certain words. A saying such as *You are a youth* can help you remember that the word *youth* contains *y-o-u*.

Remember, this is your journal! You may want to add a section all your own.

Contents

Word Study Steps

1. **Look** at the word and **say** it carefully.

2. **Picture** the word in your mind.

3. **Study** each letter in the word.

4. **Write** the word carefully.

5. **Check** the word carefully.

Did you spell the word correctly? If you made a mistake, repeat each step.

WORDS WITH Short Vowels

PHONICS PATTERNS

1. past
2. dust
3. dock
4. fist
5. gram
6. gum
7. swept
8. act
9. self
10. trust
11. sink
12. flock
13. rest
14. yet
15. rid
16. hung
17. mad
18. lift
19. love
20. done

Learn Spelling Patterns

LOOK & SAY Listen for the short vowel sound in each word.

PICTURE Close your eyes. See each word in your mind.

STUDY The letters *a, e, i, o, u* are vowels. The symbols for short vowel sounds are /a/, /e/, /i/, /o/, and /u/.

WRITE Sort the words. Which words have short vowel sounds spelled with one letter?

/a/ (1) (2) (3) (4)
/e/ (5) (6) (7) (8)
/i/ (9) (10) (11) (12)
/o/ (13) (14)
/u/ (15) (16) (17) (18)

Which words have /u/ spelled *o-e*?
(19) (20)

CHECK Did you spell each word correctly? Circle the letter or letters that stand for each short vowel sound.

Pattern Power

What letter usually spells /a/?
(21) /e/? (22) /i/? (23) /o/? (24)
/u/? (25)

Other Words

Write words you would like to add to this week's list.

_____ _____ _____ _____ _____

Practice Word Meanings

Words in Context

Write the spelling word that best completes each sentence.

1. When I am angry, I say I am _____*mad*_____.
2. Yesterday is in the ____. Tomorrow is in the future.
3. A good sleep will give you the ____ you need.
4. The sailor tied the boat to the ____.
5. The geese flew in a ____.
6. He washed his hands at the ____.
7. She took a broom and ____ the room.

Challenge Words • *Physical Education*

Write the challenge word that fits each definition.
Use the **Spelling Dictionary** on page 214 to
help you. Circle the spelling of the short vowel sound.

8. An act that shows skill or strength. ____
9. Bending or moving easily. ____
10. A steady, secure position. ____
11. Strength or eagerness to do things. ____
12. Game played by two teams of eleven players each. ____

stunt
balance
energy
soccer
limber

Spelling Tip

Use words you know how to spell to help you spell new
words. For example, if you want to spell *trust*:

✦ Listen to the sounds you hear at the beginning of the word
trust. What other word do you know how to spell that begins
with the same sounds?

✦ Listen to the sounds you hear at the end of the word *trust*.
What other word do you know how to spell that ends with
the same sounds?

✦ Put the letters that stand for the sounds together.

/tr/ **tr**ee

(trust) ⟨ ⟩ **trust**

m**ust** /ust/

List Words

past
dust
dock
fist
gram
gum
swept
act
self
trust
sink
flock
rest
yet
rid
hung
mad
lift
love
done

Challenge Words

stunt
balance
energy
soccer
limber

Review Words

sat
peg
give
tug

Build Vocabulary

Base Words

■ The main part of a word is called the **base word**. You can make new words by adding *-ed* and *-ing* to many words without changing the spelling of the base word.

dock + **ed** = docked   dock + **ing** = docking

To add *-ed* and *-ing* to words that have a single vowel followed by a final consonant, you usually double the consonant before adding the ending.

stop + **ed** = stopped   stop + **ing** = stopping

Add *-ed* and *-ing* to the base words below.

	-ed	-ing
1. dust	_____	_____
2. act	_____	_____
3. trust	_____	_____
4. lift	_____	_____
5. gum	_____	_____

■ Use words you made to complete these sentences.

6. My father _____ the furniture, and I mopped the floor.

7. My faithful friend can be _____ with our secret.

Review Words

Write the review words that have the short vowel sounds below. Circle the letters that spell the sound in each word.

/u/ 8. _____   /e/ 10. _____

/a/ 9. _____   /i/ 11. _____

sat
peg
give
tug

T A K E H O M E

Write your spelling words in three lists: words with one final consonant, more than one final consonant, and the *vowel-e* pattern. Use your lists to practice spelling the words at home.

4

Apply Spelling Skills

Dictionary Skills

In a dictionary, words are listed in alphabetical order from **A** to **Z**. Write the list words below in alphabetical order.

hung 1. ____   self 4. ____
gram 2. ____   rid 5. ____
yet 3. ____   fist 6. ____

Proofreading

Proofread the paragraph. Check spelling, capital letters, and punctuation. Then rewrite the paragraph. There are six mistakes.

> I luv to sail my yellow boat, the Sunny Max Sometimes a loud flok of birds follows my red sail. In the middle of the lake, I sail pass some small islands. When I'm done, I dok my boat

Writing • About Physical Education

PREWRITE: What is your favorite sport? Write a list of exciting adjectives that describe your favorite sport.

DRAFT: Make a poster about the sport. Use adjectives from your list.

REVISE: Check to see that you used exciting adjectives.

EDIT/PROOFREAD: Use editing marks to correct and improve your poster. Then make a clean copy of the poster.

PUBLISH: Display your posters in a classroom "sports corner."

EDITING MARKS

⬭ check spelling
≡ capital letter
/ lowercase letter
⊙ add a period
∧ add
✄ take out
¶ indent the paragraph
↪ move

For more help, see page 171.

5

WORDS WITH Short Vowels

PHONICS PATTERNS

1. pumpkin
2. attic
3. except
4. package
5. nothing
6. lettuce
7. mustard
8. bandage
9. collect
10. until
11. plastic
12. damage
13. problem
14. depend
15. accept
16. public
17. mitten
18. cabbage
19. action
20. practice

Learn Spelling Patterns

LOOK & SAY   Listen for the sounds in each word.

PICTURE   Close your eyes. See each word in your mind.

STUDY   These words have two word parts, or **syllables**. In words of two or more syllables, one syllable is usually **stressed**, or **accented**.

WRITE   Sort the words. Which words have these short vowel sounds in the accented syllable?

/a/   (1)   (2)   (3)   (4)
      (5)   (6)   (7)   (8)
/i/   (9)   (10)
/e/   (11)   (12)   (13)   (14)   (15)
/o/   (16)
/u/   (17)   (18)   (19)   (20)

CHECK   Did you spell each word correctly? Circle the letter that stands for the short vowel sound in the accented syllable.

Pattern Power

What vowel letter can spell /a/?
(21)   /i/? (22)   /e/? (23)   /o/? (24)
/u/? (25)   or   (26)

Other Words

Write words you would like to add to this week's list.

_____ _____ _____ _____ _____

Practice Word Meanings

Defining Words

Write the spelling words that match the definitions below.

To cause harm to.	1. *damage*
To bring together.	2. ____
A large, round, orange vegetable.	3. ____
A warm covering for the hand.	4. ____
Not anything.	5. ____

Accept means "to take what is given." *Except* means "other than" or "but." Write *accept* or *except* to complete each sentence below.

6. I like all vegetables ____ cabbage.

7. Yes, I ____ your offer to help me plant lettuce.

Challenge Words • *Social Studies*

Write the challenge word that best answers each question. Use the **Spelling Dictionary** on page 214 to help you. Circle the spelling of the short vowel sound in the accented syllable.

8. How long is one hundred years? ____

9. What is the story of the past? ____

10. What is another word for freedom? ____

11. What is one word for the arts, beliefs, and customs of a group of people? ____

12. What is a large land area on the earth? ____

continent
culture
century
history
liberty

Spelling Tip

Sometimes long words are easier to spell when you sound out the word one syllable at a time. Remember, each syllable must have a vowel sound. For example, to spell *pumpkin*:

✦ Listen for the first syllable. What vowel sound do you hear in the syllable?

✦ Listen for the next syllable. What vowel sound do you hear?

✦ Now write the word a syllable at a time. **pump + kin = pumpkin**

List Words

pumpkin
attic
except
package
nothing
lettuce
mustard
bandage
collect
until
plastic
damage
problem
depend
accept
public
mitten
cabbage
action
practice

Challenge Words

continent
culture
century
history
liberty

Review Words

body
ever
sandwich
window

Build Vocabulary

Base Words

■ Often you must drop the final *e* before adding an ending that begins with a vowel. Add *-ed* and *-ing* to the list words below.

	-ed	-ing
1. collect	_____	_____
2. depend	_____	_____
3. accept	_____	_____
4. package	_____	_____
5. damage	_____	_____
6. practice	_____	_____
7. bandage	_____	_____

■ Use words you made to complete these sentences.

8. I prefer to buy food that is not _____ in plastic.

9. My cabbage patch was _____ by bugs.

Review Words

Write the review words that have the short vowel sounds below in the accented syllable.

/a/ 10. _____

/e/ 11. _____

/i/ 12. _____

/o/ 13. _____

body
ever
sandwich
window

Look at each list word below. Write the review word that has the same short vowel sound in the accented syllable.

14. problem _____

15. lettuce _____

16. mitten _____

17. attic _____

TAKE HOME

Write your spelling words in two lists: those with an accent on the first syllable and those with an accent on the second syllable. Use your lists to practice at home.

Apply Spelling Skills

Dictionary Skills

If words begin with the same letter, look at the second letter to put words in alphabetical order. Write each column of spelling words below in alphabetical order.

collect   **1.** ____

until   **2.** ____

plastic   **3.** ____

cabbage   **4.** ____

public   **5.** ____

problem   **6.** ____

damage   **7.** ____

lettuce   **8.** ____

mustard   **9.** ____

action   **10.** ____

depend   **11.** ____

attic   **12.** ____

Proofreading

Check for spelling, capital letters, and punctuation. Then rewrite the paragraph. There are six mistakes.

> let us grow lettis! planting times
> dapend on where you live. in the South,
> plant in fall or winter. In the North, plant
> in spring and wait untill summer to gather
> the crop.

Writing • *About Social Studies*

PREWRITE: Imagine you are a farmer. List some of the things you do during a whole day in one of your favorite seasons.

DRAFT: Write a paragraph describing a day on your farm.

REVISE: Read your paragraph aloud to a classmate and listen to any comments. Use the **Spelling Thesaurus** on page 182 as you revise.

EDIT/PROOFREAD: Use editing marks. Write a clean copy.

PUBLISH: Illustrate your paragraph with magazine cutouts and share it with your class.

EDITING MARKS

◯ check spelling

= capital letter

/ lowercase letter

⊙ add a period

∧ add

✀ take out

¶ indent the paragraph

◯↝ move

For more help, see page 171.

3

WORDS WITH Short Vowels

PHONICS PATTERNS

1. breakfast
2. pleasant
3. instead
4. guess
5. enough
6. sweat
7. against
8. trouble
9. dead
10. deaf
11. cousin
12. ready
13. jealous
14. couple
15. ahead
16. heavy
17. lead
18. built
19. wealth
20. meant

Learn Spelling Patterns

LOOK & SAY Listen for the sounds and accented syllables in each word.

PICTURE Close your eyes. See each word in your mind.

STUDY These spelling words have /e/, /i/, or /u/ in the accented syllable. These sounds are spelled by two vowels.

WRITE Sort the words. Which words have these short vowel sounds?

/e/ (1) (2) (3) (4) (5) (6) (7) (8) (9) (10) (11) (12) (13) (14) (15)

/u/ (16) (17) (18) (19)

/i/ (20)

CHECK Did you spell each word correctly? Circle the two letters that stand for the short vowel sound.

Pattern Power

When /e/ is spelled with two vowel letters, what are usually the two letters? (21)

Other Words

Write words you would like to add to this week's list.

_____ _____ _____ _____ _____

Practice Word Meanings

Antonyms

An **antonym** is a word that is opposite or nearly opposite in meaning from another word. Write the spelling word that is the antonym of each word below.

1. destroyed *built*
2. light ____
3. for ____
4. alive ____
5. behind ____
6. unprepared ____
7. trusting ____
8. nasty ____
9. single ____

Challenge Words • *Social Studies*

Write the challenge word that best completes each sentence. Use the **Spelling Dictionary** on page 214 to help you. Circle the spelling of the short vowel sound in each word.

10. The U.S. government gave the pioneer a ____.
11. The ____ surrounds our cities and towns.
12. The Liberty Bell is a national ____.
13. A ____ may work on or own a small farm.
14. Brazil is located in the ____ hemisphere.

southern
countryside
homestead
treasure
peasant

Spelling Tip

Words that are related in meaning are often related in spelling. For example:

✦ The words *please* and *pleasant* are related in meaning.
✦ The word *please* has the long vowel sound spelled *ea*.
✦ The word *pleasant* has the short vowel sound spelled *ea*.

Remembering how to spell *please* can help you spell *pleasant*. Can you think of a word that will help you spell *meant*? How about *mean*?

List Words

breakfast
pleasant
instead
guess
enough
sweat
against
trouble
dead
deaf
cousin
ready
jealous
couple
ahead
heavy
lead
built
wealth
meant

Challenge Words

southern
countryside
homestead
treasure
peasant

Review Words

bread
again
friends
does

Build Vocabulary

Compound Words

■ A **compound word** is formed by putting two or more words together.

fire + place = fireplace

Combine a word in Column A with one in Column B to make a compound word.

A	B	
heavy	work	1. *heavyweight*
sweat	line	2. ____
dead	fast	3. ____
break	shirt	4. ____
guess	weight	5. ____

Review Words

Write the review words that have /e/ spelled with the letters below.

ea 6. ____

ai 7. ____

ie 8. ____

Write the review word that has /u/ spelled with the letters below.

oe 9. ____

Look at each list word below. Write the review word that has the same short vowel sound spelled the same way.

10. dead ____

11. against ____

bread
again
friends
does

T A K E   H O M E

Write your spelling words in two lists: words with one syllable and words with two syllables. Circle the spelling of the short vowel sound in each word's accented syllable. Use your lists to practice at home.

12

Apply Spelling Skills

Dictionary Skills

Write the list words below in alphabetical order.

meant	**1.** ___
lead	**2.** ___
instead	**3.** ___
trouble	**4.** ___
deaf	**5.** ___
wealth	**6.** ___
enough	**7.** ___
cousin	**8.** ___

Pattern Power

Look at the list words you just wrote.

- Circle the letters that spell the short vowel sound in the accented syllable of each word.

Proofreading

Check for spelling, capital letters, and punctuation. Then rewrite the paragraph. There are six mistakes.

> If I had been a pioneer I would have built a cabin out of hevy logs I would have cooked eggs for brekfast. when they were redy, I would have eaten them with my Native American neighbors.

Writing • *About Social Studies*

PREWRITE: Make a list of ideas about pioneers and the West.

DRAFT: Write a postcard from a pioneer child to a friend in the East.

REVISE: Does your postcard include ideas from your list?

EDIT/PROOFREAD: Use editing marks to correct your postcard.

PUBLISH: Display your "postcards from the past" on the bulletin board.

EDITING MARKS

◯ check spelling

≡ capital letter

/ lowercase letter

⊙ add a period

∧ add

✗ take out

¶ indent the paragraph

◯⟶ move

For more help, see page 171.

WORDS WITH /ā/ and /ē/

PHONICS PATTERNS

1. station
2. bean
3. behave
4. tray
5. lazy
6. agree
7. secret
8. believe
9. crayon
10. fail
11. cave
12. freight
13. became
14. tea
15. cape
16. rail
17. lean
18. laid
19. chief
20. cane

Learn Spelling Patterns

LOOK & SAY Listen for the sounds in each word.

PICTURE Close your eyes. See each word in your mind.

STUDY These spelling words contain /ā/ or /ē/. In the words with two syllables, /ā/ or /ē/ is in the accented syllable.

WRITE Sort the words. Which words have /ā/ spelled with the letters below?

a-e (1) (2) (3) (4) (5)
a (6) (7)
ai (8) (9) (10)
ay (11) (12)
eigh (13)

Which words have /ē/ spelled with the letters below?

ea (14) (15) (16)
ee (17)
e (18)
ie (19) (20)

CHECK Did you spell each word correctly? Circle the letters that stand for the long vowel sounds.

Pattern Power

How can /ā/ be spelled with two letters? (21) or (22) or (23) How can /ē/ be spelled with two letters? (24) or (25) or (26)

Other Words

Write words you would like to add to this week's list.

_____ _____ _____ _____ _____

Practice Word Meanings

Related Meanings

Write the spelling word that belongs with each pair of words below.

1. cabbage, carrot   *bean*
2. hidden, private   ___
3. jacket, coat   ___
4. president, captain   ___
5. train, railroad   ___
6. water, milk   ___
7. pencil, marker   ___
8. hollow, hole   ___

Challenge Words • *The Arts*

Write the challenge word that best completes each sentence. Use the **Spelling Dictionary** on page 214 to help you. Circle the spelling of /ā/or /ē/ in each word.

9. The two singers sang in ___.
10. The words *rhythm* and ___ have almost the same meaning.
11. Matt practices his ___ scales every day.
12. Popular songs often contain a repeated ___.
13. If you hum the ___, I will tell you the song.

major
melody
harmony
meter
phrase

Spelling Tip

Here's a spelling rule that you can always count on when choosing between *ei* and *ie* in spelling a word.

✦ Use *i* before *e* except after *c* or when sounded like /ā/ as in *neighbor* or *weigh*.

Which of your spelling words follow this rule?

List Words

station
bean
behave
tray
lazy
agree
secret
believe
crayon
fail
cave
freight
became
tea
cape
rail
lean
laid
chief
cane

Challenge Words

major
melody
harmony
meter
phrase

Review Words

wait
leave
awake
seem

Build Vocabulary

Rhyming Words

■ **Rhyming words** have the same middle and ending sounds. *Say* and *hay* are rhyming words. Follow the directions to write words that rhyme with the spelling words below.

1. cape	–	c	+	t	=	*tape*
2. fail	–	f	+	s	=	____
3. lean	–	l	+	m	=	____
4. behave	–	beh	+	s	=	____
5. station	–	st	+	n	=	____
6. laid	–	l	+	p	=	____
7. freight	–	fr	+	w	=	____
8. believe	–	b	+	r	=	____
9. tray	–	tr	+	s	=	____
10. lazy	–	l	+	h	=	____

Review Words

Write the review words that have the long vowel sounds below. Circle the spelling of /ā/ or /ē/ in each word.

/ā/ 11. ____

12. ____

/ē/ 13. ____

14. ____

wait
leave
awake
seem

Look at each list word below. Write the review word that has the same long vowel sound spelled the same way.

15. rail ____   17. bean ____

16. behave ____   18. agree ____

TAKE HOME

Write your spelling words in three lists: nouns, verbs, and adjectives. Some words may fit on more than one list. Circle the spelling of the long vowel sound in each word. Use your lists to practice at home.

Apply Spelling Skills

Dictionary Skills

Each dictionary page has two **guide words** to help you find a word. Imagine that the pairs of words in dark type are guide words on a dictionary page. Rewrite the list words below in alphabetical order. Underline the words that you would find on that page.

bay/bill		**cab/care**	
behave	**1.** ____	cane	**5.** ____
became	**2.** ____	crayon	**6.** ____
bean	**3.** ____	cave	**7.** ____
believe	**4.** ____	cape	**8.** ____

Proofreading

Check for spelling, capital letters, and punctuation. Then rewrite the paragraph. There are six mistakes.

Our class play takes place at a railroad stashun. Cheef joseph rescues a lazy buffalo from an oncoming fraight train We agreed to color in the scenery with creyons.

EDITING MARKS

- check spelling
- capital letter
- lowercase letter
- add a period
- add
- take out
- indent the paragraph
- move

For more help, see page 171.

Writing • *About the Arts*

PREWRITE: List some art projects you have made by yourself or with others. Think of poems, dances, plays, paintings, and music.

DRAFT: Write a paragraph that tells how you made the project.

REVISE: Read your paragraph out loud to yourself. Use the **Spelling Thesaurus** on page 182 as you revise.

EDIT/PROOFREAD: Use editing marks to correct your paragraph.

PUBLISH: Trade papers with a partner and try each other's projects.

5

Words with /ī/ and /ō/

PHONICS PATTERNS

1. hollow
2. reply
3. tomorrow
4. iron
5. crow
6. tiger
7. chose
8. pine
9. oak
10. tied
11. dive
12. groan
13. supply
14. stove
15. below
16. pile
17. note
18. roll
19. alike
20. rose

Learn Spelling Patterns

LOOK & SAY   Listen for the sounds in each word.

PICTURE   Close your eyes. See each word in your mind.

STUDY   These spelling words have /ī/ and /ō/.

WRITE   Sort the words. Which words have /ī/ spelled with the letters below?

i-e   (1)   (2)   (3)   (4)

ie   (5)

y   (6)   (7)

i   (8)   (9)

Which words have /ō/ spelled with the letters below?

oa   (10)   (11)

o-e   (12)   (13)   (14)   (15)

o   (16)

ow   (17)   (18)   (19)   (20)

CHECK   Did you spell each word correctly? Circle the letters that stand for the long vowel sounds.

Pattern Power

How can /ī/ be spelled?

(21) or (22) or (23) or (24)

How can /ō/ be spelled? (25) or (26)

or (27) or (28)

Other Words

Write words you would like to add to this week's list.

_____ _____ _____ _____ _____

Practice Word Meanings

Words in Context

Use the spelling words from the box to complete the story.

| stove   pile   hollow   tomorrow   crow   oak   tied   alike |

Ming went to explore the woods near his home. He took along some yarn. He **1.** ____ the yarn around each **2.** ____ tree he passed so he wouldn't get lost. Ming didn't notice that a **3.** ____ was pulling the yarn off to build a nest in a **4.** ____ tree. The bird had gathered a **5.** ____ of yarn by the time Ming saw what had happened. Ming headed home, but without the yarn to guide him, all the trees looked **6.** ____. He decided that **7.** ____ he would stay home and cook on the **8.** ____.

Challenge Words • *Science*

Write the challenge word that fits each clue below. Use the **Spelling Dictionary** on page 214 to help you. Circle the letter or letters that spell /ī/ or /ō/ in each word. If you hear both /ī/ and /ō/ in a word, circle the spellings of both sounds.

sparrow
pine cone
spiderweb
survive
migrate

9. Threads spun by an eight-legged animal. ____
10. Something you need fresh water to do. ____
11. What birds do when the seasons change. ____
12. A small, brown bird with a short bill. ____
13. The fruit of the pine tree, which squirrels eat. ____

Spelling Tip

Some words are difficult to spell. You can make up a saying to help you remember how to spell hard words. This sentence will help you remember that *tomorrow* has one *m* and two *r*'s:

Tom or I will **row** the boat **tomorrow.**

List Words

hollow
reply
tomorrow
iron
crow
tiger
chose
pine
oak
tied
dive
groan
supply
stove
below
pile
note
roll
alike
rose

Challenge Words

sparrow
pine cone
spiderweb
survive
migrate

Review Words

toast
lie
rope
wild

Build Vocabulary

Word Endings

■ If a base word ends in a consonant and *y*, change the *y* to *i* before adding *-ed*. The base word will not change when you add *-ing*.

reply + **ed** = replied   reply + **ing** = replying

Form new words by adding *-ed* and *-ing* to these base words. Remember that often you must drop the final *e* in a word before adding an ending that begins with a vowel.

	-ed	-ing
1. supply	_____	_____
2. dive	_____	_____
3. note	_____	_____
4. groan	_____	_____
5. iron	_____	_____
6. pile	_____	_____
7. crow	_____	_____
8. roll	_____	_____

Review Words

Write the review words that have the long vowel sounds below. Circle the spelling of /ī/ or /ō/ in each word.

/ī/   9. _____   /ō/ 11. _____

10. _____   12. _____

Look at each list word below. Write the review word that has the same long vowel sound spelled the same way.

13. tied _____   15. chose _____

14. oak _____

toast
lie
rope
wild

T A K E   H O M E

Write your words in three lists: words with one, two, or three syllables. Circle the spelling of /ī/ or /ō/ in each word. Use your lists to practice at home.

Apply Spelling Skills

Dictionary Skills

Imagine that the pairs of words in dark type are guide words. Rewrite the list words below in alphabetical order. Then underline the words that you would find on that page.

red/rope

rose 1. _____

reply 2. _____

roll 3. _____

tie/toll

tomorrow 4. _____

tiger 5. _____

tied 6. _____

Pattern Power

Look at the words you just wrote.

• Circle the spelling of /ī/ or /ō/ in each word.

Proofreading

Check for spelling, capital letters, and punctuation. Then rewrite the paragraph. There are six mistakes.

> In a pyne forest, many Birds and animals live in the trees Worms live beloe on the forest floor. they eat dead plants and suply food that helps new plants grow.

Writing • *About Science*

PREWRITE: List some creatures that live in the forest.

DRAFT: Choose one bird, insect, or animal. Write a paragraph telling about how the creature lives and what kind of food it eats.

REVISE: Exchange your paragraph with a classmate. Comment on each other's work. Use the **Spelling Thesaurus** on page 182 as you revise.

EDIT/PROOFREAD: Check your paragraph for mistakes in spelling and punctuation.

PUBLISH: Read your paragraph aloud to the class. Paint a "forest wildlife" mural based on the class's paragraphs.

EDITING MARKS

⬭ check spelling

= capital letter

/ lowercase letter

⊙ add a period

∧ add

⌇ take out

⌗ indent the paragraph

↻ move

For more help, see page 171.

6 REVIEW Spelling Patterns

Sort the words in each list. Write each word. Circle the spelling pattern.

| past | **Lesson 1** |
| dock | **Words with these short vowel sounds** |

past
dock
swept
act
trust
rest
rid
mad
love
done

Lesson 1

Words with these short vowel sounds

/a/ 1. _____   /i/ 6. _____
2. _____   /o/ 7. _____
3. _____   /u/ 8. _____
/e/ 4. _____   9. _____
5. _____   10. _____

attic
except
package
collect
until
problem
accept
public
mitten
action

Lesson 2

Words with these short vowel sounds in the accented syllable

/a/ 11. _____   /o/ 16. _____
12. _____   /ü/ 17. _____
13. _____   /e/ 18. _____
/i/ 14. _____   19. _____
15. _____   20. _____

breakfast
pleasant
guess
enough
trouble
ready
jealous
couple
built
meant

Lesson 3

Words with these short vowel sounds spelled with two letters

/e/ 21. _____   /u/ 27. _____
22. _____   28. _____
23. _____   29. _____
24. _____   /i/ 30. _____
25. _____
26. _____

station	**Lesson 4**
lazy	**Words with /ā/**
believe	**spelled**
crayon	a-e 31. _____
fail	32. _____
freight	a 33. _____
became	34. _____
lean	ai 35. _____
chief	ay 36. _____
cane	eigh 37. _____

Words with /ē/
spelled
ea 38. _____
ie 39. _____
40. _____

hollow	**Lesson 5**
tomorrow	**Words with /ō/**
tiger	**spelled**
oak	oa 41. _____
tied	42. _____
dive	o 43. _____
groan	ow 44. _____
supply	45. _____
stove	o-e 46. _____
roll	

Words with /ī/
spelled
i-e 47. _____
ie 48. _____
y 49. _____
i 50. _____

Spelling Tip

Spelling Two-Syllable Words
Two-syllable words are easier to spell
when you sound out each syllable. Say
each of the words in the circle. What
vowel sounds do you hear in the first and
second syllables of each word? Write
each word in syllables next to the vowel
sounds you hear in that word. Circle the
spelling of each vowel sound.

/ā/ and /ē/   1. _____
/a/ and /i/   2. _____
/o/ and /ō/   3. _____

attic
hollow
lazy

Word Meaning Mixed Lesson Review

attic
mitten
tomorrow
couple
dock
hollow
groan
station
breakfast
chief

Definitions
Write the spelling word that matches each definition below.

1. a deep moan of pain ___
2. the day after today ___
3. the morning meal ___
4. a warm covering for the hand ___
5. a platform where ships or boats are tied up ___
6. the leader of a group ___
7. a room or space in a house just below the roof ___
8. a regular stopping place along a route ___
9. two people or things paired together ___
10. an empty space ___

pleasant
love
believe
public
past

Antonyms
Write the spelling word that is an antonym for each word below.

11. hate ___
12. future ___
13. private ___
14. nasty ___
15. doubt ___

oak
stove
crayon
mad
tiger

Related Meanings
Write the spelling word that belongs in each group of words below.

16. pencil, paintbrush, pen ___
17. lion, cougar, cat ___
18. pine, fir, elm ___
19. angry, hurt, unhappy ___
20. fire, oven, toaster ___

Vocabulary Mixed Lesson Review

Word Endings

Add *-ed* and *-ing* to each base word below. You may have to drop the final *e* or change the final *y* to *i* before adding *-ed* or *-ing*.

	-ed	*-ing*
1. love	*loved*	*loving*
2. accept	____	____
3. dock	____	____
4. supply	____	____
5. package	____	____
6. fail	____	____
7. rest	____	____
8. believe	____	____
9. act	____	____
10. trouble	____	____

Dictionary Skills

Write the spelling words below in alphabetical order.

enough became chief freight done
jealous collect except meant

1. ____   5. ____   9. ____

2. ____   6. ____

3. ____   7. ____

4. ____   8. ____

Look at the list words you just wrote. Write the words that would be found on a dictionary page with these guide words: **door/fresh**.

10. ____   11. ____   12. ____

Spelling and Writing

A tourist pamphlet is a form of descriptive writing. The writer uses colorful words that help the reader picture a place.

EXPRESSES FEELING

Believe me, **you will love** Moab, Utah. A couple of miles from the center of town is Arches National Park. This chief tourist spot is home to the greatest number of natural stone arches in the world. **Erosion has built up and hollowed out** these huge sandstone sculptures. Hike up to "Delicate Arch." Rest under this **beautiful pale-orange structure**. Listen to the desert silence. Tomorrow, try camping out under the stars.

SPECIFIC DETAILS

VIVID DESCRIPTION

WRITING TIPS!!

Descriptive Writing
- Use words to create a vivid picture of your town.
- Use details that help readers imagine the place.
- Express a feeling about your subject.

Now write your own tourist pamphlet about where you live. Try to use spelling words in your pamphlet.

PREWRITE: What is special about your town? List some places that a visitor would enjoy seeing.

DRAFT: Write a paragraph about your town. Include interesting details about specific places, people, or historical events. Use descriptive words that will make people excited about your town.

REVISE: Share your paragraph with a classmate. Use your classmate's comments and the Writing Tips as you revise.

EDIT/PROOFREAD: Use editing marks to correct your paragraph. Rewrite a clean copy.

PUBLISH: Send your tourist pamphlets to your town's visitor center or information center for people to read.

SPELLING FUN
CUMULATIVE REVIEW

NEWSPAPER SEARCH

- Look at your words from Lessons 1–5.
- Use one page of a used newspaper or magazine. Look for as many spelling words as you can find.
- Use a highlighter or marker to highlight the spelling words you find.
- Start a class exhibition. Feature the pages with the most highlights!

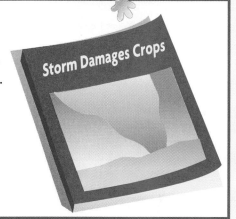

Storm Damages Crops

GUESS THE RHYME

- Choose one word from any list in Lessons 1–5.
- Select a rhyming word for your word. Tell your partner the rhyming word and have your partner guess your word.
- If your partner needs another hint, tell how many letters the word has.
- After your partner guesses the word, switch roles.

Swept

Kept

SPELLING BEE

- Divide the class into two teams. Share the job of writing 30 words from Lessons 1–5 on cards. Each team gets half of the cards.
- The first player on Team A calls out a word.
- The first player on Team B writes the word on the chalkboard or a piece of paper.

- If the word is spelled correctly, the card is taken out of the pile. If not, return the card to the pile.
- Then, the next Team B player calls out a word for the next Team A player. Continue.
- The first team to finish the other team's pile of cards wins!

7

WORDS WITH /ū/ and /ü/

1. bloom
2. ruler
3. broom
4. usual
5. roof
6. few
7. used
8. loose
9. whose
10. glue
11. clue
12. rescue
13. movie
14. human
15. avenue
16. dew
17. flute
18. due
19. tune
20. beautiful

Learn Spelling Patterns

LOOK & SAY Listen for the vowel sounds in each word.

PICTURE Close your eyes. See each word in your mind.

STUDY These spelling words have /ū/ or /ü/.

WRITE Sort the words. Which words have /ū/ or /ü/ spelled with the following letters?

u-e	(1)	(2)	(3)		
ue	(4)	(5)	(6)	(7)	(8)
u	(9)	(10)	(11)		
oo	(12)	(13)	(14)	(15)	
o	(16)	(17)			
ew	(18)	(19)			
eau	(20)				

CHECK Did you spell each word correctly? Circle the letters that stand for /ū/ or /ü/.

Pattern Power

How can /ū/ or /ü/ be spelled with one vowel? (21) or (22)

With two vowels? (23) or

(24) or (25)

Other Words

Write words you would like to add to this week's list.

_____ _____ _____ _____ _____

Practice Word Meanings

Analogies

An **analogy** compares two pairs of words. It shows how the two word pairs are similar. For example, *listen* is to *radio* as *watch* is to *television*. In other words, you listen to programs on radio and you watch programs on television. Use spelling words to complete the analogies below.

1. *Seed* is to *sprout* as *flower* is to _bloom_.
2. *Big* is to *small* as *many* is to ____.
3. *Tape* is to *paper* as ____ is to *wood*.
4. *Football* is to *stadium* as ____ is to *theater.*
5. *Hat* is to *head* as ____ is to *building.*
6. *Pen* is to *writer* as ____ is to *musician.*

Challenge Words • *Science*

Write the challenge word that best completes each sentence. Use the **Spelling Dictionary** on page 214 to help you. Circle the letters that spell /ū/ or /ü/ in each word. Note that the word *cumulus* has two different sounds that are both spelled the same way.

cumulus
humidity
lunar
monsoon
pollute

7. The ____ blew in and brought a severe rainstorm.
8. The sky is full of ____ clouds.
9. When the ____ is high, the air feels moist.
10. The smoke from that factory will ____ the air.
11. The spaceship landed on the ____ surface.

Spelling Tip

Words that are related in meaning are often related in spelling. For example:

+ The words *beauty* and *beautiful* are related in meaning.
+ The word *beauty* ends in *y*.
+ Always change a *y* to *i* before adding an ending

beauty + ful = beautiful

List Words

bloom
ruler
broom
usual
roof
few
used
loose
whose
glue
clue
rescue
movie
human
avenue
dew
flute
due
tune
beautiful

Challenge Words

cumulus
humidity
lunar
monsoon
pollute

Review Words

truth
moon
drew
boot

Build Vocabulary

Plural Nouns

■ A **singular** noun names one person, place, thing, or idea. A **plural** noun names more than one person, place, thing, or idea. You can make most nouns plural by adding -s. Write the plural of each noun below.

1. clue _____
2. ruler _____
3. movie _____
4. broom _____
5. tune _____

6. human _____
7. roof _____
8. avenue _____
9. bloom _____

■ Use words you made to complete these sentences.
10. I watched two _____ on TV.
11. We used pencils and _____ to draw straight lines.
12. The detective needs more _____ to solve the case.
13. I played some _____ on my trumpet.

Review Words

Write the review words that have /ü/ spelled with the letters below.

ew 14. _____   **oo** 16. _____
u 15. _____   17. _____

Look at each list word below. Write the review words that have the same spelling of /ü/.

broom 18. _____   dew 20. _____
      19. _____   ruler 21. _____

truth
moon
drew
boot

▲TAKE HOME◣

Write your spelling words in three groups: words with one, two, or three syllables. Circle the spelling of /ū/ or /ü/ in each word. Use your lists to practice at home.

Apply Spelling Skills

Dictionary Skills

Entry words are the words you can look up in the dictionary. They are listed in alphabetical order and printed in dark type. An entry word together with its pronunciation and meanings is called an **entry.** Look up the entry words below in the **Spelling Dictionary** on page 214. Write the first meaning given for the word.

1. loose   ____
2. whose   ____
3. dew   ____
4. usual   ____

Proofreading

Proofread the paragraph. Check spelling, capital letters, and punctuation. Then rewrite the paragraph. There are six mistakes.

> The weather was sunny and beutiful. But we needed rain to rescu the plants Before a storm was do, we put a cup outside. the next day, we usd a ruler to measure the rain in the cup.

Writing • *About Science*

PREWRITE: Visualize the four seasons. List what makes each special.

DRAFT: Choose one season and write a paragraph about it. Mention such details as its temperatures and the length of its days.

REVISE: How can you make your paragraph more interesting?

EDIT/PROOFREAD: Use editing marks. Rewrite the paragraph.

PUBLISH: Add a collage of seasonal items to your paragraph.

EDITING MARKS

⬭ check spelling
≡ capital letter
/ lowercase letter
⊙ add a period
∧ add
⤵ take out
⌐ indent the paragraph
↻ move

For more help, see page 171.

WORDS WITH Clusters

1. fry
2. grave
3. speak
4. sweet
5. bridge
6. dream
7. smoke
8. flour
9. snow
10. cream
11. flow
12. blade
13. crack
14. study
15. blanket
16. clear
17. plank
18. snap
19. drum
20. stew

Learn Spelling Patterns

LOOK & SAY Listen for the sounds in each word.

PICTURE Close your eyes. See each word in your mind.

STUDY These spelling words begin with two-letter **consonant clusters**. In a consonant cluster, each consonant stands for a single sound.

WRITE Sort the words. Which words have *l* as the second letter of the cluster?

(1) (2) (3) (4) (5) (6)

Which words have *r* as the second letter of the cluster?

(7) (8) (9) (10) (11) (12) (13)

Which words have *s* as the first letter of the cluster?

(14) (15) (16) (17) (18) (19) (20)

CHECK Did you spell each word correctly? Circle the consonant cluster at the beginning of each word.

Pattern Power

In a beginning consonant cluster, what letter often stands for the second sound you hear? (21) or (22) The first sound you hear? (23)

Other Words

Write words you would like to add to this week's list.

———— ———— ———— ———— ————

Practice Word Meanings

Words in Context

Use spelling words to complete the sentences below.

1. The workers built a ____ over the river.
2. You can grind wheat to make ____.
3. I hear the slow, steady ____ of the water.
4. The bird carried a ____ of grass.
5. The vase had a ____, but it didn't leak.
6. We heard the branch ____ before it fell.
7. I must ____ hard to pass my test.
8. The wooden sidewalk had a loose ____.
9. A white carpet of ____ covered the ground.
10. Beat out that rhythm on your ____.

Challenge Words • *Social Studies*

Write the challenge word that goes with each group of words below. Use the **Spelling Dictionary** on page 214 to help you. Circle the consonant cluster at the beginning of each word.

11. edge, border, territory ____
12. plain, mountain, valley ____
13. hurricane, tornado, earthquake ____
14. scatter, run, rush ____
15. bowl, pit, hole ____

frontier
blizzard
plateau
stampede
crater

Spelling Tip

Use words you know how to spell to help you spell new words. For example, if you want to spell *crack*:

✦ Listen to the sounds you hear at the beginning of *crack*. What word do you know how to spell that begins with the same sounds?

✦ Listen to the sound you hear at the end of *crack*. What word do you know how to spell that ends with the same sound?

✦ Put the letters that stand for the sounds together.

List Words

6 fry
11 grave
15 speak
7 sweet
19 bridge
8 dream
2 smoke
17 flour
9 snow
1 cream
12 flow
10 blade
3 crack
16 study
20 blanket
4 clear
18 plank
13 snap
5 drum
14 stew

Challenge Words

3 frontier
5 blizzard
1 plateau
4 stampede
2 crater

Review Words

cross
block
grab
spell

Build Vocabulary

Word Endings

■ When the ending -er is added to an adjective, it means "more." The ending -er is used to compare two things. When the ending -est is added to an adjective, it means "most." The ending -est is used to compare more than two things.

smart + **er** = smarter, meaning "more smart"

smart + **est** = smartest, meaning "most smart"

Add -er and -est to each adjective below. If a word ends in e, drop the e before adding the ending. If the word ends in a consonant and y, change the y to i before adding the ending.

	-er	-est
1. sweet	_____	_____
2. clear	_____	_____
3. grave	_____	_____
4. smoky	_____	_____
5. creamy	_____	_____

■ Use words you made to complete these sentences.

6. Clara wrote the _____ directions to the picnic.

7. This flower smells _____ than that one.

Review Words

Write the review words that begin with the following consonant clusters.

gr 8. _____   cr 10. _____

sp 9. _____   bl 11. _____

Look at each list word below. Write the review word that begins with the same consonant cluster.

12. speak _____   13. cream _____

cross
block
grab
spell

TAKE HOME

Write your spelling words in two lists: words with and without long vowel sounds. Circle the consonant cluster at the beginning of each word. Use your lists to practice at home.

Apply Spelling Skills

Dictionary Skills

Entry words often have spaces to show where each word can be divided. When you divide a word, write a *hyphen (-)* after the first part to show that the word has been divided. Do not divide one-syllable words. Look up each spelling word below in your **Spelling Dictionary** on page 214. Write each word, adding a hyphen to show where the word could be divided at the end of a line.

1. pleasant _____
2. breakfast _____
3. blanket _____
4. study _____

Proofreading

Check for spelling, capital letters, and punctuation. Then rewrite the paragraph. There are six mistakes.

the cowboy is cooking a creamy stue for dinner. Tonight, he'll sleep under a cleer sky. He has no one to speak to about his dreem In the morning, he'll frye eggs for breakfast.

Writing • *About Social Studies*

PREWRITE: List some of the pleasures and dangers cowboys faced as they drove cattle in the old West. Include difficult situations such as stampedes and blizzards.

DRAFT: Write a poem about the life of a cowboy.

REVISE: Did you use words that are colorful and interesting? Use the **Spelling Thesaurus** on page 182 as you revise.

EDIT/PROOFREAD: Check for spelling, capitalization, and punctuation.

PUBLISH: Hold a "cowboy poetry" festival in which you and your classmates read your poems aloud.

Pattern Power

Look at the words you just wrote.

• Circle the consonant cluster at the beginning of each word.

EDITING MARKS

⬯ check spelling
≡ capital letter
／ lowercase letter
⊙ add a period
∧ add
⤹ take out
¶ indent the paragraph
↶ move

For more help, see page 171.

WORDS WITH
Clusters

PHONICS PATTERNS

1. thread
2. steady
3. straight
4. throat
5. stretch
6. strike
7. struck
8. split
9. street
10. spray
11. stool
12. smash
13. stranger
14. style
15. strap
16. slippery
17. stroke
18. thrill
19. spill
20. spirit

Learn Spelling Patterns

LOOK & SAY Listen for the sounds in each word.

PICTURE Close your eyes. See each word in your mind.

STUDY These spelling words begin with two- or three-letter **consonant clusters**.

WRITE Sort the words. Which words have three-letter clusters?

(1) (2) (3) (4) (5)
(6) (7) (8) (9)
(10) (11) (12) (13)

Which words have two-letter clusters?

(14) (15) (16) (17)
(18) (19) (20)

CHECK Did you spell each word correctly? Circle the consonant cluster at the beginning of each word.

Pattern Power

In three-letter consonant clusters,

what letter is often the third letter?

(21)

Other Words

Write words you would like to add to this week's list.

_____ _____ _____ _____ _____

Practice Word Meanings

Related Meanings

Write the spelling word that goes with each group of words below.

1. droplets, sprinkle, splash   *spray*
2. needle, cloth, sew   ___
3. baseball, bat, pitch   ___
4. break, divide, separate   ___
5. chair, seat, bench   ___
6. ear, nose, stomach   ___
7. avenue, road, lane   ___
8. crush, break, destroy   ___
9. drip, leak, tumble   ___
10. cord, string, band   ___

Challenge Words • *Physical Education*

Write the challenge word that best completes each sentence. Use the **Spelling Dictionary** on page 214 to help you. Circle the cluster at the beginning of each word.

11. Pitching an entire baseball game can be ____.
12. The football game was held in a ____.
13. Watch how the riders ____ their horses.
14. Our coach taught us a ____ for winning.
15. The runner had a high ____ for pain.

strategy
straddle
stressful
threshold
stadium

Spelling Tip

Some words are not spelled the way you would expect them to be. For example, if you heard the word *straight,* you might expect /ā/ to be spelled *ate.* Try this hint to help you remember how to spell hard words:

✦ Figure out which part of the word gives you trouble.

✦ Pay special attention to that part every time you read or write the word.

List Words

thread
steady
straight
throat
stretch
strike
struck
split
street
spray
stool
smash
stranger
style
strap
slippery
stroke
thrill
spill
spirit

Challenge Words

strategy
straddle
stressful
threshold
stadium

Review Words

threw
spring
strong
throw

Build Vocabulary

Suffixes

■ A **suffix** is a word part that is added to the end of a base word. It changes the meaning of the base word. The suffix -er can mean "a person or thing that is or does." When -er is added to a verb, the verb becomes a noun.

dream + **er** = dreamer, meaning "a person who dreams"

Add -er to the base words below. You may have to drop the final e before adding the suffix.

1. thrill _____   3. spray _____

2. strike _____   4. stretch _____

■ Use words you made to complete these sentences.

5. Attach a _____ to the hose.

6. The injured boy was carried on a _____.

Review Words

Write the review words that begin with the consonant clusters below. Circle the cluster at the beginning of each word.

thr   7. _____

          8. _____

str   9. _____

spr   10. _____

threw
spring
strong
throw

Look at the spelling words below. Write the review words that begin with the same cluster.

thrill 11. _____   stranger 13. _____

      12. _____   spray   14. _____

T A K E   H O M E

Write your spelling words in alphabetical order. Circle the consonant cluster at the beginning of each word. Use your lists to practice at home.

Apply Spelling Skills

Dictionary Skills

At least one meaning, or **definition,** is given for each entry word in a dictionary. When a word has more than one meaning, the definitions are numbered. Use the **Spelling Dictionary** on page 214 to write the second definition for each spelling word below.

1. style ____
2. slippery ____
3. stranger ____

Proofreading

Check for spelling, capital letters, and punctuation. Then rewrite the paragraph. There are six mistakes.

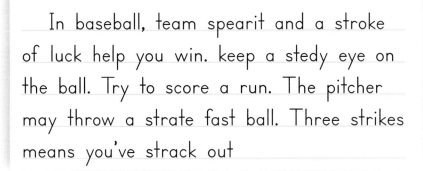

In baseball, team spearit and a stroke of luck help you win. keep a stedy eye on the ball. Try to score a run. The pitcher may throw a strate fast ball. Three strikes means you've strack out

Writing • *About Physical Education*

PREWRITE: List some group sports that you know how to play. Brainstorm special words connected to those sports.

DRAFT: Write a paragraph about one group sport. Explain how it is played.

REVISE: Trade paragraphs with a partner. Share comments. Is your paragraph written in a clear order? Use the **Spelling Thesaurus** on page 182 as you revise.

EDIT/PROOFREAD: Use editing marks to correct your paragraph. Then rewrite it.

PUBLISH: Have "sports talks." Read your paragraph aloud.

EDITING MARKS

⬭ check spelling
☰ capital letter
／ lowercase letter
⊙ add a period
⌃ add
⸆ take out
⌗ indent the paragraph
↻ move

For more help, see page 171.

10

Clusters and Digraphs

PHONICS PATTERNS

1. frost
2. smooth
3. reach
4. o'clock
5. front
6. among
7. held
8. understand
9. bent
10. path
11. breath
12. spent
13. patch
14. hang
15. blank
16. hold
17. pitch
18. belt
19. mild
20. pack

Learn Spelling Patterns

LOOK & SAY Listen for the sounds in each word.

PICTURE Close your eyes. See each word in your mind.

STUDY These spelling words end with a **consonant cluster** or a **consonant digraph**. A consonant digraph has two or more letters that together stand for a new sound.

WRITE Sort the words. Which words end with the consonant digraphs below?

th (1) (2) (3)

tch (4) (5)

ch (6)

Which words end with these clusters?

nt (7) (8) (9)

lt (10)

nk (11)

ng (12) (13)

ld (14) (15) (16)

nd (17)

ck (18) (19)

st (20)

CHECK Did you spell each word correctly? Circle the final consonant cluster or digraph.

Pattern Power

What letter is often the final letter in a consonant digraph? (21) What letter begins many final consonant clusters? (22) or (23)

Other Words

Write words you would like to add to this week's list.

_____ _____ _____ _____ _____

Practice Word Meanings

Words in Context

Use the spelling words from the box to complete the story.

reach	path	breath	o'clock	pitch	front	held

Marta ran down the **1.** _____ through the park. She stopped in **2.** _____ of a statue of George Washington. As she tried to catch her **3.** _____, she read the note she **4.** _____ in her hand. It said she could **5.** _____ in today's baseball game if she was at the field by one **6.** _____. Marta glanced at her watch. She had three minutes to get there. If she ran, she would **7.** _____ the field on time.

Challenge Words • *Science*

Write the challenge word that matches each definition below. Use the **Spelling Dictionary** on page 214 to check your answers. Circle the final consonant cluster or consonant digraph.

8. a scientist who studies rocks _____

9. letting light through so that objects on either side can be seen _____

10. to study or investigate _____

11. a basic material such as iron, oxygen, gold, or carbon _____

12. something made up of two or more parts _____

compound
element
transparent
geologist
research

Spelling Tip

Many people have trouble remembering how to spell /ch/ at the end of a word. This rule works almost all of the time.

✦ After a short vowel, spell /ch/ with the letters *tch*.

There are some words that this rule does not work with. Some examples are *rich*, *which*, and *such*. If you aren't sure whether to use *ch* or *tch*, check your dictionary.

List Words

1. frost
2. smooth
3. reach
4. o'clock
5. front
6. among
7. held
8. understand
9. bent
10. path
11. breath
12. spent
13. patch
14. hang
15. blank
16. hold
17. pitch
18. belt
19. mild
20. pack

Challenge Words

compound
element
transparent
geologist
research

Review Words

sack
lunch
wind
young

Build Vocabulary

Plurals

■ The most common way to form the plural of a noun is to add -s. When a word ends with *ch*, you must add -es to make it plural.

catch + **es** = catches

Write the plural of each spelling word below.

1. patch _____
2. blank _____
3. path _____
4. reach _____
5. belt _____
6. pack _____

Suffixes

■ Add the suffix -er to the spelling words below.

7. pitch _____
8. hang _____
9. hold _____
10. pack _____

Review Words

Write the review words that end with the consonant cluster or digraph below. Circle the final cluster or digraph in each word.

ck 11. _____
nd 12. _____
ng 13. _____
ch 14. _____

sack
lunch
wind
young

Write the review words that end with the same cluster or digraph as each spelling word below.

15. understand _____
16. reach _____
17. o'clock _____
18. among _____

TAKE HOME

Write your spelling words in short lists according to their first letters. Circle the cluster or digraph at the end of each word. Use your lists to practice at home.

Apply Spelling Skills

Dictionary Skills

Look up each word in the box in the **Spelling Dictionary** on page 214. Write the word and definition number that matches each meaning below.

| bent frost understand spent smooth |

1. Curved or crooked. ____ ____
2. To know well. ____ ____
3. Tiny ice crystals. ____ ____
4. Gentle in movement. ____ ____
5. Paid. ____ ____

P attern Power

Look at the words you just wrote.

• Circle the final consonant cluster or digraph in each word.

Proofreading

Check for spelling, capital letters, and punctuation. Then rewrite the paragraph. There are seven mistakes.

The Campers hiked along the pathe They hoped to reech their campsite soon. the day was miled, but the night would bring frost. The campers would pich their tent among wildflowers.

Writing • About Science

PREWRITE: List flowers that you have seen growing wild.

DRAFT: Choose one flower. Write a paragraph describing how the flower looks and smells and when it is in bloom.

REVISE: Did you include sensory details about the flower?

EDIT/PROOFREAD: Use editing marks to correct your paragraph.

PUBLISH: Draw a picture to go with your paragraph. Collect your class's paragraphs in a "wildflower guide book."

E DITING MARKS

◯ check spelling

≡ capital letter

/ lowercase letter

⊙ add a period

∧ add

✂ take out

¶ indent the paragraph

◯↝ move

For more help, see page 171.

Digraphs and Silent Letters

1. knuckle
2. knife
3. although
4. writer
5. limb
6. bomb
7. ought
8. comb
9. delight
10. thorough
11. whirl
12. daylight
13. unknown
14. thoughtful
15. wren
16. wreath
17. folks
18. knob
19. dumb
20. whittle

Learn Spelling Patterns

LOOK & SAY Listen for the sounds in each word.

PICTURE Close your eyes. See each word in your mind.

STUDY Some of these spelling words begin with the consonant digraph *wh*. The rest of these spelling words have one or more consonants that are *not* sounded.

WRITE Sort the words. Which words have /hw/ spelled with *wh*?

(1) (2)

Which words have these silent consonants?

k   (3) (4) (5) (6)
b   (7) (8) (9) (10)
l   (11)
gh   (12) (13) (14) (15) (16) (17)
w   (18) (19) (20)

CHECK Did you spell each word correctly? Circle the silent consonants or the letters that stand for /hw/.

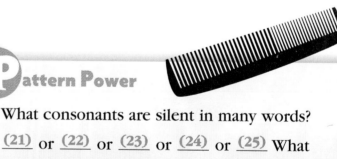

Pattern Power

What consonants are silent in many words?

(21) or (22) or (23) or (24) or (25) What

consonants spell /hw/ in many words? (26)

Other Words

Write words you would like to add to this week's list.

_____ _____ _____ _____ _____

Practice Word Meanings

Word Choice

A good writer chooses words carefully. Using the right word can mean the difference between a dull sentence and a lively description. Write the spelling word that is similar in meaning to the underlined word in each sentence below.

1. Nan heard the wind <u>twist</u> past her window in the night. ____
2. In the <u>morning</u>, she could see the storm damage. ____
3. Nan saw that a tree <u>branch</u> had smashed a car. ____
4. She found the nest of a small, brown <u>bird</u>. ____

Challenge Words • *Social Studies*

Write the challenge word that best answers each question. Use the **Spelling Dictionary** on page 214 to help you. Circle the silent consonant letters or digraph in each word.

5. What is another word for *dock*? ____
6. What do you call a building in which a dead body is placed? ____
7. Who might ride a horse and wear armor? ____
8. What causes crops to die? ____
9. What does studying and experience give you? ____

tomb
knight
knowledge
wharf
drought

Spelling Tip

Some beginning sounds can be spelled more than one way. Knowing the different spellings can help you use the dictionary to find out how to spell a word. For example, /r/ at the beginning of a word can be spelled *r* or *wr*.

✦ Look up a word that starts with /r/ under *r*.
✦ If you don't find it, try *wr*.

List Words

knuckle
knife
although
writer
limb
bomb
ought
comb
delight
thorough
whirl
daylight
unknown
thoughtful
wren
wreath
folks
knob
dumb
whittle

Challenge Words

tomb
knight
knowledge
wharf
drought

Build Vocabulary

Rhyming Words

■ Use the directions below to write the word that rhymes with each spelling word.

1. whittle   – **wh** + **l** = ____
2. knuckle   – **kn** + **b** = ____
3. ought   + **br**   = ____
4. dumb   – **d** + **cr** = ____
5. knife   – **kn** + **w** = ____
6. unknown   – **unkn** + **fl** = ____
7. folks   – **f** + **y** = ____
8. wren   – **wr** + **m** = ____
9. writer   – **wr** + **b** = ____
10. wreath   – **wr** + **ben** = ____
11. thorough   – **th** + **b** = ____

Review Words

Write the review words that contain silent consonants. Circle the silent letter or letters in each word.

12. ____   14. ____

13. ____   15. ____

Look at the spelling words below. Then write the review word that contains the same silent letter.

16. comb   ____
17. knob   ____
18. folks   ____
19. although   ____

high
knee
calf
thumb

T A K E   H O M E

Write your spelling words in two lists: words that can be used as nouns or verbs and words that are used as other parts of speech. Use your lists to practice at home.

Apply Spelling Skills

Dictionary Skills

Some words are used as more than one part of speech. The dictionary groups and labels definitions for a word according to part of speech. Locate the part of speech labels in the sample entry on page 214 of the **Spelling Dictionary.** Rewrite the words below in alphabetical order. Use the **Spelling Dictionary** to write the parts of speech for each word.

1. thoughtful ____ ____ ____

2. wreath   ____ ____

3. bomb   ____ ____

Proofreading

Check for spelling, capital letters, and punctuation. Then rewrite the paragraph. There are six mistakes.

> Legends delite readers. Some of these foke stories are about real people. Others are thorouhly made up. If you combe through our legends, you will find john Henry and Pecos bill.

Writing • *About Social Studies*

PREWRITE: Make a list of American legends and folk heroes.

DRAFT: Write your own version of one legend. Remember to introduce all the characters. Tell the plot in a logical order.

REVISE: Can you make your retelling more exciting? Use the **Spelling Thesaurus** on page 182 as you revise.

EDIT/PROOFREAD: Use editing marks to correct your mistakes.

PUBLISH: Have a "storytellers' hour" in your classroom. Take turns reading your stories to the class.

EDITING MARKS

◯ check spelling

≡ capital letter

╱ lowercase letter

⊙ add a period

⌃ add

✄ take out

¶ indent the paragraph

↻ move

For more help, see page 171.

REVIEW Spelling Patterns

Sort the words in each list. Write each word. Circle the vowel spellings, consonant clusters, digraphs, or silent letters.

---

bloom
ruler
used
loose
glue
rescue
movie
human
dew
beautiful

Lesson 7
Words with /ū/ or /ü/ spelled

u-e 1. _____   oo 6. _____

u 2. _____   7. _____

3. _____   o 8. _____

ue 4. _____   ew 9. _____

5. _____   eau 10. _____

---

grave
speak
bridge
flour
snow
study
blanket
plank
drum
stew

Lesson 8

Words with *l* or *r* as the second letter of a cluster

11. _____
12. _____
13. _____
14. _____
15. _____
16. _____

Words with *s* as the first letter of the cluster

17. _____
18. _____
19. _____
20. _____

---

thread
steady
strike
struck
spray
smash
stranger
slippery
thrill
spirit

Lesson 9

Words with 3-letter clusters

21. _____
22. _____
23. _____
24. _____
25. _____
26. _____

Words with 2-letter clusters

27. _____
28. _____
29. _____
30. _____

	Lesson 10
frost	**Lesson 10**
reach	**Words with these final digraphs or clusters**
among	
understand	th 31. _____ nk 36. _____
path	tch 32. _____ ld 37. _____
spent	ch 33. _____ nd 38. _____
blank	nt 34. _____ ck 39. _____
pitch	ng 35. _____ st 40. _____
mild	
pack	

frost
reach
among
understand
path
spent
blank
pitch
mild
pack

Lesson 10
Words with these final digraphs or clusters

th 31. _____
tch 32. _____
ch 33. _____
nt 34. _____
ng 35. _____

nk 36. _____
ld 37. _____
nd 38. _____
ck 39. _____
st 40. _____

knuckle
although
writer
comb
delight
whirl
unknown
thoughtful
folks
dumb

Lesson 11
Words with these digraphs or silent letters

wh 41. _____
w 42. _____
b 43. _____
44. _____
l 45. _____

gh 46. _____
47. _____
48. _____
k 49. _____
50. _____

Spelling Tip

Some words have unexpected spellings. Pay attention to the part of the word that is not spelled the way it sounds. Try to make up a saying that will help you remember the difficult spelling. To remember that the word *thoughtful* has the silent letters *gh*, you might say,

> **Ugh!** I'm so full of thoughts, I'm tho**ugh**tful.

Each of the spelling words below is misspelled. Rewrite each word correctly. Circle the part of each word that is not spelled the way you would expect it to be.

although
beautiful
folks
knuckle

1. byutiful _____   **3.** nuckle _____

2. altho _____   **4.** fokes _____

Word Meaning Mixed Lesson Review

dew
glue
flour
slippery
bloom

knuckle
thread
stranger
writer
drum

human
path
blanket
plank
ruler
movie
bridge
stew
writer
comb

Context Sentences

Write the spelling word that best completes each sentence.

1. You need wheat to make ____.
2. In the early morning, the grass is wet with ____.
3. Watch your step when the streets are ____.
4. By mid-summer, my rosebush is in full ____.
5. I used ____ to put together my model.

Related Meanings

Write the spelling word that belongs in each group below.

6. artist, musician, poet ____
7. knee, joint, finger ____
8. material, needle, sew ____
9. foreigner, newcomer, visitor ____
10. guitar, flute, piano ____

Analogies

Write a spelling word to complete each analogy below.

11. *Tablecloth* is to *table* as ____ is to *bed*.
12. *Singer* is to *concert* as *actor* is to ____.
13. *Brush* is to *teeth* as ____ is to *hair*.
14. *Street* is to *city* as ____ is to *woods*.
15. ____ is to *inches* as *scale* is to *pounds*.
16. ____ is to *dinner* as *cereal* is to *breakfast*.
17. ____ is to *book* as *painter* is to *picture*.
18. *Baby* is to ____ as *chick* is to *bird*.
19. *Window* is to *glass* as ____ is to *wood*.
20. *Tunnel* is to *mountain* as ____ is to *river*.

50

Vocabulary Mixed Lesson Review

Word Endings

Write the words that are formed by adding the given endings.
You may have to drop the final *e* before adding the ending.

1. loose + er   _____
2. strike + ing   _____
3. spray + ing   _____
4. thrill + ing   _____
5. rescue + ing   _____

Plurals

Write the plural of each noun below. You may have to
change *y* to *i* before adding *-es*.

6. study   _____
7. blank   _____
8. pack   _____
9. delight   _____
10. ruler   _____

Dictionary Skills

Read the dictionary entry below. Then answer the questions about it.

ruler 1. One who governs or rules. Queen Elizabeth II is the *ruler* of Great
Britain. **2.** A strip of wood, plastic, or metal that is marked off by units of measure.
I used my *ruler* to draw a straight line. **rul • er** (rü′ lər) *noun, plural* **rulers.**

1. What is the entry word? _____
2. What is the part of speech? _____
3. How many syllables does this entry word have? _____
4. What is the first definition? _____

Spelling and Writing

Directions for an arts and crafts project are one form of explanatory writing.

EXPLANATION OF PROJECT

Making a Thumbprint Mouse

Here's how to make a thumbprint mouse.

LIST OF MATERIALS

Materials you will need:

- paper
- ink pad
- crayons or markers

STEP-BY-STEP DIRECTIONS

DETAILS

Directions:

1. Press your thumb down on the ink pad. (Press hard!)
2. Press your thumb down on a sheet of paper.
3. Complete your thumbprint animal by drawing on ears, eyes, whiskers, feet, a nose, and a tail.
4. You can make other animals this way, too. Make a whole zoo full of them!

WRITING TIPS!!

Explanatory Writing

- Explain the kind of project and the materials that are needed at the beginning.
- Present directions in a logical order.
- Add details to make the explanation clear.

Now write directions for an arts and crafts project of your choosing. Try to use spelling words in your directions.

PREWRITE: What project have you done that your friends might like to do? List the materials they will need for the project and the steps they must do to complete it.

DRAFT: Write a set of directions for the project. Begin by explaining what the project is. Then write a list of materials and an explanation of how to do the project.

REVISE: Share your directions with a classmate. Use your classmate's comments and the Writing Tips as you revise.

EDIT/PROOFREAD: Use editing marks to correct your capitalization, spelling, and punctuation. Rewrite your directions neatly.

PUBLISH: Add your directions to a class arts and crafts project book.

SPELLING FUN
CUMULATIVE REVIEW

TELL ALL ABOUT IT

- Choose a noun from Lessons 1–5. Write it down the middle of a sheet of paper.
- Write some words that tell about your noun. Each word should include a different letter of the noun.
- Keep going until you've come up with a word for each letter of your noun.
- Do as many as you like. Display your work for the class.

tough
wild
growl
fierce
striped

PLAY LONG WORD, SHORT WORDS

- With a partner, choose a word at least eight letters long from any list in Lessons 7–11.
- On your own, write the word at the top of a sheet of paper.
- See how many shorter words you can make, using the letters in the long word.
- Exchange papers with your partner. Compare your lists of shorter words.

stranger
tan
ran
stare

SPELLING BEE

- Two teams share the job of writing words from Lessons 1–11 on an even number of cards. Each team gets half the cards.
- The first player on Team A calls out a word. The first player on Team B writes the word on the chalkboard.
- If the word is spelled correctly, the card is taken out of the pile and the team gets one point. If the Team B player can write another word that rhymes with the spelling word, Team B gets two extra points. If the player doesn't spell the word correctly, the card is returned to the pile.
- The teams alternate. The team that finishes first or has the most points after a given time wins.

13

WORDS WITH /f/ and /kw/

PHONICS PATTERNS

1. quilt
2. quiet
3. question
4. elephant
5. cough
6. phone
7. quite
8. rough
9. queen
10. alphabet
11. square
12. quickly
13. laugh
14. photograph
15. telephone
16. earthquake
17. quiz
18. graph
19. tough
20. equal

Learn Spelling Patterns

LOOK & SAY Listen for the sounds in each word.

PICTURE Close your eyes. See each word in your mind.

STUDY These spelling words have /f/ and /kw/.

WRITE Sort the words. Which words have /f/ spelled with the letters below?

ph (1) (2) (3)
     (4) (5) (6)

gh (7) (8) (9) (10)

Which words have /kw/ spelled *qu*?

(11) (12) (13) (14) (15)
(16) (17) (18) (19) (20)

CHECK Did you spell each word correctly? Circle the letters that stand for the /f/ and /kw/ sounds.

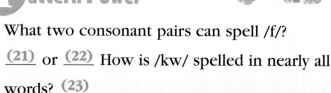

Pattern Power

What two consonant pairs can spell /f/?

(21) or (22) How is /kw/ spelled in nearly all words? (23)

Other Words

Write words you would like to add to this week's list.

___ ___ ___ ___ ___

Practice Word Meanings

Synonyms

You know that a **synonym** is a word that means the same or nearly the same as another word. Write a spelling word that is a synonym for each word below.

1. completely   ____
2. giggle   ____
3. strong   ____
4. test   ____
5. bumpy   ____
6. chart   ____
7. silent   ____
8. same   ____

Challenge Words • Math

Write the challenge word that best completes each sentence. Use the **Spelling Dictionary** on page 214 to help you. Circle the letters that spell /f/ or /kw/ in each word.

9. The ____ states that two parts are equal.
10. A basketball is the shape of a ____.
11. Chris could eat a huge ____ of spaghetti.
12. Ana recited the days of the week in ____.
13. If you divide fifteen by three, the ____ is five.

equation
sequence
quantity
quotient
sphere

Spelling Tip

Here's a spelling rule that you can always count on!

✦ The letter *q* is always followed by the letter *u*.

Find some examples in your spelling list. Did you find *question* and *quiet*? Look for some others.

List Words

quilt
quiet
question
elephant
cough
phone
quite
rough
queen
alphabet
square
quickly
laugh
photograph
telephone
earthquake
quiz
graph
tough
equal

Challenge Words

equation
sequence
quantity
quotient
sphere

Review Words

finish
quit
fit
quick

Build Vocabulary

Prefixes and Suffixes

■ The prefix *un-* means "not" or "the opposite of."

un + like = unlike

Add *un-* to the list words below.

1. quiet _____   2. equal _____

■ The suffix *-ly* means "in a certain way."

quick + **ly** = quickly

Add *-ly* to the list words below.

3. quiet _____   5. equal _____
4. square _____   6. queen _____

■ Use words you made to complete these sentences.

7. The television fit _____ in its box.

8. A pound and an ounce are _____ amounts.

9. Helen and Gail are _____ good at sports.

Review Words

Write the review words with /kw/ spelled *qu*. Circle the letters that stand for the sound in each word.

10. _____   11. _____

Write the review words that have /f/ spelled *f*.

12. _____   13. _____

Write the review word that is part of the following list word.

14. quickly _____

finish
quit
fit
quick

T A K E   H O M E

Write your spelling words in two lists: words that can be used as nouns or verbs and words that can be used as other parts of speech. Circle the spelling of /f/ or /kw/. Use your lists to practice at home.

56

Apply Spelling Skills

Dictionary Skills

A **pronunciation key** tells you how to pronounce words. Use the pronunciation key on page 215 of the **Spelling Dictionary** to figure out the first vowel sound in the words below. Write the words next to the given sounds.

| alphabet cough phone question quilt elephant |

/a/ 1. ____   /ô/ 4. ____

/e/ 2. ____   /ō/ 5. ____

3. ____   /i/ 6. ____

Pattern Power

Look at the words you just wrote.

• Circle the spelling of /f/ or /kw/ in each word.

Proofreading

Proofread the paragraph. Check for spelling, capital letters, and punctuation. Then rewrite the paragraph. There are seven mistakes.

> The earthqwak damaged 5 percent of the city's buildings. People for 20 miles could not telepfone for help hospitals quikly admitted 50 people. the photograf shows a boy receiving first aid.

Writing • About Math

PREWRITE: List some natural disasters. Think about how a reporter might use numbers to explain how many people were affected.

DRAFT: Choose one natural disaster. Write a paragraph that uses numbers to describe the event.

REVISE: Is your paragraph clear and logical? Use the **Spelling Thesaurus** on page 182 as you revise.

EDIT/PROOFREAD: Use editing marks. Then rewrite your paragraph.

PUBLISH: Pretend that you are a TV reporter or eyewitness live at the scene. Read your paragraph to the class.

EDITING MARKS

◯ check spelling

≡ capital letter

／ lowercase letter

⊙ add a period

∧ add

ℛ take out

⌗ indent the paragraph

◯↝ move

For more help, see page 171.

WORDS WITH /s/

1. famous
2. across
3. citizen
4. recess
5. science
6. chance
7. beast
8. son
9. peace
10. decide
11. exciting
12. cellar
13. police
14. beside
15. else
16. glance
17. fence
18. scene
19. press
20. mess

Learn Spelling Patterns

LOOK & SAY Listen for the sounds in each word.

PICTURE Close your eyes. See each word in your mind.

STUDY These spelling words have /s/. In two of the words, /s/ is spelled two ways.

WRITE Sort the words. Which words have /s/ spelled with the letters below?

ss	(1)	(2)	(3)	(4)
s	(5)	(6)	(7)	(8)
se	(9)			
sc	(10)	(11)		
c	(12)	(13)	(14)	(15)
	(16)			
ce	(17)	(18)	(19)	
	(20)	(21)	(22)	

CHECK Did you spell each word correctly? Circle the letter or letters that stand for /s/.

Pattern Power

How can /s/ be spelled at the beginning of a word? (23) or (24) or (25)

How can /s/ be spelled at the end of a word?
(26) or (27) or (28) or (29)

Other Words

Write words you would like to add to this week's list.

_____ _____ _____ _____ _____

Practice Word Meanings

Synonyms

Write the spelling word that is a **synonym** for the underlined word in each sentence below.

1. I think it is <u>thrilling</u> to pretend. ____
2. Sometimes, I pretend I have captured a horrible <u>animal</u>. ____
3. I put the creature in my <u>basement</u>. ____
4. Every hour, I <u>look</u> at it. ____
5. I become <u>well-known</u> when my story is in the papers. ____
6. My picture appears <u>next to</u> the story. ____
7. Tomorrow, I will pretend something <u>different</u>. ____

Challenge Words • *Social Studies*

Write the challenge word that best completes each sentence. Use the **Spelling Dictionary** on page 214 to help you. Circle the spelling of /s/.

8. All the visitors live in a nearby ____.
9. The judge makes sure that people receive ____.
10. The ____ makes the laws for the state.
11. We attended a marriage ____.
12. At the first meeting, we planned the second ____.

ceremony
session
congress
justice
district

Spelling Tip

Here are some hints for spelling /s/ followed by a vowel.

✦ The sound /s/ followed by *a, o,* or *u* is always spelled *s*.

✦ The sound /s/ is spelled *c* only when *c* is followed by *i, e,* or *y*.

Which words on your spelling list follow these rules?

List Words

famous
across
citizen
recess
science
chance
beast
son
peace
decide
exciting
cellar
police
beside
else
glance
fence
scene
press
mess

Challenge Words

ceremony
session
congress
justice
district

Review Words

pass
asleep
race
sorry

Build Vocabulary

Finding Base Words

■ Write the spelling word that is the base word of each word listed below.

1. peaceful _____
2. pressed _____
3. beastly _____
4. chances _____
5. scenes _____

6. undecided _____
7. fences _____
8. recesses _____
9. sons _____
10. messes _____

■ Use the words you wrote to complete the following sentences.

11. What can people do to bring about world _____?
12. I have decided to clean up the _____ in my room.
13. My aunt painted the _____ in front of our house.
14. I appear in the first _____ in our class play.

Review Words

Write the review words that have /s/ spelled with the letters below.

s 15. _____
   16. _____
ce 17. _____
ss 18. _____

Write a review word that has the same number of syllables and the same spelling of /s/ as each of the list words below.

19. mess _____
20. famous _____   21. _____
22. peace _____

pass
asleep
race
sorry

T A K E   H O M E

Write your spelling words in short lists. Each list should be in alphabetical order. Circle the spelling of /s/ in each word. Use your lists to practice at home.

Apply Spelling Skills

Dictionary Skills

The symbol ə stands for a vowel sound called a *schwa*. The schwa sound occurs in many syllables that are not accented. For example, the *o* in *police* and the *ou* in *famous* are spellings of /ə/. Write the list word that each respelling below stands for. Then circle the letter or letters that spell the schwa sound in each word. Use the **Spelling Dictionary** on page 214 to help you.

1. (sel′ər) _____
2. (ə krôs′) _____
3. (sit′ə zən) _____
4. (sī′əns) _____

Proofreading

Check for spelling, capital letters, and punctuation. Then rewrite the paragraph. There are six mistakes.

> i'm writing an exsiting news story about my dog Ruff. Ruff got trapped in a neighbor's celler The neighbor heard him bark and decided to call the polise for help. Now Ruff is famus.

Writing • *About Social Studies*

PREWRITE: List some interesting things in your town. You might include activities, news events, or places of interest.

DRAFT: Write a news article about one item on your list. Tell *who, what, why, where,* and *when* about the topic.

REVISE: Is your article interesting? Does it describe your choice completely? Use the **Spelling Thesaurus** on page 182 as you revise.

EDIT/PROOFREAD: Check your article for spelling, grammar, and punctuation. Then rewrite your paragraph.

PUBLISH: Assemble the class's articles into a newspaper.

EDITING MARKS

◯ check spelling
≡ capital letter
/ lowercase letter
⊙ add a period
∧ add
✀ take out
¶ indent the paragraph
↻ move

For more help, see page 171.

15

Words with /ou/

PHONICS PATTERNS

1. pound
2. powder
3. owl
4. underground
5. scout
6. outdoors
7. downtown
8. aloud
9. allow
10. however
11. stout
12. county
13. frown
14. growl
15. bounce
16. dollhouse
17. trout
18. noun
19. tower
20. gown

Learn Spelling Patterns

LOOK & SAY Listen for the sounds in each word.

PICTURE Close your eyes. See each word in your mind.

STUDY These spelling words have /ou/.

WRITE Sort the words. Which words have /ou/ spelled with the letters below?

ou (1) ___ (2) ___ (3) ___
(4) ___ (5) ___ (6) ___
(7) ___ (8) ___ (9) ___
(10) ___ (11) ___

ow (12) ___ (13) ___ (14) ___
(15) ___ (16) ___ (17) ___
(18) ___ (19) ___ (20) ___

CHECK Did you spell each word correctly? Circle the letters that stand for /ou/.

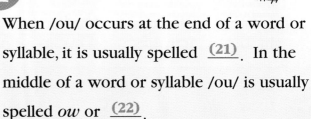

attern Power

When /ou/ occurs at the end of a word or syllable, it is usually spelled (21) ___ . In the middle of a word or syllable /ou/ is usually spelled *ow* or (22) ___ .

Other Words

Write words you would like to add to this week's list.

___ ___ ___ ___ ___

Practice Word Meanings

Antonyms and Compound Words

Write the spelling word that is the **antonym,** or means the opposite, of each word below.

1. countryside ____
2. forbid ____
3. smile ____
4. thin ____
5. silently ____
6. indoors ____

Make a compound word. Combine a word in Column A with a word in Column B.

A	B	
doll	ground	7. ____
down	ever	8. ____
under	house	9. ____
how	town	10. ____

Challenge Words • *Science*

Write the challenge word that best answers each question. Use the **Spelling Dictionary** on page 214 to help you. Circle the letters that spell /ou/.

11. Where can plants and seedlings grow? ____
12. What swims in the sea? ____
13. Which way does water flow? ____
14. Which animal has a day named after it? ____
15. What might happen on a cloudy day? ____

flounder
groundhog
greenhouse
shower
downstream

Spelling Tip

Sometimes you can hear a small word that you know in a longer word. You can use the small word to help you spell the longer word. For example:

✦ Listen to the word *county.* You can hear the small word *count.*

✦ Add the ending *y.* **count + y = county**

Find other small words in the new words on your spelling list. Use them to help you remember how to spell the new words.

List Words

pound
powder
owl
underground
scout
outdoors
downtown
aloud
allow
however
stout
county
frown
growl
bounce
dollhouse
trout
noun
tower
gown

Challenge Words

flounder
groundhog
greenhouse
shower
downstream

Review Words

mouth
hour
crown
clown

Build Vocabulary

Adding -ed and -ing

■ Form the past tense of a verb by adding -ed to the verb. Add -ing to a verb to show that an action is continuing.

growl + **ed**   The dog **growled** yesterday.

growl + **ing**   The dog is **growling** right now.

Add -ed and -ing to the words below. If a word ends with e, you may have to drop the final e before adding the ending.

	-ed	-ing
1. frown	____	____
2. tower	____	____
3. bounce	____	____
4. allow	____	____
5. scout	____	____
6. pound	____	____
7. powder	____	____

Review Words

Write the review words that have /ou/ spelled with the letters below. Circle the letters that stand for /ou/ in each word.

ou 8. ____   **ow** 10. ____

9. ____   11. ____

Write the review words that have /ou/ spelled the same way as the list words below.

trout 12. ____   frown 14. ____

13. ____   15. ____

*mouth
hour
crown
clown*

TAKE HOME

Write your spelling words in two lists: words that are five letters or less and words that are six letters or more. Circle the spelling of /ou/ in each word. Use your lists to practice at home.

Apply Spelling Skills

Dictionary Skills

Imagine that the pairs of words in dark type are **guide words** on a dictionary page. Write the spelling word that could be found on each page.

1. **noisy/octopus** ____
2. **travel/twice** ____
3. **over/pack** ____
4. **alley/along** ____
5. **furious/great** ____
6. **circle/cow** ____

Pattern Power

Look at the list words you just wrote.

- Circle the letters that spell /ou/ in each word.

Proofreading

Check for spelling, capital letters, and punctuation. Then rewrite the paragraph. There are six mistakes.

What do you hear in the great owtdoors You may hear a bear groel or an owl hoot. You might hear trowt splashing in a stream. What would happen if you said alowd, Hello"?

Writing • *About Science*

PREWRITE: List some animals, birds, and fish.

DRAFT: Choose three creatures whose sounds interest you. Write a poem that describes the calls these animals make.

REVISE: Reread your poem aloud. Did you use words that are colorful and fun to hear? Use the **Spelling Thesaurus** on page 182 as you revise.

EDIT/PROOFREAD: Use editing marks to correct your poem and then rewrite it.

PUBLISH: Have a "calls of the wild" day. Read your poem aloud.

EDITING MARKS

⬭ check spelling

≡ capital letter

/ lowercase letter

⊙ add a period

∧ add

✄ take out

¶ indent the paragraph

↻ move

For more help, see page 171.

WORDS WITH /ô/ or /ôr/

PHONICS PATTERNS

1. hawk
2. daughter
3. toward
4. form
5. torn
6. brought
7. already
8. always
9. important
10. forty
11. board
12. author
13. report
14. cord
15. awful
16. haul
17. sauce
18. roar
19. office
20. offer

Learn Spelling Patterns

LOOK & SAY   Listen for the sounds in each word.

PICTURE   Close your eyes. See each word in your mind.

STUDY   These spelling words have /ô/ or /ôr/.

WRITE   Sort the words. Which words have /ô/ spelled with the letters below?

a   (1)   (2)
augh   (3)
au   (4)   (5)   (6)
aw   (7)   (8)
o   (9)   (10)
ough   (11)

Which words have /ôr/ spelled with the letters below?

or   (12)   (13)   (14)   (15)   (16)   (17)
oar   (18)   (19)
ar   (20)

CHECK   Did you spell each word correctly? Circle the letters that stand for /ô/ or /ôr/.

Pattern Power

How can /ô/ be spelled? (21) or (22) or (23) or (24) or (25) or (26)

How can /ôr/ be spelled? (27) or (28) or (29)

Other Words

Write words you would like to add to this week's list.

_____ _____ _____ _____ _____

Practice Word Meanings

Rhyming Words

Write a spelling word to complete each sentence below. The last two words in each sentence should rhyme.

1. A yellow vegetable with a rip in it is _torn_ corn.
2. A car full of things from a shopping trip is a mall ____.
3. If you don't know much about your topic, write a short ____.
4. The number one salsa is boss ____.
5. Heavy string with nothing to do is bored ____.
6. The sound a lion makes at night is a ____ snore.
7. If a plank flew away, you might say the ____ soared.

Challenge Words • Health

Write the challenge words that match the definitions. Use the **Spelling Dictionary** on page 214 to help you. Circle the spelling of /ô/ or /ôr/.

8. Close care; watchfulness. ____
9. Having a rough or harsh, deep sound. ____
10. The state of being painful. ____
11. A body part that does a specific job. ____
12. Injury caused by exposure to extreme cold. ____

organ
caution
soreness
frostbite
hoarse

Spelling Tip

Sometimes you can hear small words or word parts that you know how to spell in a longer word. These words or word parts can help you spell the longer word. Try this with the word *offer.*

+ Say the word out loud.
+ Listen for the smaller word *off.*
+ Listen for the word part *er.*

   off + er = offer

List Words

hawk
daughter
toward
form
torn
brought
already
always
important
forty
board
author
report
cord
awful
haul
sauce
roar
office
offer

Challenge Words

organ
caution
soreness
frostbite
hoarse

Review Words

law
sport
song
order

Build Vocabulary

Forming Words by Adding -s

■ You know how to make a noun plural by adding -s. An -s ending on a verb means that the subject of the sentence is *third person singular—he, she,* or *it—* and that the action is happening in the present.

They *board* the plane.

He *boards* the plane.

Add -s to the nouns and verbs below.

Nouns		Verbs	
1. hawk	____	6. roar	____
2. daughter	____	7. report	____
3. author	____	8. haul	____
4. sauce	____	9. offer	____
5. office	____	10. form	____

■ Use words you made to complete these sentences.

11. The cook's ____ are a tasty treat.

12. He ____ round cookies with the top of a glass.

Review Words

Write the review words that have the sounds /ô/ or /ôr/. Circle the letters that stand for /ô/ or /ôr/ in each word.

/ô/ 13. ____

14. ____

/ôr/ 15. ____

16. ____

law
sport
song
order

TAKE HOME

Write your spelling words in two lists: words with one syllable and words with more than one syllable. Circle the spelling of /ô/ or /ôr/ in each word. Use your lists to practice at home.

Apply Spelling Skills

Dictionary Skills

The **respelling**, used together with the pronunciation key, tells you how to say a word. Write the list words for the respellings below. Use the pronunciation key on page 214 of the **Spelling Dictionary** to help you.

1. (tə wôrd′ or tôrd) _____

2. (ôl red′ē) _____

3. (brôt) _____

4. (ô′fəl) _____

5. (tôrn) _____

Proofreading

Check spelling, capital letters, and punctuation. Then rewrite the paragraph. There are six mistakes.

> The awthor read from her new health book Fourty people listened quietly. She made some impourtant points about ending world hunger. her readings are alwaes popular.

EDITING
MARKS

⬭ check spelling

≡ capital letter

╱ lowercase letter

⊙ add a period

∧ add

✄ take out

¶ indent the paragraph

↻ move

For more help, see page 171.

Writing • *About Health*

PREWRITE: Make a list of healthful foods.

DRAFT: Write a menu for a healthful meal using foods from your list. Try to make your meal interesting as well as healthful.

REVISE: Have you created a balanced, enjoyable meal?

EDIT/PROOFREAD: Use editing marks to correct spelling, capital letters, and punctuation. Write a clean copy.

PUBLISH: Collect a photocopy of each classmate's menu. Take the menus home and share them with your family.

Words With /är/

PHONICS PATTERNS

1. farther
2. army
3. hardly
4. starve
5. carpet
6. cart
7. argue
8. scarf
9. marbles
10. barnyard
11. cardboard
12. barber
13. carnival
14. garbage
15. garden
16. farmer
17. spark
18. harm
19. harsh
20. yarn

Learn Spelling Patterns

LOOK & SAY Listen for the sounds in each word.

PICTURE Close your eyes. See each word in your mind.

STUDY These spelling words have /är/.

WRITE Sort the words. Which one-syllable words have /är/ spelled *ar*?

ar (1) (2) (3) (4)
    (5) (6) (7)

Which words with more than one syllable have /är/ spelled *ar*?

ar (8) (9) (10) (11)
    (12) (13) (14)
    (15) (16) (17)
    (18) (19) (20)

CHECK Did you spell each word correctly? Circle the letters that stand for /är/.

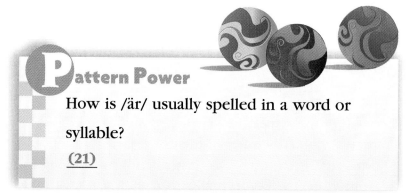

Pattern Power

How is /är/ usually spelled in a word or syllable?

(21)

Other Words

Write words you would like to add to this week's list.

_____ _____ _____ _____ _____

Practice Word Meanings

Synonyms and Antonyms

You know that **synonyms** are words with the same or nearly the same meaning and that **antonyms** are words with opposite meanings.

Write the spelling word that is an antonym for each word below.

1. closer _____
2. gentle _____
3. help _____
4. feed _____
5. always _____

Write a spelling word that is a synonym for each word below.

6. flash _____
7. wagon _____
8. festival _____
9. farmyard _____
10. rug _____

Challenge Words • *Social Studies*

Write the challenge word that best completes each sentence. Use the **Spelling Dictionary** on page 214 to help you. Circle the spelling of /är/.

11. Mr. Edgars has a small jam shop at the _____.
12. Jodi put a _____ on her horse.
13. The farm's main crop is _____.
14. There is an _____ about the rodeo in the newspaper.
15. The town _____ says that no one can fish in the river.

harness
barley
article
bazaar
charter

Spelling Tip

Some words with unusual letter combinations can be hard to spell. For example, the word *argue* ends with a silent *e* that some people forget to add. Try this to get a hard word right:

✦ Figure out which part of the word gives you trouble.
✦ Pay special attention to that part of the word every time you read or write it.

List Words

farther
army
hardly
starve
carpet
cart
argue
scarf
marbles
barnyard
cardboard
barber
carnival
garbage
garden
farmer
spark
harm
harsh
yarn

Challenge Words

harness
barley
article
bazaar
charter

Review Words

apart
card
art
shark

Build Vocabulary

Rhyming Words

■ Follow the directions to write the word that rhymes with each spelling word below.

1. cart   –   **c**   +   **p**   =   _____
2. harm   –   **h**   +   **f**   =   _____
3. starve   –   **st**   +   **c**   =   _____
4. spark   –   **sp**   +   **b**   =   _____
5. yarn   –   **y**   +   **b**   =   _____
6. garden   –   **g**   +   **h**   =   _____
7. harsh   –   **h**   +   **m**   =   _____
8. marbles   –   **m**   +   **g**   =   _____

Review Words

Write the review words in alphabetical order. Circle the letters that spell /är/.

9. _____

10. _____

11. _____

12. _____

Look at the list words below. Write the review word that begins with the same letter and has the same number of syllables as the list word.

13. scarf _____

14. argue _____

15. cart _____

Write the review word that you see within the list word below.

16. cart _____

apart
card
art
shark

T A K E H O M E

Write your spelling words in short lists according to their first letters. Circle the letters that spell /är/ in each word. Use your lists to practice at home.

72

hawk
toward
brought
already
forty
board
author
report
sauce
offer

Lesson 16

Words with /ô/ spelled

a 32. ____

au 33. ____

34. ____

aw 35. ____

o 36. ____

ough 37. ____

Words with /ôr/ spelled

or 38. ____

39. ____

oar 40. ____

ar 41. ____

army
cart
argue
scarf
marbles
carnival
garbage
farmer
harm
harsh

Lesson 17

Words with /är/ spelled ar in alphabetical order

42. ____

43. ____

44. ____

45. ____

46. ____

47. ____

48. ____

49. ____

50. ____

51. ____

Spelling Tip

Finding small words or word parts in longer words can help you spell words with more than one syllable. Try this with the word *farmer.*

✦ Say the word out loud.

✦ Listen for the smaller word *farm.*

✦ Listen for the word part *er.*

Rewrite each spelling word below. Circle one or two smaller words within each list word you wrote.

across
beside
carnival
already

1. carnival ____

2. already ____

3. across ____

4. beside ____

75

Word Meaning Mixed Review

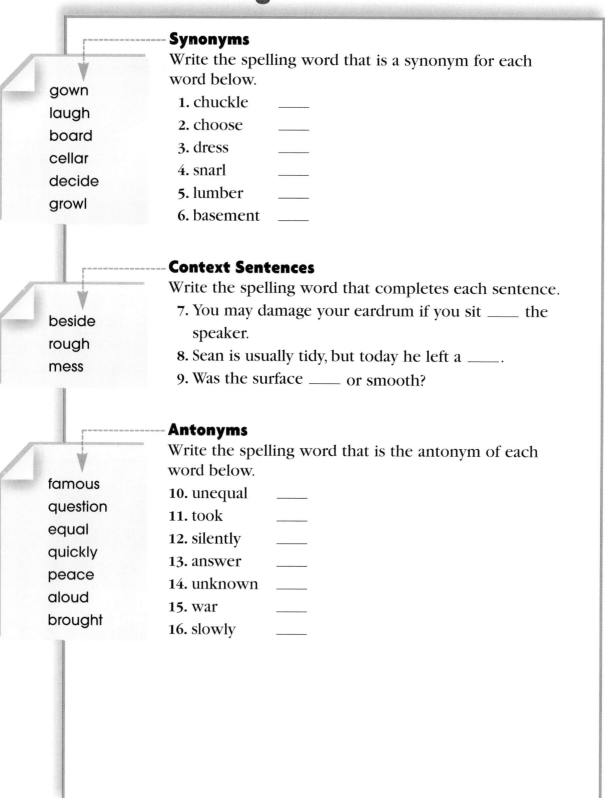

gown
laugh
board
cellar
decide
growl

Synonyms
Write the spelling word that is a synonym for each word below.

1. chuckle _____
2. choose _____
3. dress _____
4. snarl _____
5. lumber _____
6. basement _____

beside
rough
mess

Context Sentences
Write the spelling word that completes each sentence.

7. You may damage your eardrum if you sit _____ the speaker.
8. Sean is usually tidy, but today he left a _____.
9. Was the surface _____ or smooth?

famous
question
equal
quickly
peace
aloud
brought

Antonyms
Write the spelling word that is the antonym of each word below.

10. unequal _____
11. took _____
12. silently _____
13. answer _____
14. unknown _____
15. war _____
16. slowly _____

Vocabulary Mixed Review

Write Singular and Plural Possessives

Write the singular and plural possessive forms for each noun below.

	Singular Possessive	Plural Possessive
1. elephant	*elephant's*	*elephants'*
2. graph	_____	_____
3. scene	_____	_____
4. scout	_____	_____
5. gown	_____	_____
6. hawk	_____	_____
7. powder	_____	_____
8. farmer	_____	_____
9. scarf	_____	_____
10. author	_____	_____
11. cellar	_____	_____
12. dollhouse	_____	_____

Dictionary Skills

Use the pronunciation key in the **Spelling Dictionary** on page 214 to write the list words for the respellings below.

1. (rüf) _____
2. (ə krôs′) _____
3. (fā′məs) _____
4. (koun′tē) _____
5. (är′mē) _____
6. (pə lēs′) _____

Spelling and Writing

TOPIC

To compare and contrast means to list similarities and differences between two things. This can make your writing more exciting and more informative. The writer uses specific examples to compare and contrast.

MAIN IDEA

CONTRAST DETAILS

COMPARISON DETAILS

The African elephant and the polar bear are quite different, though they share some traits. Elephants, who travel in herds, eat plants and do not harm other animals. Polar bears usually live alone and feed mainly on seals and smaller mammals. Both of these huge beasts are equally fond of water. Elephants drink about forty gallons of water at a time. Polar bears hunt in the sea. Both animals move quickly. A polar bear swims at about six miles per hour. An elephant walks along at about five miles per hour.

WRITING TIPS!!

Comparison/Contrast

- State the main idea at the beginning.
- Present comparisons in a clear order.
- Give details and examples to support your main idea.

Now write your own compare and contrast paragraph. Write about two animals. Try to use some of the spelling words in your description.

PREWRITE: Choose two animals to compare and contrast. Then list similarities and differences.

DRAFT: Write a paragraph comparing and contrasting the two animals. Begin with a sentence that introduces the two animals you are writing about. Include facts about each animal.

REVISE: Read over your paragraph. Did you include all the similarities and differences that you listed?

EDIT/PROOFREAD: Use editing marks to correct your capitalization, spelling, and punctuation. Rewrite your paragraph neatly.

PUBLISH: Find or draw a picture of each animal to illustrate your paragraph. Add your page to a class "animal facts" book.

SPELLING FUN
CUMULATIVE REVIEW

MAKE A HAIKU

- A haiku is a poem that has seventeen syllables in three lines, five in the first and last lines and seven in the middle line. Japanese haiku often describe something in nature or refer to a season of the year.

- Write your own haiku. Choose some words from Lessons 1–11 to include in your poem.

- Use your best handwriting to copy your poem on a piece of unlined paper.

- Draw a picture to go with your haiku. Contribute your poem and drawing to a class book of haiku.

PLAY WORD CODE

- With a partner, write each letter of the alphabet and give each letter a different number. Number the letters beginning with 1.

- Use the numbers to send a coded message to your partner. Use at least four words from Lessons 13–17 in your message.

- Use the code to figure out what your partner's numbered message spells in letters. When you are both finished, check to see that you and your partner have decoded each message correctly.

1 2 3
a b c

SPELLING BEE

- Work in two teams. Each team should write twenty words from Lessons 1–17 on separate cards.

- Team A challenges Team B to spell a word from Team A's stack. Team members should take turns spelling the words.

- If a word is spelled correctly, the card is taken out of the pile. If the word is spelled incorrectly, the card is returned to the bottom of the pile and the team that spelled the word incorrectly loses its turn.

- The first team to finish the other team's pile wins!

19

WORDS WITH /ûr/

PHONICS PATTERNS

1. perfect
2. furniture
3. birth
4. further
5. germ
6. worth
7. turkey
8. purpose
9. worst
10. firm
11. sir
12. curl
13. skirt
14. dessert
15. insert
16. fern
17. curve
18. burst
19. nurse
20. worry

Learn Spelling Patterns

LOOK & SAY Listen for the sounds in each word.

PICTURE Close your eyes. See each word in your mind.

STUDY These spelling words have /ûr/.

WRITE Sort the words. Which words have /ûr/ spelled with the letters below?

ur   (1)   (2)   (3)   (4)
     (5)   (6)   (7)   (8)

or   (9)   (10)

er   (11)   (12)   (13)   (14)   (15)

ir   (16)   (17)   (18)   (19)

orr   (20)

CHECK Did you spell each word correctly? Circle the letter or letters that stand for /ûr/.

Pattern Power

How can /ûr/ be spelled? (21) or (22) or (23) or (24) or (25)

Other Words

Write words you would like to add to this week's list.

_____ _____ _____ _____ _____

Practice Word Meanings

Related Meanings

Write the word from each pair that relates to the word in dark print.

1. **bend** curve carve   *curve*
2. **gentleman** sir sore   ____
3. **chairs** rooms furniture   ____
4. **terrible** worst worth   ____
5. **plant** furniture fern   ____
6. **best** perfect project   ____
7. **add** insist insert   ____
8. **explode** burst brush   ____

Challenge Words • *Health*

Write the challenge word that best completes each sentence. Use the **Spelling Dictionary** on page 214 to help you. Circle the spelling of /ûr/ in each word.

9. He had ____ to remove his tonsils.
10. The loud claps of thunder made me feel ____.
11. Exercising daily will improve your blood ____.
12. The hospital ____ was filled with newborn babies.
13. Salt has been used as a ____ for thousands of years.

nervous
preservative
circulation
surgery
nursery

Spelling Tip

Here's a rule you can count on almost all of the time.

✦ When you hear /ûr/ after /w/ at the beginning of a word, /ûr/ is spelled *or*.

Find some spelling words that follow this rule.

perfect

furniture

birth

further

germ

worth

turkey

purpose

worst

firm

sir

curl

skirt

dessert

insert

fern

curve

burst

nurse

worry

Challenge Words

nervous

preservative

circulation

surgery

nursery

Build Vocabulary

Word Endings

■ You know that when a word ends with *y* after a consonant, you often change the *y* to *i* before adding an ending. When a word ends with *y* after a vowel, do not change the base word to add an ending.

donkey + s = donkeys

Add the given endings to each spelling word below.

1. turkey + s ____

2. worry + ed ____

3. worth + y ____

4. germ + s ____

5. curl + ed ____

■ Use words you made to complete these sentences.

6. He was ____ about finishing his work on time.

7. It takes two ____ to feed my huge family.

■ Follow the directions to write the word that rhymes with each spelling word below.

8. insert − in + des = ____

9. burst − bu + wo = ____

10. worth − wo + bi = ____

11. germ − ge + fi = ____

Review Words

Write the review words that have /ûr/ spelled with the letters below.

er 12. ____   **or** 14. ____

ir 13. ____   **ur** 15. ____

burn
world
person
thirsty

TAKE HOME

Write your spelling words in three lists: nouns, verbs, and adjectives. Some words might fit on more than one list. Circle the spelling of /ûr/. Use your lists to practice at home.

Apply Spelling Skills

Dictionary Skills

You know that many words have multiple meanings. The dictionary numbers the different meanings. Look up these entry words in the **Spelling Dictionary** on page 214. Read the meaning for each word. Write 1 or 2 to show which meaning of the underlined word is used in each sentence below. Then rewrite the spelling word.

1. The baby <u>burst</u> into tears. ____ ____
2. It was the <u>birth</u> of a new era. ____ ____

Pattern Power

Look at the list words you just wrote.

• Circle the letters that spell /ûr/ in each word.

Proofreading

Proofread the paragraph. Check for spelling, capital letters, and punctuation. Then rewrite the paragraph. There are six mistakes.

My mother works in a Hospital as a nirse. She calms people who wurry about their health. That is not her only purrpose She has made firther contributions to improve health care.

EDITING MARKS

⬭ check spelling

= capital letter

/ lowercase letter

⊙ add a period

∧ add

⤴ take out

¶ indent the paragraph

↻ move

For more help, see page 171.

Writing • *About Health*

PREWRITE: List some things you do that keep you in good health, such as taking vitamins and getting enough sleep.

DRAFT: Write a paragraph about one item on your list.

REVISE: Reread your paragraph. Use the **Spelling Thesaurus** on page 182 to help you revise.

EDIT/PROOFREAD: Use editing marks. Then write a clean copy.

PUBLISH: Collect class paragraphs into a "health handbook."

20

Words With /ù/ and /yù/

PHONICS PATTERNS

1. woolen
2. cure
3. handful
4. wooden
5. fully
6. during
7. bull
8. sure
9. furious
10. tour
11. footprint
12. cookies
13. goodness
14. overlook
15. pulley
16. crooked
17. bulldozer
18. curious
19. butcher
20. pure

Learn Spelling Patterns

LOOK & SAY Listen for the sounds in each word.

PICTURE Close your eyes. See each word in your mind.

STUDY These spelling words have /ù/ or /yù/.

WRITE Sort the words. Which words have /ù/ spelled with the letters below?

u (1) _____ (2) _____ (3) _____ (4) _____
   (5) _____ (6) _____ (7) _____

u-e (8) _____

oo (9) _____ (10) _____ (11) _____ (12) _____
    (13) _____ (14) _____ (15) _____

ou (16) _____

Which words have /yù/ spelled with the letters below?

u (17) _____ (18) _____

u-e (19) _____ (20) _____

CHECK Did you spell each word correctly? Circle the letter or letters that stand for these sounds.

Pattern Power

How can /ù/ be spelled?

(21) _____ or (22) _____ or (23) _____ or (24) _____ How can /yù/ be spelled? (25) _____ or (26) _____

Other Words

Write words you would like to add to this week's list.

_____ _____ _____ _____ _____

Practice Word Meanings

Words in Context

Write a spelling word to complete each sentence.

1. The doctor set my broken arm so that it would not be ____.
2. My friend was ____ when I lost her favorite hat.
3. Do you ____ understand what Virginia said?
4. The scientist discovered a ____ for the disease.
5. Gabriel flattened the building with a big ____.
6. There are a lot of people, so don't ____ Adam.
7. We went to buy meat from the ____.
8. On our ____ of France, we saw the Eiffel Tower.
9. The ____ charged at the bullfighter's cape.
10. "My ____, you are tall!" said my grandmother.

Challenge Words • *The Arts*

Write the challenge word that best answers each question. Use the **Spelling Dictionary** on page 214 to help you. Circle the spelling of /ù/ or /yù/.

11. Where would you look to find a recipe? ____
12. To sit on something soft, what could you make? ____
13. What kind of craft is a carpenter good at? ____
14. Where can you store sweaters and socks? ____
15. What do you call something that lasts a long time? ____

bureau
cushion
woodwork
cookbook
durable

Spelling Tip

Words that are related in meaning are often related in spelling.

+ The words *pull* and *pulley* are related in meaning.
+ When you need to write the word *pulley*, remember to add *-ey* to *pull*.
+ How is the meaning of *pull* related to the meaning of *pulley*?

List Words

woolen
cure
handful
wooden
fully
during
bull
sure
furious
tour
footprint
cookies
goodness
overlook
pulley
crooked
bulldozer
curious
butcher
pure

Challenge Words

bureau
cushion
woodwork
cookbook
durable

Review Words

wolf
push
stood
wool

Build Vocabulary

Prefixes

■ The prefixes *un-* and *im-* mean "not" or "the opposite of."

im + possible = impossible, meaning "not possible"

■ Add the given prefix to each word below, to make a word with the given meaning.

un-	*im-*
1. not sure ____	2. not pure ____

■ Use words you made to complete these sentences.

3. We can't drink the water because it is ____.

4. I am ____ of the answer to that question.

Review Words

Write the words that have /ù/ spelled with the letters below.

u   5. ____

oo   6. ____

      7. ____

o   8. ____

wolf
push
stood
wool

Read each list word below. Then write the review word or words that have /ù/ spelled the same way.

butcher   9. ____

crooked   10. ____

           11. ____

Write this list word. Then circle the review word you see in it.

12. woolen ____

TAKE HOME

Write your spelling words in three lists: one-, two-, and three-syllable words. Circle the spelling of /ù/ or /yù/ in each word. Use your lists to practice at home.

Apply Spelling Skills

Dictionary Skills

Dictionaries often use an **example sentence** to explain the meaning of a word. If the meaning is not clear after you have read a word's definition, look for an example sentence. Look up the list words below in the **Spelling Dictionary** on page 214. Write the first example sentence given for each word. If two sentences are given, write the first one.

1. **pulley** ——
2. **footprint** ——
3. **curious** ——

Proofreading

Check for spelling, capital letters, and punctuation. Then rewrite the paragraph. There are six mistakes.

> During winter a handfull of students started a new project. They created large cookys, cakes, and fruit out of different materials Some pieces were woodin. Others were made of clay

Writing • *About the Arts*

PREWRITE: List some art objects you have made, such as necklaces, clay animals, or model airplanes.

DRAFT: Choose your favorite art project. Write step-by-step directions telling how you made the object.

REVISE: Make sure your directions are in the correct order.

EDIT/PROOFREAD: Use editing marks to correct your spelling and punctuation.

PUBLISH: Make a classroom arts folder. Choose someone else's art project, and try to do it yourself.

EDITING MARKS

⬯ check spelling
= capital letter
/ lowercase letter
⊙ add a period
∧ add
℘ take out
❡ indent the paragraph
↻ move

For more help, see page 171.

21

WORDS WITH /oi/

PHONICS PATTERNS

1. voyage
2. noisy
3. moist
4. pointed
5. avoid
6. royalty
7. choice
8. destroy
9. annoy
10. employ
11. joint
12. enjoyment
13. topsoil
14. coil
15. disappoint
16. oily
17. soybean
18. broil
19. loyal
20. appointment

Learn Spelling Patterns

LOOK & SAY   Listen for the sounds in each word.

PICTURE   Close your eyes. See each word in your mind.

STUDY   These spelling words have /oi/.

WRITE   Sort the words. Which words have /oi/ spelled with the letters below?

oi   (1) ____ (2) ____ (3) ____
(4) ____ (5) ____ (6) ____
(7) ____ (8) ____ (9) ____
(10) ____ (11) ____ (12) ____

oy   (13) ____ (14) ____ (15) ____
(16) ____ (17) ____ (18) ____
(19) ____ (20) ____

CHECK   Did you spell each word correctly? Circle the letters that stand for /oi/.

Pattern Power

How is /oi/ usually spelled in the middle of a word or syllable? (21) ____ How is /oi/ usually spelled at the end of a word or syllable? (22) ____

Other Words

Write words you would like to add to this week's list.

____ ____ ____ ____ ____

Practice Word Meanings

Synonyms and Antonyms

Write the spelling word that is a **synonym** or an **antonym** for each word below. Then write *synonym* or *antonym* after the word.

1. faithful ___ ___
2. cook ___ ___
3. dry ___ ___
4. journey ___ ___
5. pleasure ___ ___
6. selection ___ ___
7. quiet ___ ___
8. dull ___ ___

Challenge Words • *Science*

Write the challenge word that best answers each question. Use the **Spelling Dictionary** on page 214 to help you. Circle the spelling of /oi/.

9. What is a small planet that circles the sun? ___
10. What makes something wet? ___
11. What is like a fingerprint? ___
12. What is a word for when liquid boils? ___
13. What do you put on your skin to heal it? ___

asteroid
moisture
boiling point
voiceprint
ointment

pelling Tip

Sometimes you can hear a small word that you know how to spell in a longer word. The small word can help you spell the longer word.

✦ Say the word *enjoyment*. You can hear the small word *joy* in the middle.
✦ Add the beginning letters *en*
✦ Add the ending letters *ment*.

en + joy + ment = enjoyment

Find other new words on your spelling list that have small words to help you spell the new words.

voyage

noisy

moist

pointed

avoid

royalty

choice

destroy

annoy

employ

joint

enjoyment

topsoil

coil

disappoint

oily

soybean

broil

loyal

appointment

Challenge Words

asteroid

moisture

boiling point

voiceprint

ointment

Review Words

boy

noise

joy

point

Build Vocabulary

Suffixes

■ The suffix -*ment* means "the act of" or "state of being."

agree + **ment** = agreement

Write the list words that have the suffix -*ment*.

1. _____ 2. _____

Add -*ment* to the list words below.

3. employ _____ 4. disappoint _____

■ The suffix -*ness* means "the quality or state of being."

cute + **ness** = cuteness

Add -*ness* to the list words below. You may need to change *y* to *i* before adding this ending.

5. noisy _____ 6. oily _____

■ Use words you made to complete these sentences.

7. Her sad look showed her _____.

8. I could not hear because of the crowd's _____.

Review Words

Write the review words that have /oi/ spelled with the letters below.

oy 9. _____   **oi** 11. _____

10. _____   12. _____

Write the review word you see in each list word below.

13. pointed _____

14. enjoyment _____

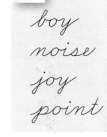

boy

noise

joy

point

TAKE HOME

Write your spelling words in three lists: nouns, verbs, and adjectives. Some words may fit on more than one list. Circle the spelling of /oi/ in each word. Use your lists to practice at home.

Apply Spelling Skills

Dictionary Skills

Write the list words for the respellings below. Use the pronunciation key in the **Spelling Dictionary** on page 215 to help you.

1. (joint)   _____
2. (tŏp′soil′) _____
3. (koil)   _____
4. (ə noi′)   _____
5. (roi′əl tē) _____
6. (soi′bēn′) _____

Pattern Power

Look at the list words you just wrote.

• Circle the letters that spell /oi/ in each word.

Proofreading

Check for spelling, capital letters, and punctuation marks. Then rewrite the paragraph. There are six mistakes.

> You and I have a choyce about the garbage we make. we should avoyd wasting foil and paper. we can give old toys to a younger boy or girl Let's save our planet and not destroi it.

Writing • About Science

PREWRITE: List ways you can help the environment.

DRAFT: Choose one thing to do. Write a paragraph that will convince your classmates to join you.

REVISE: Ask a classmate to comment on your paragraph. Use the **Spelling Thesaurus** on page 182 as you revise.

EDIT/PROOFREAD: Use editing marks. Then rewrite your paragraph.

PUBLISH: Post your paragraph on the bulletin board.

EDITING MARKS

◯ check spelling
≡ capital letter
/ lowercase letter
⊙ add a period
∧ add
⊱ take out
⫯ indent the paragraph
↻ move

For more help, see page 171.

22

WORDS WITH /ər/ and /chər/

PHONICS PATTERNS

1. feather
2. honor
3. nature
4. either
5. picture
6. capture
7. motor
8. rather
9. number
10. matter
11. humor
12. neither
13. owner
14. pasture
15. lumber
16. finger
17. danger
18. favor
19. visitor
20. enter

Learn Spelling Patterns

LOOK & SAY Listen for the sounds in each word.

PICTURE Close your eyes. See each word in your mind.

STUDY These spelling words have /ər/ or /chər/.

WRITE Sort the words. Which words have /ər/ spelled with the letters below?

er (1) (2) (3) (4)
(5) (6) (7) (8)
(9) (10) (11)

or (12) (13) (14) (15)
(16)

Which words have /chər/ spelled with the letters below?

ture (17) (18) (19) (20)

CHECK Did you spell each word correctly? Circle the letters that stand for /ər/ or /chər/.

Pattern Power

How can /ər/ be spelled at the end of a word? (21) or (22) How can /chər/ be spelled at the end of a word? (23)

Other Words

Write words you would like to add to this week's list.

_____ _____ _____ _____ _____

Practice Word Meanings

Analogies

Write a spelling word to complete each analogy below.

1. *Write* is to *story* as *draw* is to ____.
2. *Exit* is to *out* as ____ is to *in*.
3. *Water* is to *lake* as *grass* is to ____.
4. *Wind* is to *windmill* as *gasoline* is to ____.
5. *Concrete* is to *sidewalk* as ____ is to *tree house*.
6. *Toe* is to *foot* as ____ is to *hand*.
7. *Fur* is to *cat* as ____ is to *bird*.
8. *Yes* is to *no* as ____ is to ____.

Challenge Words • *Social Studies*

Write the challenge word that best completes each sentence. Use the **Spelling Dictionary** on page 214 to help you. Circle the spelling of /ər/ or /chər/.

9. The ____ saved the cows from the burning barn.
10. Workers ____ products in large factories.
11. Today, the voters of our city will elect a new ____.
12. Certain chemicals can ____ animals and birds.
13. The ship's captain looked for a calm and safe ____.

manufacture
endanger
firefighter
mayor
harbor

Spelling Tip

Here's a spelling rule that you can count on.

✦ When you hear /chər/ at the end of a word, it is usually spelled *ture*.

What spelling words can you find that follow this rule?

feather
honor
nature
either
picture
capture
motor
rather
number
matter
humor
neither
owner
pasture
lumber
finger
danger
favor
visitor
enter

Challenge Words

manufacture
endanger
firefighter
mayor
harbor

Build Vocabulary

Prefixes

■ The prefix *re-* usually means "again."

> ***re*** + appear = reappear, meaning "appear again"

Add *re-* to the words below.

1. enter _____   3. number _____

2. capture _____

■ The prefix *dis-* usually means "not" or "the opposite of."

> ***dis*** + agree = disagree, meaning "not agree"
>
> ***dis*** + appear = disappear, meaning "the opposite of appear"

Add *dis-* to the words below.

4. honor _____   5. favor _____

■ Use words you made to complete these sentences.

6. Please be quiet when you _____ the classroom.

7. The cheating students brought _____ to their class.

Review Words

Write the review words that have /ər/ spelled with the letters below. Circle the letters that spell /ər/ in each word.

er   8. _____

9. _____

or 10. _____

ar 11. _____

mirror
pitcher
silver
dollar

Read each list word below. Then write the review word or words that have /ər/ spelled the same way.

visitor 12. _____   danger 13. _____   14. _____

TAKE HOME

Write your spelling words in alphabetical order. Circle the letters that spell /ər/ or /chər/ in each word. Use your lists to practice spelling the words at home.

Apply Spelling Skills

Dictionary Skills

Write the spelling word that matches the given dictionary definition. Check your answers in the **Spelling Dictionary** on page 214.

1. Chance of injury. ____
2. A person who visits; guest. ____
3. The funny part of something. ____
4. Logs that have been sawed into boards. ____
5. Anything that takes up space and has weight. ____

Proofreading

Check for spelling, capital letters, and punctuation. Then rewrite the paragraph. There are six mistakes.

> My dad is the ownr of a farm. We have a rathur small amount of land. The nachure of our work is very important? Someday our farming methods may help a great numbr of Farmers.

Writing • *About Social Studies*

PREWRITE: List activities you do in both the city and the country.

DRAFT: Write a paragraph about one activity. For example, in the city you separate your trash and then it is collected. In the country, you bring your trash to a dump and then separate it.

REVISE: Have a parent or other adult review your paragraph. Use the **Spelling Thesaurus** on page 182 to help you revise.

EDIT/PROOFREAD: Use editing marks to correct the paragraph.

PUBLISH: Read your paragraph in class.

EDITING MARKS

◯ check spelling
≡ capital letter
/ lowercase letter
⊙ add a period
∧ add
ℊ take out
ℋ indent the paragraph
◯ move

For more help, see page 171.

23

WORDS WITH /əl/

PHONICS PATTERNS

1. terrible
2. general
3. model
4. settle
5. possible
6. gentle
7. jungle
8. hospital
9. simple
10. evil
11. several
12. label
13. level
14. uncle
15. final
16. puddle
17. total
18. festival
19. battle
20. castle

Learn Spelling Patterns

LOOK & SAY   Listen for the sounds in each word.

PICTURE   Close your eyes. See each word in your mind.

STUDY   These spelling words have /əl/.

WRITE   Sort the words. Which words have /əl/ spelled with the letters below?

le
(1)____ (2)____ (3)____ (4)____
(5)____ (6)____ (7)____ (8)____
(9)____ (10)____

al   (11)____ (12)____ (13)____ (14)____
(15)____ (16)____

el   (17)____ (18)____ (19)____

il   (20)____

CHECK   Did you spell each word correctly? Circle the letters that stand for /əl/.

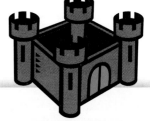

Pattern Power

How can /əl/ be spelled at the end of a word? (21)____ or (22)____ or (23)____ or (24)____

Other Words

Write words you would like to add to this week's list.

_____ _____ _____ _____ _____

Practice Word Meanings

Related Meanings

Write the spelling word that goes with each group of words below.

1. holiday, celebration, carnival _____
2. aunt, cousin, nephew _____
3. flat, even, smooth _____
4. splash, water, trickle _____
5. forest, woods, bushes _____
6. awful, dreadful, alarming _____
7. tag, marker, sticker _____
8. kind, calm, sweet _____
9. harmful, wicked, cruel _____
10. many, some, various _____

Challenge Words • *Social Studies*

Write the challenge word that best completes each sentence. Circle the spelling of /əl/. Use the **Spelling Dictionary** on page 182 to help you.

11. Paris is the _____ of France.
12. A ship is a seagoing _____.
13. The queen was of _____ birth.
14. It is a crime to _____ illegal goods into the United States.
15. The right to vote is a _____ right.

noble
capital
civil
vessel
smuggle

Spelling Tip

Some beginning sounds like /j/ can be spelled more than one way at the beginning of a word.

✦ The sound /j/ followed by *a, o,* or *u* is always spelled *j.*

✦ The sound /j/ is spelled *g* only when *g* is followed by *i, e,* or *y.*

Which spelling words follow these rules?

List Words

terrible
general
model
settle
possible
gentle
jungle
hospital
simple
evil
several
label
level
uncle
final
puddle
total
festival
battle
castle

Challenge Words

noble
capital
civil
vessel
smuggle

Review Words

purple
able
royal
turtle

Build Vocabulary

Related Words

■ How are these words similar in spelling and meaning?

locality   local

Say each word and listen to the sound of the letter *a*. How does the pronunciation of the *a* in *locality* help you to spell the /ə/ sound in *local*?

Write each word. Then write the spelling word that you see in each word. Circle the letter in the longer word that helps you spell the /ə/ sound in the list word. Use the **Spelling Dictionary** on page 214 to help you.

1. totality   _____
2. hospitality _____
3. finality   _____
4. generality _____

■ Use the list words you wrote to complete each sentence.

5. We spent a _____ of thirty dollars.
6. I had my tonsils out in the _____.

Review Words

Write the review words in alphabetical order. Circle the letters that spell /əl/ in each word.

7. _____   9. _____
8. _____   10. _____

Look at each list word below. Then write the review word or words that have /əl/ spelled with the same letters.

jungle 11. _____   12. _____   13. _____
festival 14. _____

purple
able
royal
turtle

⌂ T A K E ⌂ H O M E ▸

Write your spelling words in two lists: two- and three-syllable words. Circle the spelling of /əl/ in each word. Use your lists to practice spelling the words at home.

Apply Spelling Skills

Dictionary Skills

After an entry word's definitions, you may find other forms of the word such as **plurals**, **verb forms**, and **adjective forms**. These types of words contain the entry word plus a word ending, such as *-ing* or *-ed*. Look up the list words below in the **Spelling Dictionary** on page 214. Write the other forms of these entry words.

1. settle _____   _____
2. simple _____   _____
3. battle _____   _____   _____

Proofreading

Check for spelling, capital letters, and punctuation. Then rewrite the paragraph. There are seven mistakes.

> Centuries ago, kings and queens lived in castels In Class, we built a modil of one of these buildings. In genral, they were made of stone? It was possibul for us to use wood instead.

Writing • *About Social Studies*

PREWRITE: List some events in American history, such as the signing of the Declaration of Independence.

DRAFT: Draw a funny or serious cartoon that illustrates one event. Write a caption for your cartoon.

REVISE: Are the details accurate? Do the picture and words show what you want to say?

EDIT/PROOFREAD: Use editing marks to correct your caption. Prepare a clean copy of your cartoon.

PUBLISH: Make a "book of historical cartoons" for your classroom.

EDITING MARKS

◯ check spelling
= capital letter
/ lowercase letter
⊙ add a period
∧ add
✒ take out
¶ indent the paragraph
↻ move

For more help, see page 171.

24 REVIEW Spelling Patterns

Sort the words in each list. Write each word. Circle the spelling pattern.

perfect	**Lesson 19**
furniture	**Words with** /ûr/ **spelled**
birth	
further	ur 1. _____
worst	2. _____
dessert	3. _____
insert	4. _____
curve	ir 5. _____
nurse	
worry	

or 6. _____
er 7. _____
8. _____
9. _____
orr 10. _____

handful	**Lesson 20**
wooden	**Words with** /u̇/ **spelled**
during	
sure	u 11. _____
tour	12. _____
cookies	13. _____
pulley	ou 14. _____
crooked	u-e 15. _____
curious	
pure	

oo 16. _____
17. _____
18. _____

Words with /yu̇/ **spelled**
u 19. _____
u-e 20. _____

voyage	**Lesson 21**
noisy	**Words with** /oi/ **spelled**
moist	
destroy	oi 21. _____
employ	22. _____
joint	23. _____
enjoyment	24. _____
coil	25. _____
disappoint	
loyal	

oy 26. _____
27. _____
28. _____
29. _____
30. _____

feather
nature
picture
motor
rather
owner
finger
danger
favor
visitor

Lesson 22
Words with /ər/ spelled

er 31. ____
32. ____
33. ____
34. ____
35. ____

or 36. ____
37. ____
38. ____

Words with /chər/ spelled

ture 39. ____
40. ____

---

terrible
model
jungle
hospital
evil
uncle
final
puddle
total
castle

Lesson 23
Words with /əl/ spelled

le 41. ____
42. ____
43. ____
44. ____
45. ____

al 46. ____
47. ____
48. ____

el 49. ____

il 50. ____

Spelling Tip

Spelling Long Words

Remember: Long words are easier to spell when you divide them into syllables. Say each of the words respelled below. What syllables do you hear? Listen for prefixes and suffixes you know how to spell. Try writing the words one syllable at a time. Circle any prefix or suffix you find.

hospital
enjoyment
handful

1. /hand′fŭl′/ ____

2. /en joi′mənt/ ____

3. /hos′pit′əl/ ____

Word Meaning Mixed Review

total
voyage
loyal
evil
noisy
curve
castle
terrible
final
worst

Synonyms and Antonyms

Write the spelling word that is a **synonym** or an **antonym** for each word below. Then write synonym or antonym after each word pair.

1. good _____ _____
2. loud _____ _____
3. straight _____ _____
4. whole _____ _____
5. journey _____ _____
6. unfaithful _____ _____
7. palace _____ _____
8. wonderful _____ _____
9. best _____ _____
10. last _____ _____

finger
uncle
crooked
jungle
hospital

Context Sentences

Write a spelling word to complete each sentence below.

11. Lola went to the _____ for an operation.
12. Many wild animals live in the _____.
13. Janet could not straighten the _____ picture.
14. My aunt's husband is my _____.
15. He wore a ring on his _____.

destroy
motor
picture
feather
danger

Related Meanings

Write the spelling word that belongs with each group of words below.

16. tires, hood, trunk _____
17. break, smash, crush _____
18. flood, poison, risk _____
19. beak, wing, bird _____
20. photo, painting, drawing _____

Vocabulary Mixed Review

Identify Prefixes, Suffixes, and Base Words

Write the prefix, base word, and suffix of the words below. Not all the words have a prefix and a suffix.

	Prefix	Base Word	Suffix
1. disloyal	*dis*	*loyal*	_____
2. disappointment	___	___	___
3. perfectly	___	___	___
4. unsure	___	___	___
5. curiously	___	___	___
6. disfavor	___	___	___
7. rebirth	___	___	___
8. enjoyment	___	___	___
9. crookedness	___	___	___
10. remodel	___	___	___

loyal
disappoint
perfect
sure
curious
favor
birth
enjoyment
crooked
model

Dictionary Skills

Read the dictionary entry and complete the items below.

worry 1. To feel or cause to feel uneasy or troubled. The parents *worried* when their children did not call. **2.** To pull or bite at something with the teeth. The puppy *worried* the rug. *Verb.*
—Something that causes an uneasy or troubled feeling. Their biggest *worry* was that they did not have enough money. *Noun.* **wor•ry** (wûr′ē) *verb,* **worried, worrying**; *noun, plural* **worries.**

1. Write the parts of speech for *worry.* ___ ___

2. Write the verb forms for *worry.* ___ ___

3. Write the first example sentence for *worry* used as a verb. ___

Spelling and Writing

A personal narrative is a story about something that happened in your own life. An event at your school is one topic you might choose for a personal narrative.

REAL PEOPLE

TIME WORDS

PLACE

Last Friday afternoon, our class held a bake sale to raise money for the annual Fourth Grade Spring Festival. The sale took place in the **gym**. We sold several kinds of baked goods. Our biggest sellers were the cookies, cakes, and other dessert items. We earned a grand total of $501! With that much money to spend on our festival, it is sure to disappoint no one!

Now write your own story about a real event that happened at your school. (You might want to write about a sports event, a school fair, or a class play, for example.) Try to use spelling words in your story.

PREWRITE: What events have taken place at your school this year? Choose an event and list some details about it.

DRAFT: Write a story about the event. Begin with a topic sentence that tells what event you'll be writing about. Describe the event.

REVISE: Share your paragraph with a classmate. Use your classmate's comments and the Writing Tips on the left as you revise.

EDIT/PROOFREAD: Use editing marks to correct your capitalization, spelling, and punctuation. Rewrite your paragraph neatly.

PUBLISH: Add your story to a class newsletter.

WRITING TIPS!!

Personal Narrative

- Tell about yourself and real people around you.
- Set the story in a specific time and place.
- Make sure the story events are in an order that readers can follow.

Spelling Fun
CUMULATIVE REVIEW

PICTURE THIS

- Choose a word from Lessons 1–17 that suggests a picture.
- Find your own way of writing the word to show its meaning.
- See how creative you can be!
- Do as many as you like. Start a class gallery.

PLAY BEETLE

- Choose one word from Lessons 19–23.
- To begin, draw a circle. Write the spelling pattern for your word in the center.
- Make one blank for each letter of your word.
- Your partner names a letter. If it is in your word, fill in the correct blank. If not, add a body part, leg, or antenna to the beetle.
- When you're done, switch roles.

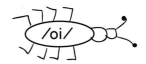

c   h   o   i   c   e

SPELLING BEE

- Two teams share the job of writing words from Lessons 1–23 on cards. Each team gets half of the cards.
- The first player on Team A calls out a word.
- The first player on Team B writes the word on the board.
- If the word is spelled correctly, the card is taken out of the pile. If not, correct the word and return the card to the pile.
- Then, the next Team B player calls out the word for the next Team A player. Continue on.
- The first team to finish the other team's pile wins!

25

Words with /ən/

PHONICS PATTERNS

1. ribbon
2. cotton
3. kitchen
4. lion
5. fountain
6. women
7. reason
8. chicken
9. common
10. sudden
11. dragon
12. eleven
13. gallon
14. listen
15. open
16. siren
17. button
18. oven
19. wagon
20. lemon

Learn Spelling Patterns

LOOK & SAY   Listen for the sounds in each word.

PICTURE   Close your eyes. See each word in your mind.

STUDY   These spelling words end with /ən/.

WRITE   Sort the words. Which words have /ən/ spelled with the following letters?

en	(1)	(2)	(3)
	(4)	(5)	(6)
	(7)	(8)	(9)
ain	(10)		
on	(11)	(12)	(13)
	(14)	(15)	(16)
	(17)	(18)	(19)
	(20)		

CHECK   Did you spell each word correctly? Circle the letters that stand for /ən/.

Pattern Power

How can /ən/ be spelled at the end of a word? (21) or (22) or (23)

Other Words

Write words you would like to add to this week's list.

_____ _____ _____ _____ _____

Practice Word Meanings

Words in Context

Write the list word that best completes each sentence.

1. The ____ laid two eggs today.

2. I won a blue ____ for one event in the horse show.

3. On hot days, I wear ____ shirts.

4. I tasted the ____, and it was very sour.

5. When taking a test, it is ____ to feel nervous.

6. Four quarts are equal to one ____.

7. A ____ is a make-believe animal.

8. The mother ____ took good care of her cubs.

9. Tell me the ____ why you were late.

10. We baked a pumpkin pie in the ____.

11. Yesterday, I lost a ____ from my coat.

Challenge Words • *Physical Education* ----------------

Write the challenge word that is a synonym for each word below. Use the **Spelling Dictionary** on page 214 to help you. Circle the spelling of /ən/ in each word.

12. winner ____

13. picked ____

14. build up ____

15. leader ____

16. partner ____

captain
strengthen
chosen
champion
companion

pelling Tip

Sometimes a word is not spelled the way it sounds. You can make up a saying to help you remember the spelling.

✦ When I need to spell *listen*, I make a *list*.

List Words

ribbon

cotton

kitchen

lion

fountain

women

reason

chicken

common

sudden

dragon

eleven

gallon

listen

open

siren

button

oven

wagon

lemon

Challenge Words

captain

strengthen

chosen

champion

companion

Review Words

lesson

certain

woman

happen

Build Vocabulary

Forming Plurals and Possessives

■ You know how to make a singular noun possessive by adding an apostrophe and *s (button's)*. You know how to make a plural noun that ends in *s* possessive by adding an apostrophe after the *s (chickens')*. You can make a plural noun that does not end in *s* possessive by adding an apostrophe and *s*.

women   women**'s**

Read each sentence below. Decide whether the spelling word in dark type should be a plural noun, a singular possessive, or a plural possessive. Write the word correctly with *s, s',* or *'s.*

wagon   1. What color is your ____ handle?

siren   2. The ____ announce the beginning of the game

women   3. The ____ right to vote was won in 1920.

fountain 4. Six ____ pipes have been cleaned.

kitchen 5. The ____ new floor is white.

■ Use words you made to complete each sentence.

6. The ____ dresses were bright and colorful.

7. We heard the fire engine's ____ .

Review Words

Write the review words that have the /ən/ spelled with the letters below. Circle the letters that stand for /ən/ in each word.

ain 8. ____   **on** 10. ____

en 9. ____   **an** 11. ____

lesson
certain
woman
happen

TAKE HOME

Write your spelling words in three lists: nouns, verbs, and adjectives. Some words may fit on more than one list. Circle the spelling of /ən/ in each word. Use your lists to practice at home.

Apply Spelling Skills

Using the Thesaurus

A **thesaurus** is a special dictionary for writers. It lists synonyms for an entry word. Look at the **Spelling Thesaurus** on page 182. List words are red. Synonyms are black. Use the index to find the list word for each of these synonyms in your **Spelling Thesaurus**.

1. uncovered _____
2. hear _____
3. unexpected _____

Proofreading

Proofread the paragraph. Check for spelling, capital letters, and punctuation. Then rewrite the paragraph. There are six mistakes.

At age elevun I began to play basketball. Do not lissen to people who say you must be tall. Short players make suddain moves. they find opin spots and score baskets.

Pattern Power

Look at the words you just wrote.

• Circle the spelling of /ən/ in each word.

Writing • *About Physical Education*

PREWRITE: List several athletes whom you admire.

DRAFT: Choose one person. Write a paragraph about why you admire this person's skill.

REVISE: Reread your draft. Will readers understand why you admire this person? Use the **Spelling Thesaurus** on page 182 as you revise.

EDIT/PROOFREAD: Check and then rewrite your paragraph.

PUBLISH: Imagine that you are a TV sportscaster. Read your paragraph to the class.

EDITING MARKS

◯ check spelling
≡ capital letter
/ lowercase letter
⊙ add a period
∧ add
✗ take out
¶ indent the paragraph
◯ move

For more help, see page 171.

26

WORDS WITH /âr/

PHONICS PATTERNS

1. share
2. dairy
3. hair
4. careful
5. wear
6. pear
7. dare
8. spare
9. stare
10. bare
11. scarce
12. repair
13. upstairs
14. scare
15. fair
16. unfair
17. hare
18. glare
19. fare
20. anywhere

Learn Spelling Patterns

LOOK & SAY   Listen for the sounds in each word.

PICTURE   Close your eyes. See each word in your mind.

STUDY   These spelling words have /âr/.

WRITE   Sort the words. Which words have /âr/ spelled with the following letters?

are   (1)__ (2)__ (3)__
     (4)__ (5)__ (6)__
     (7)__ (8)__ (9)__
     (10)__

air   (11)__ (12)__ (13)__
     (14)__ (15)__ (16)__

ear   (17)__ (18)__

ere   (19)__

ar   (20)__

CHECK   Did you spell each word correctly? Circle the letters that stand for /âr/.

Pattern Power

How can /âr/ be spelled? (21)__ or (22)__ or (23)__ or (24)__ or (25)__

Other Words

Write words you would like to add to this week's list.

_____ _____ _____ _____ _____

Practice Word Meanings

Homophones

Homophones are two or more words that sound alike but have different spellings and different meanings.

stare and *stair*

Write the spelling word that is a homophone for each word below.

1. bear ____
2. pair ____
3. hair ____
4. fare ____

Related Meanings

Anywhere means "in, at, or to any place." *Somewhere* means "in, at, or to some place not known or named." Write *anywhere* or *somewhere* to complete each sentence.

5. In a jet, you can go ____ in the world.
6. The lightning hit ____ near the television tower.

Challenge Words • *Social Studies*

Write the challenge word that answers each question below. Use the **Spelling Dictionary** on page 214 to help you. Circle the spelling of /âr/ in each word.

7. What is another word for announce? ____
8. What happens when two countries fight? ____
9. What government program helps needy people? ____
10. Where do store owners keep products? ____
11. What do you call the excitement of a crowd that is hearing an important speech? ____

declare
fanfare
welfare
warfare
warehouse

Spelling Tip

Here's a spelling rule you can rely on.

✦ The only words or word parts in which /âr/ is spelled *ere* are *there* and *where*!

Which one of your spelling words follows this rule?

List Words

share
dairy
hair
careful
wear
pear
dare
spare
stare
bare
scarce
repair
upstairs
scare
fair
unfair
hare
glare
fare
anywhere

Challenge Words

declare
fanfare
welfare
warfare
warehouse

Review Words

care
airport
airplane
stairs

Build Vocabulary

Word Endings

■ Add -ed and -ing to these verbs. If the verb ends in e, drop the e before adding -ed or -ing.

	-ed	-ing
1. share	____	____
2. dare	____	____
3. spare	____	____
4. stare	____	____
5. scare	____	____
6. repair	____	____
7. glare	____	____

■ Use words you made to complete these sentences.

8. Anna was ____ the broken chain on her bike.

9. We ____ a sandwich when we stopped for lunch.

Review Words

Write the review words that have /âr/ spelled with the letters below. Circle the letters that stand for /âr/ in each word.

air 10. ____

11. ____

12. ____

are 13. ____

care
airport
airplane
stairs

Write the review words that have the same spelling of /âr/ and the same number of syllables as each list word below.

dairy 14. ____   **fair** 16. ____

15. ____   **hare** 17. ____

TAKE HOME

Write your spelling words in three lists: words with one, two, and three syllables. Circle the spelling of /âr/ in each word. Use your lists to practice at home.

Apply Spelling Skills

Dictionary Skills

Use the **Spelling Dictionary** on page 214 to look up the definition of each pair of homophones below. Decide which homophone best completes each sentence, and write it.

1. **hair, hare**   The child has curly brown _____.
2. **fair, fare**   I went to the crafts _____ to buy a ring.
3. **stair, stare**   I was told not to _____ at the sun.
4. **where, wear**   What will you _____ to the party?

Proofreading

Check for spelling, capital letters, and punctuation. Then rewrite the paragraph. There are six mistakes.

> I think its unfare. When jobs are skairce, I must work at the family's dairy. I want to be a lifeguard. i went upstares to the office to apply. I filled out the form cairefully.

Writing • *About Social Studies*

PREWRITE: Imagine that you are a teenager who wants a summer job. List the jobs you would like.

DRAFT: Choose one job. Then write a letter telling why you would be a good person for the job.

REVISE: Reread your letter. Is it polite? Are your ideas clear? Use the **Spelling Thesaurus** on page 182 as you revise.

EDIT/PROOFREAD: Use editing marks. Then write a clean copy.

PUBLISH: Read your letter aloud to your classmates.

EDITING MARKS

◯ **check spelling**

≡ **capital letter**

╱ **lowercase letter**

⊙ **add a period**

∧ **add**

✓ **take out**

¶ **indent the paragraph**

◯~ **move**

For more help, see page 171.

WORDS WITH /îr/

1. year
2. sincerely
3. disappear
4. fear
5. deer
6. cheer
7. here
8. dear
9. tear
10. spear
11. near
12. hear
13. fierce
14. period
15. weary
16. rear
17. gear
18. beard
19. weird
20. cereal

Learn Spelling Patterns

LOOK & SAY Listen for the sounds in each word.

PICTURE Close your eyes. See each word in your mind.

STUDY These spelling words have /îr/.

WRITE Sort the words. Which words have /îr/ spelled with the following letters?

ear	(1)	(2)	(3)
	(4)	(5)	(6)
	(7)	(8)	(9)
	(10)	(11)	(12)
eer	(13)	(14)	
ere	(15)	(16)	
er	(17)	(18)	
ier	(19)		
eir	(20)		

CHECK Did you spell each word correctly? Circle the letters that stand for /îr/.

Pattern Power

How can /îr/ be spelled?

(21) or (22) or (23) or (24) or (25) or (26)

Other Words

Write words you would like to add to this week's list.

_____ _____ _____ _____ _____

Practice Word Meanings

Analogies

You know that an **analogy** compares pairs of related words. Write a list word to complete each analogy.

1. *Hot* is to *cold* as *gentle* is to ____.
2. *Agree* is to *disagree* as *appear* is to ____.
3. *Laughing* is to *crying* as *front* is to ____.
4. *Sad* is to *happy* as *far* is to ____.
5. *Pair* is to *pear* as *dear* is to ____.
6. *Hair* is to *hare* as *hear* is to ____.
7. *Steak* is to *meat* as *oatmeal* is to ____.
8. *Tool* is to *hammer* as *weapon* is to ____.
9. *Seven days* is to a *week* as *365 days* is to a ____.

Challenge Words • *Science*

Write the challenge word that matches each definition below. Use the **Spelling Dictionary** on page 214 to help you. Circle the spelling of /îr/.

10. layer of gas around the earth ____
11. a person who designs roads or bridges ____
12. part of the ear that sends sound waves to the hearing nerves ____
13. what something is made out of or used for ____
14. a thin, clear liquid that can help to heal a person who has an illness ____

atmosphere
engineer
serum
eardrum
material

Spelling Tip

Here's a spelling rule that you can almost always count on when choosing between *ei* and *ie* in spelling a word.

✦ Use *i* before *e* except after *c* or when sounded like /ā/ as in *neighbor* or *weigh*.

Which spelling word follows the rule? Which spelling word is an exception?

List Words

year
sincerely
disappear
fear
deer
cheer
here
dear
tear
spear
near
hear
fierce
period
weary
rear
gear
beard
weird
cereal

Challenge Words

atmosphere
engineer
serum
eardrum
material

Review Words

nearby
clear
we're
ear

Build Vocabulary

Suffixes

■ The suffix -*ful* means "full of."

care + **ful** = careful, meaning "full of care"

Add the suffix -*ful* to each underlined word below to make a word that fits the given meaning.

1. full of <u>cheer</u> _____
2. full of <u>fear</u> _____
3. full of <u>tear(s)</u> _____

■ The suffix -*less* means "without."

care + **less** = careless, meaning "without care"

Add -*less* to the spelling words below.

4. tear _____   6. cheer _____
5. beard _____   7. fear _____

■ Use words you made to complete these sentences.

8. When my dog hears the lawn mower, she is _____.
9. The losing team was _____.

Review Words

Write the review words that have /îr/ spelled with the letters below. Circle the spelling of /îr/ in each word.

ear 10. _____   12. _____
11. _____   **e're** 13. _____

Look at the list word below. Write the review words that have /îr/ spelled the same way.

dear 14. _____   15. _____   16. _____

nearby
clear
we're
ear

T A K E H O M E

Write your spelling words in two lists: words that rhyme with *ear* and words that do not. Write each list in alphabetical order. Circle the spelling of /îr/. Use your lists to practice at home.

Apply Spelling Skills

Dictionary Skills

Use the pronunciation key on page 214 of your **Spelling Dictionary** to write the list words for the respellings below.

1. (sin sîr′lē) _____
2. (wîrd) _____
3. (pîr′ē əd) _____
4. (wîr′ē) _____
5. (fîrs) _____
6. (gîr) _____

Pattern Power

Look at the list words you just wrote.

- Circle the spelling of /îr/ in each word.

Proofreading

Check for spelling, capital letters, and punctuation. Then rewrite the paragraph. There are six mistakes.

Deer Dr Gomez

    I here you will be in town soon. Will you call me when you arrive

           Sinceerly,

Writing • *About Science*

PREWRITE: List ways that your sight and hearing help you.

DRAFT: Choose your sight or your hearing. Write a paragraph that explains why your sight or hearing is important.

REVISE: Did you start with your best reason first? Did you use convincing words? Use the **Spelling Thesaurus** on page 182 as you revise.

EDIT/PROOFREAD: Edit and then rewrite your paragraph.

PUBLISH: Read your paragraph to the class. Make a chalkboard chart that shows how many students chose *sight* and how many chose *hearing*.

EDITING MARKS

- ⬭ check spelling
- ≡ capital letter
- / lowercase letter
- ⊙ add a period
- ∧ add
- ℐ take out
- ⌙ indent the paragraph
- ↻ move

For more help, see page 171.

28

DAYS AND Months

1. March
2. May
3. Sunday
4. October
5. November
6. July
7. February
8. Saturday
9. Wednesday
10. calendar
11. January
12. April
13. September
14. June
15. Tuesday
16. August
17. December
18. Monday
19. Friday
20. Thursday

Learn Spelling Patterns

LOOK & SAY Listen for the sounds in each word.

PICTURE Close your eyes. See each word in your mind.

STUDY These spelling words include the names of the months and days of the week.

WRITE Sort the words according to these headings.

Months of the year, in time order:

(1) (2) (3) (4) (5) (6)
(7) (8) (9) (10) (11) (12)

Days of the week, in time order:

(13) (14) (15) (16) (17) (18) (19)

The word that is *not* a proper noun: (20)

CHECK Did you spell each word correctly? Circle any capital letters.

Pattern Power

What kind of letter begins the name

of a month or a day of the week?

(21)

Other Words

Write words you would like to add to this week's list.

_____ _____ _____ _____ _____

Practice Word Meanings

Word Origins

Our names of the months came from the Roman calendar, which had only ten months. Originally, the first month was March. Some names of months come from Roman numbers. Others are based on ancient gods, emperors, and rituals. Use the clues below to write the list word for each month.

1. *Janus,* the Roman god with two faces, one facing the new year and one facing the old *January*
2. *novem,* the Latin word for "nine" ____
3. *decem,* the Latin word for "ten" ____
4. the month of the emperor *Julius Caesar* ____
5. *Mars,* the Roman god of war ____
6. *septem,* the Latin word for "seven" ____
7. *Juno,* queen of the Roman gods ____

Challenge Words • *Math*

Write the challenge word that best completes each sentence below. Use the **Spelling Dictionary** on page 214 to help you.

8. I heard the clock strike ____.
9. Raking ____ leaves is a chore I actually like.
10. The owl hoots in the ____ at about 7 P.M.
11. We spent our winter ____ ice-skating.
12. We go to the ____ picnic every year.

holiday
autumn
annual
midnight
evening

ⓢpelling Tip

Making up a way to pronounce a hard word can help you remember how to spell it.

+ *Wednesday* is hard to spell because the first *d* is not pronounced.
+ When you need to write *Wednesday*, say *wed nes day* to yourself in order to remember all of the letters in the word.

List Words

March
May
Sunday
October
November
July
February
Saturday
Wednesday
calendar
January
April
September
June
Tuesday
August
December
Monday
Friday
Thursday

Challenge Words

holiday
autumn
annual
midnight
evening

Review Words

afternoon
outside
inside
tonight

Build Vocabulary

Forming Plurals and Possessives

■ Write the plural of each noun below.

1. Friday _____   5. calendar _____
2. Monday _____   6. Thursday _____
3. Saturday _____   7. Tuesday _____
4. Wednesday _____   8. Sunday _____

■ Write the possessive form of each noun below.

9. May _____   12. April _____
10. June _____   13. January _____
11. August _____   14. February _____

■ Use words you made to complete these sentences.

15. We made some _____ for next year in art class.
16. On _____ we get a lot of homework, because we get the next two days off.
17. New Year's Day is _____ first holiday.

Review Words

Write the review words that refer to time.

18. _____
19. _____

Write the review words that refer to place.

20. _____
21. _____

*afternoon
outside
inside
tonight*

TAKE HOME

Write your spelling words in alphabetical order. Circle any capital letters at the beginning of a word. Use your lists to practice spelling the words at home.

Apply Spelling Skills

Dictionary Skills

Dictionaries tell you the history, or **etymology**, of some words. Look up *Friday* in the **Spelling Dictionary** on page 214. A "Word History" box tells you the origin of the word *Friday.* Use the **Spelling Dictionary** to write the history of the words below.

	Original Language	Meaning
1. Friday	*Old English*	*"Frigga's day"*
2. Wednesday	___	___
3. Thursday	___	___
4. Tuesday	___	___

Proofreading

Check for spelling, capital letters, and punctuation. Then rewrite the paragraph. There are five mistakes.

> We used a calender to make a graph of our birthdays. more students were born in october than in any other month. More of us were born on Thersday than on any other day

Writing • *About Math*

PREWRITE: Imagine that there are no clocks or calendars. List some ways that you might keep track of time.

DRAFT: Write a one-paragraph explanation of your method. Explain how you could tell time without a clock or calendar.

REVISE: Reread your explanation. Is the order of ideas clear?

EDIT/PROOFREAD: Use editing marks. Write a clean copy.

PUBLISH: Collect your paragraphs into a "time-telling" book.

EDITING MARKS

◯ check spelling

≡ capital letter

/ lowercase letter

⊙ add a period

∧ add

⅌ take out

⌗ indent the paragraph

◠ move

For more help, see page 171.

29

HOLIDAYS

1. Thanksgiving
2. Martin Luther King Day
3. weekend
4. Fourth of July
5. Veterans Day
6. vacation
7. Valentine's Day
8. Flag Day
9. Mother's Day
10. Father's Day
11. Labor Day
12. Presidents' Day
13. Memorial Day
14. May Day
15. New Year's Day
16. Columbus Day
17. Washington's Birthday
18. Groundhog Day
19. Earth Day
20. Election Day

Learn Spelling Patterns

LOOK & SAY   Listen for the sounds in each word.

PICTURE   Close your eyes. See each word in your mind.

STUDY   These spelling words include proper nouns.

WRITE   Sort the words according to these headings.

Names of holidays from January through June:

(1)   (2)   (3)   (4)   (5)   (6)

(7)   (8)   (9)   (10)   (11)   (12)

Names of holidays from July through December:

(13)   (14)   (15)   (16)   (17)   (18)

Words that are not names of holidays.

(19)   (20)

CHECK   Did you spell each word correctly? Circle any capital letters in the holidays.

Pattern Power

What kind of letter do you use to begin each main word in the name of a holiday? (21)

Other Words

Write words you would like to add to this week's list.

_____   _____   _____   _____   _____

Practice Word Meanings

Context Clues

Write the name of the holiday that matches each clue.

1. We remember soldiers who died in wars.
   Memorial Day
2. Fireworks are set off. ____
3. People celebrate the gifts of nature. ____
4. We honor a civil rights leader. ____
5. We celebrate spring. ____
6. We welcome a new calendar year. ____
7. United States' citizens vote. ____
8. We celebrate an early explorer. ____
9. We honor our first president. ____

Challenge Words • *Social Studies*

Write the challenge word that answers each question below. Use the **Spelling Dictionary** on page 214 to help you.

10. Who travels to a special place? ____
11. What might you do on your birthday? ____
12. What do you wear in a school play? ____
13. What do you do when you obey a rule or follow a tradition? ____
14. Where do we see marching? ____

observe
celebrate
pilgrim
costume
parade

Spelling Tip

Some of the holidays are spelled with an apostrophe.

+ Most of the time, the apostrophe comes before the *s*.
+ *Presidents' Day* has an apostrophe after the *s* because this holiday honors two presidents, George Washington and Abraham Lincoln.

List Words

Thanksgiving
Martin Luther King Day
weekend
Fourth of July
Veterans Day
vacation
Valentine's Day
Flag Day
Mother's Day
Father's Day
Labor Day
Presidents' Day
Memorial Day
May Day
New Year's Day
Columbus Day
Washington's Birthday
Groundhog Day
Earth Day
Election Day

Challenge Words

observe
celebrate
pilgrim
costume
parade

Review Words

weather
winter
summer
season

Build Vocabulary

Suffixes and Possessives

■ The suffixes -er and -or can mean "a person who is or does."

collect + **or** = collector, meaning "a person who collects"

quilt + **er** = quilter, meaning "a person who quilts"

Add -or or -er to each word below. You may need to drop the final e or change y to i before adding the suffix.

1. believe _____   4. photograph _____
2. act _____   5. garden _____
3. worry _____   6. vacation _____

■ Fill in the singular or plural possessive form.

Singular	Plural
7. mother's	_____
8. _____	presidents'
9. year's	_____
10. father's	_____

Review Words

Write the review words that have the vowel sounds.

/ē/ 11. _____   /i/ 13. _____
/e/ 12. _____   /u/ 14. _____

15. On Memorial Day, the _____ is often warm.

16. Valentine's Day and Presidents' Day are _____ holidays.

weather
winter
summer
season

TAKE HOME

Write your spelling words in three lists: proper nouns made up of three or more words, proper nouns made up of two words, and any nouns that are single words. Use your lists to practice at home.

Apply Spelling Skills
Dictionary Skills

Some words have more than one accented syllable. In the respelling, a **primary accent mark** in dark type shows which syllable is said with the most force. A **secondary accent mark** in light type shows which syllable is said with less force. Use the **Spelling Dictionary** on page 214 to write each word in syllables. Draw a heavy accent mark after the most heavily stressed syllable and a lighter mark after the syllable that is said with less force.

1. Groundhog Day   _____
2. Thanksgiving   _____
3. Valentine's Day   _____

Pattern Power

Look at the words you just wrote.

• Circle any capital letters in the words.

Proofreading

Check for spelling, capital letters, and punctuation. Then rewrite the paragraph. There are six mistakes.

> My family enjoys holidays and vacashuns. On Veterens Day, my father marches in a parade. On labor Day, presidents Day, and Memorial Day, we go away for long weekends.

Write • *About Social Studies*

PREWRITE: Create a new holiday. Write notes about the holiday.

DRAFT: Create a poster for your holiday. Use words and pictures that will make people want to share your holiday.

REVISE: Look at your poster again. Have you used colorful words? Will people want to know more about your holiday?

EDIT/PROOFREAD: Use editing marks to correct your writing. Rewrite a clean copy of your poster.

PUBLISH: Display your holiday posters in the classroom.

EDITING MARKS

⬭ check spelling
≡ capital letter
╱ lowercase letter
⊙ add a period
∧ add
✗ take out
¶ indent the paragraph
↻ move

For more help, see page 171.

30 REVIEW Spelling Patterns

Sort the words in each list. Write each word. Circle the spelling pattern or capital letters.

---

ribbon
kitchen
fountain
chicken
common
dragon
listen
oven
button
lemon

Lesson 25
Words with /ən/ spelled

en   1. _____   on   6. _____
     2. _____   7. _____
     3. _____   8. _____
     4. _____   9. _____
ain 5. _____   10. _____

---

share
dairy
careful
wear
stare
scarce
repair
fair
glare
anywhere

Lesson 26
Words with /âr/ spelled

air 11. _____   are 16. _____
     12. _____   17. _____
     13. _____   18. _____
ear 14. _____   19. _____
ar   15. _____   ere 20. _____

---

sincerely
disappear
cheer
here
dear
fierce
weary
rear
weird
cereal

Lesson 27
Words with /îr/ spelled

ear 21. _____   ere 26. _____
     22. _____   27. _____
     23. _____   er   28. _____
     24. _____   ier 29. _____
eer 25. _____   eir 30. _____

October	**Lesson 28**
July	
February	**Names of months in alphabetical order**
Wednesday	
Sunday	31. _____
January	32. _____
Tuesday	33. _____
August	34. _____
Friday	35. _____
Thursday	

Names of days in alphabetical order

36. _____
37. _____
38. _____
39. _____
40. _____

Thanksgiving	**Lesson 29**
Martin Luther King Day	**Names of holidays in alphabetical order**
Valentine's Day	41. _____
Mother's Day	42. _____
Father's Day	43. _____
Memorial Day	44. _____
Washington's Birthday	45. _____
New Year's Day	46. _____
Columbus Day	
Election Day	

47. _____
48. _____
49. _____
50. _____

Spelling Tip

Making up a way to pronounce a hard word can help you remember how to spell the word.

✦ *February* is hard to spell because many people forget to pronounce the first *r*.

✦ When you need to write *February*, say each syllable to yourself (*Feb ru ar y*) in order to remember each letter in the word.

Tuesday
disappear
Memorial Day
sincerely

Write each of the spelling words below in syllables. Include capital letters for words that are proper nouns. Use the **Spelling Dictionary** on page 214 to check your answers.

1. Memorial Day _____   3. disappear _____

2. sincerely _____   4. Tuesday _____

127

Word Meaning Mixed Lesson Review

stare
kitchen
fierce
Friday
Martin Luther
  King Day
here
lemon
share

Analogies
Write a spelling word to complete each analogy below.

1. *Lettuce* is to *vegetable* as ____ is to *fruit.*
2. *Sleep* is to *bedroom* as *cook* is to ____.
3. *Monday* is to *Tuesday* as ____ is to *Saturday.*
4. *Columbus* is to *Columbus Day* as *Martin Luther King* is to ____.
5. *Short* is to *long* as *glance* is to ____.
6. *Kitten* is to *gentle* as *lion* is to ____.
7. *Stingy* is to *keep* as *generous* is to ____.
8. *Far* is to *away* as *near* is to ____.

August
January
October
February
Thursday

Word Histories
Write a spelling word next to the source of its name.

9. *Februa,* a Roman feast ____
10. *Janus,* a god with two faces, one facing the new year and one facing the old ____
11. *Thor,* the ancient god of thunder ____
12. *octo,* the Latin word for "eight" ____
13. the month of the Roman emperor *Caesar Augustus* ____

fountain
anywhere
New Year's Day
repair
dairy

Context Words
Write a spelling word to complete each sentence below.

14. On the first of January, we celebrate ____.
15. You can go ____ in Boston by train.
16. We sat near the cool water of the ____.
17. I milked a cow at the ____ farm.
18. A carpenter will ____ the broken chair.

Vocabulary Mixed Lesson Review

Form Plurals and Possessives

Write the singular and the plural possessive form for each word. You may have to change the *y* to *i* before adding *-es* to form the plural of some words.

		Singular Possessive	Plural Possessive
1.	lemon	*lemon's*	*lemons'*
2.	cereal	_____	_____
3.	dairy	_____	_____
4.	Tuesday	_____	_____
5.	dragon	_____	_____
6.	Friday	_____	_____
7.	ribbon	_____	_____
8.	Sunday	_____	_____
9.	kitchen	_____	_____
10.	fair	_____	_____

Dictionary Skills

Read the dictionary entry and complete the items below.

> **weird** Strange or mysterious; odd. *Weird* sounds came from the scary old house.
> **weird** (wîrd) *adjective,* **weirder, weirdest.**

1. Write the part of speech for the entry word. _____
2. Write the example sentence given for *weird*. _____
3. Write three synonyms for weird. _____ _____ _____
4. Write the respelling for *weird*. _____

Spelling and Writing

QUESTION ABOUT TOPIC An advice column on health is a form of writing a report. The writer gives information based on facts.

Dear Healthful Habits:

How much sleep do I need? My parents make me go to bed at 8:30. I am nine years old. Going to bed so early makes me feel like a baby. Please help!

Sincerely,

Annie Peña

MAIN IDEA

Dear Annie: **Research shows that weary children do less well in school and are less healthy than children who sleep enough.** Many experts think that **nine year olds should sleep about nine-and-one-half hours a night.** (Babies commonly need about 12 hours of sleep.) If you get up at six in the morning, you are getting the proper rest. Maybe you could stay up late on the weekend if you can sleep later in the morning. **Be careful to get enough sleep.**

FACTS

CONCLUSION

WRITING TIPS!!

Reports

- Ask a question about your topic.
- Introduce the main idea about your topic.
- Present the facts in logical order.
- End with a strong conclusion.

Now write your own newspaper column that gives advice about healthful habits. Try to use some spelling words in your writing.

PREWRITE: What healthful habits would you like to know more about? Choose one health issue, and look up facts about it.

DRAFT: Write a report about healthful habits, using a newspaper advice column format. Write the question and the answer. Use facts to support your answer.

REVISE: Exchange reports with a classmate. Use your classmate's comments and the Writing Tips as you revise.

EDIT/PROOFREAD: Use editing marks to correct your capitalization, spelling, and punctuation. Rewrite your newspaper column neatly.

PUBLISH: Add your "healthful habits" column to a class "health journal."

SPELLING FUN
CUMULATIVE REVIEW

WORD WEB

- Choose a word from Lessons 1-23. Write it on a piece of paper.
- Use each letter in the word to write a spelling word that starts with that letter.
- Then find a spelling word that begins with one of the letters in each of the new words you wrote.
- You can stop now, or you can continue your Word Web!

Knuckle
number
insert
festival
elephant

PLAY EEEE-GADS

- Choose four words from the lists in Lessons 25-29. Each word must include the letter *e*. Make one blank for each letter of each word.
- Write the *e*'s on the blanks, in the places they should appear in each word.
- Switch papers with your partner. Try to figure out which word fits in each of the blanks.

- When both of you have made your guesses, show your partner your secret words. How did you do? Were there two or more words that could have fit in the blanks?

_ _ _ e̲   ____

_ e̲ _ _   ____

_ e̲ e̲ _   ____

_ _ _ _ _ e̲ _ e̲   ____

SPELLING BEE

- Two teams each list 15 words from Lessons 1-29 on a sheet of paper.
- The first player on Team A calls out the first word.
- The first player on Team B spells the word.
- If the word is spelled correctly, the Team A player places a check next to the word. If not, an *o* is placed next

to the word. Then the next player on Team B attempts to spell the word. Once the word is spelled correctly, a check is placed next to the word.

- Team B calls out the first word on their list. Continue on.
- The team that has received the fewest *o*'s wins!

31

COMPOUND Words

1. grandmother
2. bedroom
3. newspaper
4. sunshine
5. overcome
6. grandfather
7. railroad
8. herself
9. somewhere
10. playground
11. fireplace
12. anyway
13. backyard
14. homemade
15. everybody
16. bedspread
17. bathtub
18. bathroom
19. homework
20. within

Learn Spelling Patterns

LOOK & SAY Listen for the sounds in each word.

PICTURE Close your eyes. See each word in your mind.

STUDY These spelling words are compound words.

WRITE Sort the words. Which words contain the words below?

with	(1)	**home**	(11)
bath	(2)		(12)
	(3)	**news**	(13)
bed	(4)	**sun**	(14)
	(5)	**over**	(15)
fire	(6)	**any**	(16)
grand	(7)	**every**	(17)
	(8)	**her**	(18)
back	(9)	**some**	(19)
play	(10)	**rail**	(20)

CHECK Did you spell each word correctly? Circle each word within the compound word.

Pattern Power

How many words does a compound word usually contain? (21)

Other Words

Write words you would like to add to this week's list.

_____ _____ _____ _____ _____

Practice Word Meanings

Related Meanings

Write the spelling word that belongs in each group of words.

1. mother, son, grandfather ____
2. magazine, book, letter ____
3. rain, wind, snow ____
4. toothbrush, sink, soap ____
5. myself, yourself, himself ____
6. fence, garden, lawn ____
7. nobody, anybody, somebody ____
8. highway, river, runway ____
9. quilt, blanket, sheet ____
10. school, books, paper ____

Challenge Words • *Health*

Write the challenge word that best completes each sentence. Use the **Spelling Dictionary** on page 214 to help you. Circle the words that make up each compound word.

11. Some bread got stuck in Uncle Max's ____.
12. Every year, I go to my doctor for a ____.
13. The baby's ____ felt hot.
14. The nurse said a rest would help my ____.
15. It is not healthy to be ____.

headache
underweight
windpipe
checkup
forehead

Spelling Tip

A computer spellchecker will find words that are misspelled. If words are not misspelled, but are used incorrectly, the spellchecker can't help you!

✦ The spellchecker will not correct the spelling *grand mother* even if you mean *grandmother*, because both shorter words are spelled correctly.

Only the writer knows which spelling fits the meaning of a word or words.

List Words

grandmother

bedroom

newspaper

sunshine

overcome

grandfather

railroad

herself

somewhere

playground

fireplace

anyway

backyard

homemade

everybody

bedspread

bathtub

bathroom

homework

within

Challenge Words

headache

underweight

windpipe

checkup

forehead

Review Words

anyone

everyone

maybe

without

Build Vocabulary

Forming Compound Words

■ New compound words can be formed by replacing one word in a compound word with a new word.

$$\text{fire} + \textit{house} = \text{firehouse}$$

$$\text{fire} + \textit{place} = \text{fireplace}$$

Replace the underlined word in each compound word with a word from the box.

work how mate your due out

1. home<u>made</u> ＿＿＿

2. any<u>way</u> ＿＿＿

3. play<u>ground</u> ＿＿

4. over<u>come</u> ＿＿＿

5. <u>her</u>self ＿＿＿

6. with<u>in</u> ＿＿＿

■ Use words you made to complete these sentences.

7. My brother can cross the street ＿＿＿ me.

8. My library books are ＿＿＿.

Review Words

Write the review words that contain the words below. Circle the two words in each compound.

one 9. ＿＿＿

10. ＿＿＿

with 11. ＿＿＿

may 12. ＿＿＿

Look at the list words below. Write the review word that contains the same word.

13. within ＿＿＿

14. anyway ＿＿＿

15. everybody ＿＿＿

anyone

everyone

maybe

without

▲TAKE HOME▲

Write your spelling words in short lists according to their first letters. Circle the words within each compound word. Use your lists to practice at home.

Apply Spelling Skills

Dictionary Skills

Write the spelling word that matches the definition below. Use the **Spelling Dictionary** on page 214 to check your answers.

1. Space at the rear of a house. ____
2. An opening in a chimney to hold a fire. ____
3. The father of one's father or mother. ____
4. A room used for sleeping. ____
5. A tub in which to bathe. ____
6. In, at, or to some place not known or named. ____

Pattern Power

Look at the words you just wrote.

- Circle each word within the compound word.

Proofreading

Proofread the paragraph. Check for spelling, capital letters, and punctuation. Then rewrite the paragraph. There are six mistakes.

My grand mother has several rules for taking care of herselve. First, She gets plenty of sunshien and rest. Second, she finds somewere to exercise every day. Third, she eats homade food.

Writing • *About Health*

PREWRITE: List some healthy habits that you think are important.

DRAFT: Write a poster that encourages students to keep healthy.

REVISE: What details do you need to add or take out? What should be shown with pictures?

EDIT/PROOFREAD: Look for spelling and punctuation mistakes.

PUBLISH: Exhibit your posters outside your classroom or the school nurse's office.

EDITING MARKS

⬯ check spelling
≡ capital letter
/ lowercase letter
⊙ add a period
∧ add
⤳ take out
⌗ indent the paragraph
↻ move

For more help, see page 171.

32

PLURALS WITH -s and -es

1. errands
2. patches
3. buckets
4. monkeys
5. matches
6. ideas
7. ranches
8. engines
9. socks
10. brushes
11. shadows
12. bricks
13. sales
14. addresses
15. parents
16. foxes
17. peaches
18. pillows
19. coaches
20. mixes

Learn Spelling Patterns

LOOK & SAY — Listen for the sounds in each word.

PICTURE — Close your eyes. See each word in your mind.

STUDY — These spelling words are **plurals.**

WRITE — Sort the words. Write the plural words that have been formed in the following ways.

base word + s

(1) (5) (9)
(2) (6) (10)
(3) (7) (11)
(4) (8)

base word + es

(12) (15) (18)
(13) (16) (19)
(14) (17) (20)

CHECK — Did you spell each word correctly? Circle the letter or letters that make the base word plural.

Pattern Power

What letter is added to form the plural of most nouns? (21) What letters are added to form the plural of nouns that end with *s*, *sh*, *ch*, or *x*? (22)

Other Words

Write words you would like to add to this week's list.

_____ _____ _____ _____ _____

Practice Word Meanings

Related Meanings

Write the spelling words that are related in meaning to each word below.

1. zoo ____
2. think ____
3. feet ____
4. teams ____
5. streets ____
6. cattle ____
7. fires ____
8. children ____
9. cars ____
10. pails ____
11. duties ____
12. crayons ____
13. beds ____
14. plums ____

Challenge Words • The Arts

Write the challenge word that best completes each sentence. Use the **Spelling Dictionary** on page 214 to help you. Circle -*s* or -*es* to show how each plural word has been formed.

15. The art students used ____ to hold their paintings.
16. They made pencil ____ of trees before painting them.
17. At the fair, sculptors and other ____ showed their works.
18. Many ____ on the lawn were made of marble.
19. Mary ____ gardens for public parks throughout the United States.

sketches
designs
artists
easels
statues

Spelling Tip

Here's a rule to remember when adding -*s* to the end of a word that ends in *y*.

✦ When a word ends in a vowel followed by -*y*, add -*s* after the *y*.

Which spelling word fits this rule?

List Words

errands
patches
buckets
monkeys
matches
ideas
ranches
engines
socks
brushes
shadows
bricks
sales
addresses
parents
foxes
peaches
pillows
coaches
mixes

Challenge Words

sketches
designs
artists
easels
statues

Review Words

buses
shells
boxes
branches

Build Vocabulary

Singular Forms

■ Write the spelling words that rhyme with the words below. Then write the singular form of each spelling word.

	Rhyming Word	Singular Form
1. locks	_socks_	_sock_
2. chicks	_____	_____
3. bales	_____	_____
4. boxes	_____	_____
5. patches	_____	_____
6. beaches	_____	_____
7. willows	_____	_____
8. fixes	_____	_____

■ Use words you made to complete these sentences.

9. The _____ wall is covered with ivy.

10. He _____ three colors together to make brown.

Review Words

Write the review words that have plurals formed in the following ways. Circle the letter or letters that make the word plural.

base word + s

11. _____

base word + es

12. _____

13. _____

14. _____

buses
shells
boxes
branches

TAKE HOME

Write your spelling words in three lists: one-, two-, and three-syllable words. Circle the letter or letters that make each word plural. Use your lists to practice at home.

Apply Spelling Skills

Using the Thesaurus

Some words are overused. A thesaurus can help you find a more exact word. Use the index in the **Spelling Thesaurus** on page 182 to find the best word to replace the underlined word in each sentence.

1. The cardinals found worms in the <u>darkness</u> under a tree. _____
2. The quilter <u>repairs</u> the holes in the bedspread. _____

Proofreading

Check for spelling, capital letters, and punctuation. Then rewrite the paragraph. There are six mistakes.

georgia O'Keeffe lived near mountains and ranchs in New Mexico. She often took brushs and paint with her and worked outdoors You can see shadowes of hills in some of her paintings

Writing • *About the Arts*

PREWRITE: List paintings, sculptures, or photographs you like.

DRAFT: Choose one. Write a paragraph telling what the artwork means to you.

REVISE: Read your paragraph aloud. Use the **Spelling Thesaurus** on page 182 as you revise.

EDIT/PROOFREAD: Use editing marks. Then write a clean copy.

PUBLISH: Make a sketch of the artwork you wrote about. Attach it to your paragraph. Exhibit your work in a class art show.

EDITING MARKS

◯ check spelling

≡ capital letter

／ lowercase letter

⊙ add a period

⌃ add

✄ take out

¶ indent the paragraph

↷ move

For more help, see page 171.

33

PLURALS WITH Spelling Changes

1. mice
2. geese
3. leaves
4. enemies
5. wives
6. batteries
7. thieves
8. groceries
9. companies
10. puppies
11. knives
12. shelves
13. calves
14. hobbies
15. wolves
16. elves
17. families
18. cherries
19. pennies
20. cavities

Learn Spelling Patterns

LOOK & SAY Listen for the sounds in each word.

PICTURE Close your eyes. See each word in your mind.

STUDY These spelling words are **plurals** that change the spelling of the base words.

WRITE Sort the words. Write the plural words that have been formed in the following ways.

y changes to i before adding -es

(1) (2) (3) (4) (5)

(6) (7) (8) (9) (10)

f changes to v before adding -es

(11) (12) (13) (14)

(15) (16) (17) (18)

middle letters change

(19) (20)

CHECK Did you spell each word correctly? Circle the letters that make the base word plural.

Pattern Power

What letter does *y* change to at the end of a word before you add -es? (21) What letter may *f* change to at the end of a word before you add -es? (22)

Other Words

Write words you would like to add to this week's list.

_____ _____ _____ _____ _____

Practice Word Meanings

Words in Context

Write spelling words to complete the sentences below.

1. In the wilderness, we heard the howling of a pack of ____.
2. The flock of ____ flew south.
3. My dog gave birth to six ____.
4. Baby cows are called ____.
5. One female mouse had four baby ____.

Related Meanings

Write the spelling word that belongs with each word below.

6. steal ____
7. fruit ____
8. teeth ____
9. electricity ____

Challenge Words • *Science*

Write the challenge word that completes each analogy below. Use the **Spelling Dictionary** on page 214 to help you. Circle the letter or letters that make the words plural. Underline the word that is the same in both the singular and plural.

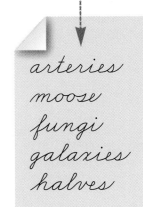

arteries
moose
fungi
galaxies
halves

10. ____ are to *antlers* as *cows* are to *horns*.
11. ____ are to *hearts* as *hoses* are to *hydrants*.
12. ____ are to *wholes* as *eighths* are to *quarters*.
13. *Stars* are to ____ as *trees* are to *forests*.
14. *Plums* are to *fruits* as *mushrooms* are to ____.

Spelling Tip

Remember the following rule when you write the plural of a noun ending in *y*.

✦ When a word ends in a consonant followed by *-y*, change *y* to *i* and add *-es*.

Which spelling words fit this rule?

List Words

mice

geese

leaves

enemies

wives

batteries

thieves

groceries

companies

puppies

knives

shelves

calves

hobbies

wolves

elves

families

cherries

pennies

cavities

Challenge Words

arteries

moose

fungi

galaxies

halves

Build Vocabulary

Singular Forms

■ You know that some base words change spellings when they are made plural. Use what you know about these spelling changes to write the singular form of the spelling words below. Use the **Spelling Dictionary** on page 214 to help you.

1. cavities _____

2. knives _____

3. families _____

4. shelves _____

5. elves _____

6. enemies _____

7. groceries _____

8. companies _____

9. leaves _____

10. wives _____

11. hobbies _____

12. pennies _____

■ Use words you made to complete these sentences.

13. Stamp collecting is my favorite _____.

14. She came to the party in an _____ costume.

15. My brother works in the meat section of the _____ store.

Review Words

Write the review words in alphabetical order. Circle the letter or letters that make each base word plural.

16. _____

17. _____

18. _____

19. _____

Write the review word that goes with the spelling word *leaves*.

20. _____

baskets

trees

pockets

wishes

■ T A K E H O M E

Write your spelling words in two lists: words with /ē/ as in *green* and words without /ē/. Circle the letter or letters that make each base word plural. Use your lists to practice at home.

Apply Spelling Skills

Dictionary Skills

Some words stay the same in the plural form or have more than one correct plural form.

moose (müs) *noun, plural* **moose**.

The **Spelling Dictionary** on page 214 gives the plurals of most nouns at the end of the entry. Write the plural form or forms of the words below. Check the answers in the **Spelling Dictionary.**

1. scarf _____
2. turkey _____
3. roof _____
4. trout _____
5. hare _____
6. self _____

Proofreading

Check for spelling, capital letters, and punctuation. Then rewrite the paragraph. There are six mistakes.

> The storm knocked down all the leafs from the trees. Many familys had no electricity. stores stayed open so that people could get grocaries. People also needed to buy candles and batteryes

Writing • *About Science*

PREWRITE: List the many ways you use electricity in daily life.

DRAFT: Write a paragraph about what your day would be like without electricity. What would be different from an ordinary day? What would be the same?

REVISE: Did you use enough descriptive words? Use the **Spelling Thesaurus** on page 182 as you revise.

EDIT/PROOFREAD: Use editing marks to correct your paragraph.

PUBLISH: Read your paragraph aloud to your class.

EDITING MARKS

- ⬭ check spelling
- ≡ capital letter
- / lowercase letter
- ⊙ add a period
- ⌃ add
- ✄ take out
- ¶ indent the paragraph
- ↻ move

For more help, see page 171.

34

HOMOPHONES and Homographs

1. beat
2. weak
3. pupil
4. lying
5. beet
6. fan
7. bowl
8. tire
9. punch
10. week
11. post
12. pale
13. tail
14. shed
15. tale
16. drill
17. deal
18. pail
19. bury
20. berry

Learn Spelling Patterns

LOOK & SAY Listen for the sounds in each word.

PICTURE Close your eyes. See each word in your mind.

STUDY Words that sound alike but have different spellings and meanings are called **homophones**. Words that are spelled alike but have completely different meanings are called **homographs**.

WRITE Sort the words. Which word pairs sound the same but have different spellings and meanings? Write the words side by side.

(1)___ (2)___ (3)___ (4)___ (5)___
(6)___ (7)___ (8)___ (9)___ (10)___

Write the remaining words. Can you think of two completely different meanings for each word ?

(11)___ (12)___ (13)___ (14)___ (15)___
(16)___ (17)___ (18)___ (19)___ (20)___

CHECK Did you spell each word correctly?

Pattern Power

What kind of words sound alike but have different meanings and spellings?

(21)___

Other Words

Write words you would like to add to this week's list.

___ ___ ___ ___ ___

Practice Word Meanings

Riddles

A **riddle** can be a funny question that makes you think about the meaning of words. Use a spelling word or words in the answer for each riddle below.

1. What does seven days without food make? It makes one _____.

2. When is it cold at a baseball game? when there are a lot of _____

3. What kind of story would you find at the top of the Empire State Building? a tall _____

4. What kind of vegetable do you feel like at the end of a long day? _____

5. What do squirrels do to store fruit? They _____ a _____.

Challenge Words • *Social Studies*

Write the challenge word that is a homophone of each word below.

6. cruise _____
7. martial _____
8. boy _____
9. morn _____
10. air _____

heir

crews

mourn

marshal

buoy

Spelling Tip

A computer spellchecker can tell you whether a homophone is spelled correctly. It cannot tell you if you have used the wrong homophone.

✦ If you wrote, "My heart *beet* quickly," the spellchecker would not correct you, because *beet* is a correctly spelled word.

Only the writer knows which homophone is correct in meaning.

List Words

beat

weak

pupil

lying

beet

fan

bowl

tire

punch

week

post

pale

tail

shed

tale

drill

deal

pail

bury

berry

Challenge Words

heir

crews

mourn

marshal

buoy

Review Words

plain

wood

plane

would

Build Vocabulary

Word Endings

■ Form new words by adding *-ed* and *-ing* to these verbs. You know that you may need to drop the final *e*, change *y* to *i*, or double the final consonant before adding *-ed* or *-ing*.

	-ed	-ing
1. fan	___	___
2. bowl	___	___
3. tire	___	___
4. bury	___	___
5. drill	___	___
6. post	___	___
7. punch	___	___

■ Write the spelling word that has the ending *-ing*.

8. ___

■ Use words you made to complete these sentences.

9. The long plane trip was quite ___.

10. I ___ a letter from Mexico City.

Review Words

Write the word pairs that are homophones. Underline the letters in each pair of words that are different.

11. ___ ___

12. ___ ___

plain
wood
plane
would

TAKE HOME

List the word pairs that are homophones in alphabetical order. Circle the word pairs. Then list the words that are homographs in alphabetical order. Use your lists to practice at home.

Apply Spelling Skills

Dictionary Skills

Homographs have a small, raised number after them in the dictionary to show that the word has more than one entry. Use the **Spelling Dictionary** on page 214 to write a homograph for each definition below.

1. A student.____
2. A round opening in the eye.____
3. To make or become weak from too much work or use.____
4. A band of rubber that fits around a wheel. ____

Proofreading

Check spelling, capital letters, and punctuation. Then rewrite the paragraph. There are six mistakes.

> You can't beet the rocky Mountains for a great vacation! Our cabin looks like a shedd. We carry water in a pale. We see a great deel of beautiful animals. last night I saw a deer's tail.

Writing • *About Social Studies*

PREWRITE: Imagine you are taking a trip to a place you have always wanted to visit. List the things you want to see.

DRAFT: Write a postcard telling a friend some interesting details about the place you are visiting.

REVISE: Read your postcard over to yourself. Have you used exciting, descriptive words?

EDIT/PROOFREAD: Use editing marks. Then write a clean copy.

PUBLISH: Make a postcard. Draw a picture on the back. Then "send" your postcard to someone in your class.

EDITING MARKS

◯ check spelling
≡ capital letter
/ lowercase letter
⊙ add a period
∧ add
↗ take out
⸮ indent the paragraph
↺ move

For more help, see page 171.

35

CONTRACTIONS

1. wouldn't
2. weren't
3. I'd
4. there's
5. he'll
6. let's
7. what's
8. they'd
9. who's
10. we've
11. here's
12. couldn't
13. he's
14. she'll
15. it'll
16. where's
17. he'd
18. she'd
19. didn't
20. hadn't

Learn Spelling Patterns

LOOK & SAY Listen for the sounds in each word.

PICTURE Close your eyes. See each word in your mind.

STUDY In these spelling words, two words have been joined and shortened to form a **contraction.** An apostrophe shows where one or more letters have been left out.

WRITE Sort the words. Which words have the following underlined letters left out?

is/has   (1)   (2)   (3)   (4)   (5)   (6)
not   (7)   (8)   (9)   (10)   (11)
will   (12)   (13)   (14)
have   (15)
would/had   (16)   (17)   (18)   (19)
us   (20)

CHECK Did you spell each word correctly? Circle the apostrophe in each word.

Pattern Power

What letters does an apostrophe replace when *is* or *has* is combined with a word to form a contraction? (21) or (22) When *not* is combined with a verb to form a contraction? (23)

Other Words

Write words you would like to add to this week's list.

_____   _____   _____   _____   _____

Practice Word Meanings

Words in Context

Write a spelling word from the box below to complete each sentence.

where's	it'll	didn't	there's	couldn't	I'd

1. _____ like to do a report on birds.
2. What would we do if we _____ have birds?
3. I'm sure _____ be my best report ever.
4. Do you think _____ a good book on birds in the library?
5. Angela _____ think of a topic for her report.
6. _____ the best place for bird watching?

Challenge Words • *Language Arts*

Write the challenge words in which an apostrophe shows that the underlined letters have been left out. Use the **Spelling Dictionary** on page 214 to help you. Circle each apostrophe.

<u>is</u> or **has**   7. _____
will   8. _____
n<u>o</u>t   9. _____
have   10. _____
                    11. _____

what'll
should've
how's
you've
mustn't

Spelling Tip

In a contraction, be sure to put the apostrophe where the missing letter or letters would be.

✦ Most of the time, the letters that are dropped are at the beginning of the second word of the contraction.

✦ When a contraction is made with *not*, the *n* is usually connected to the first word, and the apostrophe takes the place of the *o*.

List Words

wouldn't

weren't

I'd

there's

he'll

let's

what's

they'd

who's

we've

here's

couldn't

he's

she'll

it'll

where's

he'd

she'd

didn't

hadn't

Challenge Words

what'll

should've

how's

you've

mustn't

Review Words

I'll

we'll

I'm

it's

Build Vocabulary

Forming Contractions

■ Write a spelling word that is a contraction for each word pair below.

1. he is _____   7. she will _____

2. had not _____   8. we have _____

3. were not _____   9. she would _____

4. he will _____   10. he would _____

5. let us _____   11. here is _____

6. who is _____   12. they would _____

■ When a word is used in several contractions, usually the same letter or letters are replaced by an apostrophe. In the examples below, the *i* in *is* is replaced by an apostrophe.

he + *is* = he's   she + *is* = she's   that + *is* = that's

Write the contraction that is formed when each pair of words below is combined.

13. I + have _____   15. they + have _____

14. I + will _____   16. you + will _____

■ Use words you made in **13–16** to complete these sentences.

17. _____ see you after school at the soccer game.

18. Do you think _____ finished practice yet?

Review Words

Write the review words in which an apostrophe shows that the underlined letters have been left out. Circle the apostrophes in each contraction.

am 19. _____   21. _____

will 20. _____   **is** or **has** 22. _____

I'll
we'll
I'm
it's

▲T A K E◆H O M E▲

Write your spelling words in alphabetical order. Circle the apostrophe in each word. Use your lists to practice spelling the words at home.

Apply Spelling Skills

Dictionary Skills

You can locate a contraction in the dictionary by looking up the contraction in alphabetical order. Use the **Spelling Dictionary** on page 214 to find the entry word that comes right before each contraction below.

1. it'll _iron_
2. she'd ____
3. he'd ____
4. let's ____
5. what's ____
6. I'm ____

Pattern Power

Look at the contractions in the dictionary activity.

• Circle any words you wrote that are contractions.

Proofreading

Check spelling, capital letters, and punctuation. Then rewrite the poem. There are six mistakes.

Whats up at three
Wheres he going to be?
Why coudnt he hurry
Why wouldnt she scurry?

Writing • *About Language Arts*

PREWRITE: List some rhyming words and contractions that would be fun to use in a nonsense poem.

DRAFT: Write a nonsense poem with at least two contractions.

REVISE: Exchange poems with a classmate. Help each other think of more rhymes for your poems.

EDIT/PROOFREAD: Use editing marks. Then rewrite your poem.

PUBLISH: Read your poem aloud in a class poetry reading.

EDITING MARKS

⬯ check spelling

≡ capital letter

/ lowercase letter

⊙ add a period

⌃ add

✗ take out

¶ indent the paragraph

↻ move

For more help, see page 171.

36 REVIEW Spelling Patterns

Sort the words in each list. Write each word.

grandmother newspaper sunshine overcome somewhere homemade everybody bathroom homework within	**Lesson 31** **Compound words in alphabetical order** Circle two smaller words within the compounds. 1.____ 6.____ 2.____ 7.____ 3.____ 8.____ 4.____ 9.____ 5.____ 10.____

patches buckets monkeys matches ranches shadows sales addresses parents coaches	**Lesson 32** **Plurals with -s and -es** Circle endings and spelling changes in plurals. -s 11. ____ -es 16. ____ 12. ____ 17. ____ 13. ____ 18. ____ 14. ____ 19. ____ 15. ____ 20. ____

mice geese leaves enemies thieves knives shelves families cherries pennies	**Lesson 33** **Plurals with spelling changes in alphabetical order** Circle endings and spelling changes in plurals. 21.____ 26.____ 22.____ 27.____ 23.____ 28.____ 24.____ 29.____ 25.____ 30.____

weak	
pupil	
bowl	
tire	
week	
post	
shed	
drill	
bury	
berry	

Lesson 34
Homophones and homographs in alphabetical order

31._____   36._____

32._____   37._____

33._____   38._____

34._____   39._____

35._____   40._____

weren't
he'll
let's
who's
we've
here's
it'll
where's
he'd
didn't

Lesson 35
Contractions in alphabetical order
Circle apostrophes in contractions.

41._____   46._____

42._____   47._____

43._____   48._____

44._____   49._____

45._____   50._____

Spelling Tip

In a contraction, an apostrophe takes the place of a missing letter or group of letters.

✦ Usually the letters that are dropped are at the beginning of the second word of the contraction.

✦ When *not* is part of a contraction, the only letter that is dropped is *o*. You usually connect the *n* to the first word in the contraction.

Write contractions for the following words.

1. who + is = _____

2. were + not = _____

3. where + is = _____

where's
who's
weren't

153

Word Meaning Mixed Lesson Review

everybody
weren't
monkeys
who's
post
he'd
bury

Context Sentences

Write the spelling word that can replace the underlined word or words in each sentence.

1. We saw the <u>apes</u> in the zoo. ____
2. <u>Who is</u> watching the zoo animals? ____
3. The squirrel will <u>cover</u> the pine cones. ____
4. The bananas <u>were not</u> quite ripe. ____
5. James said <u>he would</u> help me. ____
6. The animals are enjoyed by <u>all people</u>. ____
7. The sign was nailed to a <u>pole</u>. ____

thieves
bowl
somewhere
sunshine
pupil
didn't

Synonyms and Antonyms

Write the spelling word that is a synonym or an antonym for each word below. Then write *synonym* or *antonym* after each word pair.

8. darkness ____ ____
9 robbers ____ ____
10. student ____ ____
11. did ____ ____
12. nowhere ____ ____
13. container ____ ____

he'll
pennies
bathroom
berry
leaves

Related Meanings

Write the spelling word that belongs with each group of words below.

14. seed, nut, fruit ____
15. kitchen, den, bedroom ____
16. she'll, they'll, I'll ____
17. roots, trees, stems ____
18. money, dollars, change ____

Vocabulary Mixed Lesson Review

Identify the Singular Form

Write the singular form of each spelling word below.

1. coaches _____
2. matches _____
3. sales _____
4. geese _____
5. buckets _____
6. mice _____
7. thieves _____
8. cherries _____
9. shelves _____
10. addresses_____

Dictionary Skills

Read the dictionary entries and complete the items below.

> **shed**[1] A small building. The *shed* was used as a storage space.
> **shed** (shed) *noun, plural* **sheds**.
>
> **shed**[2] **1.** To pour forth. Don't *shed* tears over your mistakes.
> **2.** To let drop or fall. Does your dog *shed* much hair?
> **shed** (shed) *verb*, **shed**, **shedding**.

1. Entry words like those above are called _____.
2. The part of speech for **shed**[1] is _____.
3. The part of speech for **shed**[2] is _____.
4. Write the definition for **shed**[1]. _____

Spelling and Writing

A letter to the editor is a form of persuasive writing. The writer gives facts and reasons to support his or her opinion.

OPINION

EXAMPLES

PERSUASIVE WORDS

May 23, 1997

To the Editor:

Instead of a new mini-mall, **our town needs a new park!** We have only one small park within the town. Children need a park with safe playground equipment. **Older people need somewhere to enjoy the sunshine. People who jog or bicycle have to use the streets.** If we build a park, families could use it to relax together outdoors. The town already has lots of stores, and the big mall is only five miles away. **Let's use the land for the good of everybody.**

Jason Cisneros

Student, Elmwood Elementary School

Now write your own persuasive letter to the editor. Try to use some of the spelling words in your letter.

PREWRITE: How could you make your town better? Write your opinion about the issue.

DRAFT: Write a paragraph about your issue. Begin with a topic sentence that states your opinion. Give reasons and facts to support your opinion.

REVISE: Did you use persuasive words? Did you support your opinion?

EDIT/PROOFREAD: Use editing marks to correct your capitalization, spelling, and punctuation. Rewrite your paragraph neatly.

PUBLISH: Contribute your letter to the editor to a class newspaper.

WRITING TIPS!!

Persuasive Writing

- Use examples to make your letter convincing.
- Use facts and persuasive words to make your point.
- Give your opinions.

Spelling Fun
CUMULATIVE REVIEW

SILLY SENTENCES

- Choose words from Lessons 1–29.
- Write four silly sentences. In each sentence, use a noun, a verb, and an adjective from your spelling words.
- Be as silly as you like. You can also make more than four sentences if you like.
- Read your sentences during a class comedy show.

PLAY GUESS MY WORD

My word is "grandmother"

- Choose one word from any list in Lessons 31–35.
- Tell your partner the word's spelling pattern.
- Have your partner try to guess your word by asking you questions about how many letters your word has, whether your word rhymes with another word, what kind of ending your word has, and so on.
- After your partner guesses your word, switch roles.

SPELLING BEE

- Team A writes one word each from Lessons 1–17 (15 words) on cards. (Skip review lessons.) Team B writes one word each from Lessons 19–35 (15 words) on cards.
- Team A calls out a word.
- The first player on Team B writes the word on a piece of paper.
- If the word is spelled correctly, the word is taken out of the pile and Team B scores 1 point. If not, the word is returned to the pile.
- Play continues as Team B calls out a word for the first player on Team A to spell.
- The first team to get 15 points wins.

CONTENTS OF
Handbook

Spelling Resources

Writing Handbook

Common Spelling Patterns

Below is a list of sounds and different ways sounds are spelled. Use this list when you can't find a word in the dictionary to see how else the sound may be spelled.

/a/	a	act, bat	/ir/	ear	fear, eardrum	/th/	th	smooth, they
/ā/	a	able, lazy		eer	cheer, deer	/th/	th	path, thing
	a-e	cave, ate		ere	here, sincere	/u/	u	lump, up
	ai	rail, wait		er	period, cereal		ou	trouble, cousin
	ay	say, maybe	/k/	c	coil, act	/ù/	u	pull, push
	eigh	neighbor,		k	kitchen, dark		oo	book, took
		weigh		ck	knuckle, back	/ü/	ew	drew, grew
/är/	ar	hard, part		lk	folks, yolk		ue	glue, true
/âr/	are	share, care	/kw/	qu	quilt, equal		oo	too,
	air	repair, stairs	/n/	n	newspaper			monsoon
	ear	pear, wear		kn	knives, knob		o	do, to
	ere	where, there	/o/	o	socks, hospital	/ū/	u	pupil, music
	eir	their	/ō/	o	roll, noble		ew	few, nephew
/ch/	ch	such, chance		o-e	those, phone		ue	rescue, fuel
	tch	patch, match		oa	groan, coaches	/ûr/	er	perfect, her
/e/	e	let's, rest		ow	grow, owner		ir	firm, stir
	ea	meant, jealous	/ô/	a	all, although		or	word, work
/ē/	e	me, she, he		au	haul, taught		ur	curve, nurse
	y	study, city		aw	awful, law	/yù/	u	curious,
	ee	sweet, knee		o	cross, song			bureau
	ea	mean, repeat	/oi/	oi	moist, broil		u-e	cure, pure
	e-e	scene, these		oy	annoy, boy	/əl/	al	hospital, loyal
	ie	piece, chief	/ôr/	or	order, cord		el	model, level
/f/	f	famous, leaf		ore	soreness, store		il	evil, April
	ff	office, stuff		oar	soar, board		le	rattle, giggle
	gh	laugh, cough	/ou/	ou	county, aloud	/ən/	on	ribbon, button
	ph	phone, graph		ow	anyhow, owl		en	chicken,
/hw/	wh	whirl, which	/r/	r	rescue, already			kitchen
/i/	i	lift, pitch		wr	wrap, writer		an	woman, organ
/ī/	i	I, idea	/s/	s	secret, outside		ain	fountain,
	i-e	decide, mine		ss	press, across			captain
	y	supply, try		c	decide, pencil	/ər/	er	enter, matter
	ie	tie, lie		ce	race, peace		or	color, doctor
				sc	scene, science		ar	grammar, cellar

Spelling Tips: Rules

Learning these spelling rules can help you spell many words.

1. When words end in silent *e*, drop the *e* when adding an ending that begins with a vowel. *(argue + ed = argued)* When adding an ending that begins with a consonant, keep the silent *e*. *(like + ly = likely)*

2. When a base word ends with a consonant followed by *y*, change the *y* to *i* when adding any ending except endings that begin with *i*. *(cry + es = cries; cry + ing = crying)*

3. When a base word ends with a vowel followed by *y*, do not change the *y* when adding endings. *(monkey + s = monkeys)*

4. When a one-syllable word ends in one vowel followed by one consonant, double the consonant before adding an ending that begins with a vowel. *(run + ing = running)*

5. The letter *q* is always followed by *u*. *(quilt, quiet)*

6. Add *-s* to most words to form plurals or to change the tense of verbs. Add *-es* to words ending in *x*, *z*, *s*, *sh*, or *ch*. *(cup + s = cups; laugh + s = laughs; glass + es = glasses)*

7. To make plurals of words that end with one *f* or *fe*, usually change the *f* or *fe* to *v* and add *-es*. *(wife + es = wives)*

8. When choosing *ei* or *ie*, remember that *i* comes before *e* except after *c* or when sounded like /ā/ as in *neighbor* or *weigh*.

9. When *s* is spelled *c*, *c* is always followed by *e*, *i*, or *y*. *(peace, citizen, fancy)*

10. When /j/ is spelled *g*, *g* is always followed by *e*, *i*, or *y*. *(gem, engine, energy)*

11. If the /ch/ immediately follows a short vowel in a one-syllable word, it is spelled *tch*. *(clutch, sketch)* There are a few exceptions in English: *much*, *such*, *which*, and *rich*.

12. The /f/ sound at the end of a word may be spelled *f*, *ph*, or *gh*. *(chief, graph, laugh)*

Spelling Tips: Strategies

These strategies can help you become a better speller.

1. Learn common homophones and make sure you have used the correct homophone in your writing.

   They brought *their* own books. Move the books over *there*. *It's* a sunny day. The earth gets *its* light from the sun.

2. Think of a word you know that has the same spelling pattern as the word you want to spell, such as a rhyming word. *(blue, clue, glue)*

3. Use words that you know how to spell to help you spell new words. *(flower + clock = flock)*

4. Make up clues to help you remember the spelling. *(u and i build a house; a piece of pie; the principal is your pal)*

5. Think of a related word to help you spell a word with a silent letter or a hard-to-hear sound. *(sign-signal; relative-related)*

6. Divide the word into syllables. *(sub scrip tion)*

7. Learn to spell prefixes and suffixes you use often in writing.

8. Look for word chunks or smaller words that help you remember the spelling of the word. *(hippopotamus = hippo pot am us)*

9. Change the way you say the word to yourself to help with the spelling. *(knife = /kə nīf/; beauty = /bē ə ū tē/)*

10. Think of times you may have seen the word in reading, on signs, or in a textbook. Try to remember how it looked. Write the word in different ways. Which one looks correct? *(havy, hevy, heavy)*

11. Keep an alphabetical Personal Word List in your Spelling Journal. Write words you often have trouble spelling.

12. One more strategy will always help you: Become familiar with the dictionary and use it often.

Computer Tip:

Use the spell-check, but read your writing carefully, too. The computer can't tell if you used a wrong word, such as *your* instead of *you're* or *it's* instead of *its*.

Spelling and Meaning Connections

Many words, like *poem* and *poetic*, are close in meaning. They are also close in spelling. Such words are called related words. Sometimes two related words can have different pronunciations but the same spelling. You can use this fact to help you remember how to spell many related words.

1. The underlined letter in the first word in each group below stays the same in other words in the group. How does the sound change?

electri<u>c</u>
electri<u>c</u>ity—a form of energy that uses electric power
electri<u>c</u>ian—a person who repairs electrical objects

mathemati<u>c</u>s
mathemati<u>c</u>ian—someone who studies and teaches mathematics

musi<u>c</u>
musi<u>c</u>ian—someone who plays music

publi<u>c</u>
publi<u>c</u>ity—information given to attract public attention to a person or thing

In each group, the sound of the letter *c* changes from /k/ to /s/ or /sh/.

- To remember how to spell *electricity*, think of the related word *electric*.

- If you know that *electric* ends with the letter *c*, it can help you remember to spell /s/ in *electricity* with the letter *c*.

- Use this tip with other related words that follow the same pattern as *electric* and *electricity*.

2. Here's another sound-letter pattern. What changes about the underlined letter in each word in the group? What stays the same?

ac<u>t</u>
ac<u>t</u>ion—the process of acting

coopera<u>t</u>e
coopera<u>t</u>ion—the act or process of cooperating

crea<u>t</u>e
crea<u>t</u>ion—the act or process of creating something

decora<u>t</u>e
decora<u>t</u>ion—the act or process of decorating

depar<u>t</u>
depar<u>t</u>ure—the act of departing

direc<u>t</u>
direc<u>t</u>ion—the act or process of directing or instructing

fac<u>t</u>
fac<u>t</u>ual—having the quality of being based on facts

habi<u>t</u>
habi<u>t</u>ual—being done by habit

inven<u>t</u>
inven<u>t</u>ion—something that is invented

loca<u>t</u>e
loca<u>t</u>ion—where something is located or can be found

narra<u>t</u>e
narra<u>t</u>ion—the act or process of narrating or telling something

objec<u>t</u>
objec<u>t</u>ion—the act of objecting or protesting something

In all the words you just read, the sound of the letter *t* changes from /t/ to /sh/ or /ch/.

- To remember how to spell *action*, think of the related word *act*.

- If you know that *act* ends with the letter *t*, it can help you remember to spell /sh/ with the letter *t*.

- Use this tip with other related words that follow the same pattern as *act* and *action*.

Spelling and Meaning Connections

3. Look at the letter that is underlined in the words in each group below. How does the sound of that letter change from the first word in the group to the other word or words?

auto<u>n</u>mal—having to do with
   autumn
autum<u>n</u>
autum<u>n</u>s

colum<u>n</u>ist—someone who
   writes a column for a
   newspaper or magazine
colum<u>n</u>
colum<u>n</u>s

crum<u>b</u>le—to break into pieces
   or crumbs
crum<u>b</u>
crum<u>b</u>s

fas<u>t</u>—firmly attached; securely
   fastened
fas<u>t</u>en
fas<u>t</u>ener
unfas<u>t</u>en

has<u>t</u>e—speed or hurry
has<u>t</u>y—quick
has<u>t</u>en

mus<u>c</u>ular—having strong or
   well-developed muscles
mus<u>c</u>le
mus<u>c</u>les

mois<u>t</u>—slightly wet; damp
mois<u>t</u>en

signal—a light, movement, or
   other form of communication
si<u>g</u>n

sof<u>t</u>—easy to shape; not hard
sof<u>t</u>en
sof<u>t</u>ener

In each group, the underlined letter is sounded in the first word and silent in the word or words that follow.

■ To remember how to spell *autumn,* think of the sound of the related word *autumnal.*

■ You can hear the *n* in *autumnal.* That sound can help you remember to spell final /m/ in *autumn* with *mn.*

■ Use this tip with other related words that have silent and sounded letters.

4. Each word in this group has one or more vowels underlined. Decide how the vowels change in other words in the group.

br<u>ea</u>the—to draw air, or breath, into the lungs and let it out again
br<u>ea</u>th
br<u>ea</u>thless

c<u>a</u>ve—a hole or hollow in the ground or in a mountainside
c<u>a</u>vity
c<u>a</u>vern

cl<u>ea</u>n—not dirty
cl<u>ea</u>nse
cl<u>ea</u>nser

comp<u>e</u>te—to try to win or gain something
comp<u>e</u>tition
comp<u>e</u>titive

d<u>ea</u>l—a bargain or arrangement
d<u>ea</u>lt

h<u>ea</u>l—to get better or make something get better
h<u>ea</u>lth
h<u>ea</u>lthy

m<u>ea</u>n—to have in mind
m<u>ea</u>nt

m<u>i</u>nus—less, decreased by
m<u>i</u>nimum

n<u>a</u>tion—a country that has its own government
n<u>a</u>tional
intern<u>a</u>tional

n<u>a</u>ture—all the things, like trees, that are not made by people
n<u>a</u>tural
unn<u>a</u>tural

pl<u>ea</u>se—to give pleasure to
pl<u>ea</u>sure
pl<u>ea</u>sant

w<u>i</u>se—having or showing good judgment
w<u>i</u>sdom

A long vowel sound in one word can sometimes change to a short vowel sound in a related word, without a change in spelling.

- *Breathe* and *breath* are related in meaning.
- *Breathe* has the long vowel sound spelled *ea.*
- *Breath* has the short vowel sound spelled *ea.*
- Remembering how to spell *breathe* can help you spell *breath.*
- Can you think of a word that will help you spell *dreamt*?

5. The underlined letter in the first word in each group has /ə/. What kind of vowel sound does the underlined letter spell in the other words in each group?

ability—the condition of being able

able

unable

admiration—the act of admiring

admire

admirer

composition—a piece of writing or music that is composed

compose

composer

definition—a phrase or sentence that defines a word

define

indefinable

relative—a person, like a sister or cousin, who is related to you

relate

related

In related words, /ə/ in one word can sometimes change to a long vowel sound in a related word, without a change in spelling.

■ *Ability* and *able* are related words.

■ *Ability* has /ə/ spelled with the letter *a*.

■ *Able* has a long vowel sound spelled with the letter *a*.

■ Remembering how to spell *able* can help you spell *ability*.

■ Can you think of a word that will help you spell *alternative?*

6. The underlined letter in the first word in each group has /ə/. What kind of vowel sound does the underlined letter spell in the other word or words in each group?

democr<u>a</u>cy—a form of government that recognizes people's rights
democr<u>a</u>tic
democr<u>a</u>t

fin<u>a</u>l—last
fin<u>a</u>lity
fin<u>a</u>lities

hum<u>a</u>n—having to do with people
hum<u>a</u>nity

individu<u>a</u>l—one person
individu<u>a</u>lity

leg<u>a</u>l—done according to the law
leg<u>a</u>lity

loc<u>a</u>l—nearby, within this area or community
loc<u>a</u>lity

met<u>a</u>l—a hard, shiny material, like gold or iron
met<u>a</u>llic
nonmet<u>a</u>llic

norm<u>a</u>l—ordinary, regular
norm<u>a</u>lity

perf<u>e</u>ct—without fault or flaw
perf<u>e</u>ction
imperf<u>e</u>ction

In related words, /ə/ in one word can sometimes change to a short vowel sound in a related word, without a change in spelling.

- *Democracy* and *democrat* are related words.
- *Democracy* has /ə/ spelled with the letter *a*.
- *Democrat* has a short vowel sound spelled with the letter *a*.
- Remembering how to spell *democrat* can help you spell *democracy.*
- Can you think of a word that will help you spell *personal?*

Difficult Words

Easily Confused Words

Easily confused words are words that are often mistaken for other words because they are spelled similarly or sound alike. These words have different definitions and can mix up the meaning of a sentence. Make sure you know the meaning of the words in each pair.

accept	all together	breath	ever	of	trail
except	altogether	breathe	every	off	trial
accuse	angel	cloth	expect	picture	use
excuse	angle	clothe	suspect	pitcher	used
advice	any more	costume	farther	quiet	weather
advise	anymore	custom	further	quite	whether
affect	any way	dairy	lay	recent	were
effect	anyway	diary	lie	resent	where
all ready	bean	desert	loose	though	your
already	been	dessert	lose	through	you're

Troublesome Words

Some words are hard to spell for many writers. Use this list to check your spelling or to test yourself to see how many of these words you can spell correctly.

a lot	break	except	interesting	once	there's
address	brought	favorite	into	opened	tomorrow
again	busy	finally	knew	other	took
against	caught	first	know	our	trouble
all right	children	found	library	outside	until
already	country	friend	maybe	people	upon
always	cousin	front	might	probably	usually
answer	different	guess	minute	really	vacation
beautiful	doesn't	happened	morning	since	watch
because	dollar	heard	myself	something	we're
before	done	hospital	nickel	sometimes	when
believe	enough	house	none	straight	whole
birthday	especially	hundred	off	stuff	woman
bought	every	instead	often	swimming	women

Common Homophones

Homophones are words with the same pronunciation but with different meanings and spellings. *Cent* and *sent* are homophones.

ad	cent	flour	heard	oh	their
add	sent	flower	herd	owe	there
aisle	scent				they're
I'll	chews	forth	hole	*pail	
	choose	fourth	whole	*pale	threw
allowed					through
aloud	coarse	groan	in	pare	
	course	grown	inn	pear	wade
ate					weighed
eight	creak	guessed	its	passed	
	creek	guest	it's	past	wail
bare					whale
bear	days	hair	loan	peace	
	daze	hare	lone	piece	*weak
base					*week
bass	dew	hall	made	peer	
	do	haul	maid	pier	
*beat					
*beet	fair	heal	meat	*plain	
	fare	heel	meet	*plane	
*berry					
*bury	flea	hear	missed	*tail	
	flee	here	mist	*tale	

Words printed in color appear in spelling lessons.
* These homophones appear in Lesson 34.

Writing Plan

Writing is a way to share facts, ideas, or feelings. Follow these steps to create good, clear writing.

Prewrite

Choose your topic.
Decide who will be your audience.
What is your purpose for writing?

- to express feelings
- to describe a person, place, thing, or event
- to give information
- to persuade

Jot down what you already know about your topic. Then learn more about it.

- Read books, magazines, and newspapers. Use the computer Internet.
- Talk to people. Ask questions. Interview an expert.
- Look at the real thing! Take a field trip if you need to.

How will you remember details you see and organize information?

- Take notes.
- Create a story map.
- Make a word web.
- Make a list or outline.
- Draw pictures.
- Draw a chart or graph.
- Make a diagram.

Draft

After you have gathered and organized your information, write it in sentence form. Just let your thoughts flow. Get them all down on paper.

Revise

Read over your writing. Think about your audience and purpose.

- Did you cover the important points?
- Did you present your ideas in a logical order? Do you need to move, take out, or add anything?
- Does your writing have a clear beginning, middle, and end?
- Do your sentences express complete thoughts?

You could also ask a friend to read what you wrote.

Writing Plan

Edit/Proofread

Reread your writing, looking carefully at these things:

- spelling
- punctuation—commas, apostrophes, quotation marks, end marks
- capital letters—to start a sentence and for proper nouns
- indenting of paragraphs
- handwriting—dotting *i*'s and *j*'s, crossing *t*'s and *x*'s.

Use these editing marks as you revise, edit, and proofread.

> ⌐Jupiter is the largest Planet^in our ⟨soler⟩ solar
> system. It rotates much faster than earth.
> A day on Jupiter is ~~only~~ ten hours long ⟨only⟩.
>
>   Jupiter is the largest planet in our solar
> system. It rotates much faster than Earth.
> A day on Jupiter is only ten hours long.

EDITING MARKS

- ◯ **check spelling**
- ≡ **capital letter**
- / **lowercase letter**
- ⊙ **add a period**
- ∧ **add**
- ⤸ **take out**
- ⌐ **indent the paragraph**
- ◯⤳ **move**

Publish

Think about your audience as you put your writing into final form. How do you want to share your work?

- Read it aloud.
- Hang it on the wall.
- Record it on tape.
- Give it to a friend.
- Create a book.
- Mail it.

Types of Writing

Here are things to think about for different types of writing you may do.

Narrative Writing

A story is narrative writing—writing that tells about something that happens.

- Will the action, or events, be interesting to readers?
- Are the events in an order that readers can follow?
- Do the characters face an interesting challenge?
- When the characters talk, does their dialog help tell the story?
- Will readers get a clear picture of the setting, or the time and place of the story?

Report

A report gives information about a subject. It presents facts in a clear, organized way.

- Does your report begin with an introduction to the main idea?
- Have you ordered your facts logically in the body of the report?
- Does your report end with a clear summary of the facts?

Explanatory Writing

Explanatory writing tells how to make or do something.

- Did you express your purpose at the beginning?
- Did you present the information and details in the right order?
- Do you need to add details to make the explanation clearer?
- Do you need a picture or diagram?

Persuasive Writing

Persuasive writing tries to get the audience to do something or to share an opinion. Advertising, movie reviews, letters to a newspaper, and book reports are kinds of persuasive writing.

- Did you use facts and forceful words like *should* to make your point?
- What is the most convincing part of your writing?
- Will readers share your opinion?

Comparison/Contrast Writing

Comparison/contrast writing presents facts about two things to show how they are alike and how they are different.

- Do you begin with a main idea?
- Are your comparisons and contrasts clear? Are they in an order that is easy to understand?
- Do the comparisons and contrasts help express the main idea?
- Is your conclusion clear and strong?

Descriptive Writing

Descriptive writing creates a word picture of a person, place, thing, or event. The words help readers use all their senses to "get the picture."

- Have you used vivid words that help readers see, hear, and touch what you describe?
- When possible, have you used more exact words, such as *rushed* instead of *ran,* to make your details clearer?
- Does your writing express a feeling about the subject?

Capitalization and Punctuation Tips

Abbreviation An abbreviation is a short form of a word. Most abbreviations begin with a capital letter and end with a period. *Dec.* is the abbreviation for *December*.

Use abbreviations for titles of people, addresses, days of the week, and months of the year. **Dr. Zato   15 Oak Ave.   Thurs.   Sept.** Some abbreviations, such as the U.S. Postal Service abbreviations for the names of states, contain all capital letters and no periods.

Alabama—AL	Missouri—MO
Alaska—AK	Montana—MT
Arizona—AZ	Nebraska—NE
Arkansas—AR	Nevada—NV
California—CA	New Hampshire—NH
Colorado—CO	New Jersey—NJ
Connecticut—CT	New Mexico—NM
Delaware—DE	New York—NY
District of	North Carolina—NC
Columbia—DC	North Dakota—ND
Florida—FL	Ohio—OH
Georgia—GA	Oklahoma—OK
Hawaii—HI	Oregon—OR
Idaho—ID	Pennsylvania—PA
Illinois—IL	Rhode Island—RI
Indiana—IN	South Carolina—SC
Iowa—IA	South Dakota—SD
Kansas—KS	Tennessee—TN
Kentucky—KY	Texas—TX
Louisiana—LA	Utah—UT
Maine—ME	Vermont—VT
Maryland—MD	Virginia—VA
Massachusetts—MA	Washington—WA
Michigan—MI	West Virginia—WV
Minnesota—MN	Wisconsin—WI
Mississippi—MS	Wyoming—WY

Apostrophe
An apostrophe is a punctuation mark used to show possession.

Use an apostrophe with *s* after a person's name to show possession.

Cary's scarf   the scarf that belongs to Cary

Use an apostrophe alone to form the possessive of a plural noun that ends in -*s*.

the girls' shoes   the shoes that belong to the girls

Use an apostrophe to show where letters have been left out in a contraction.   **don't** = do not

Capitalization
Capitalization is the writing of the first letter of a word in its upper case form.

Capitalize the first word in a sentence.

Both of the dogs like cheese.

Capitalize the first letter of a proper noun.

George   Ms. Singh   Japan

Capitalize days of the week, months, and holidays.

Friday   April   Thanksgiving Day

Colon
A colon is a punctuation mark used to introduce a list, an explanation, or an example.

These are the origami shapes I can make: the crane, the bell, the box, and the crab.

A colon is also used to separate hours and minutes when writing time in numerals.

The movie starts at 3:30.

Capitalization and Punctuation Tips

Comma A comma is a punctuation mark that indicates a pause or separation between parts of a sentence.

Use a comma between the city and the state in an address.

Topeka, Kansas

Use a comma between the day and year in a date.

May 29, 1998

Use commas to separate three or more items in a series.

Javier enjoys swimming, running, and basketball.

Use a comma after the greeting in a friendly letter and the closing in all letters.

Dear Eddie,   Sincerely yours,

End punctuation The punctuation mark at the end of a sentence tells you what kind of sentence it is.

A **period** is used at the end of a statement, a mild command, or a polite request.

Leila built a birdhouse.   Please pass the salt.

An **exclamation mark** is used at the end of a strong command or an exclamatory sentence.

Don't touch that!   What an exciting game this is!

A **question mark** is used at the end of a question.

Are you going to the beach?

Hyphen Use a hyphen to show the division of a word at the end of a line. Divide the word between syllables.

Where have you put the ad-dresses of the new members?

Quotation Marks In a direct quotation, quotation marks go before and after the exact words that someone said.

Bernardo said, "I am learning how to swim."

Grammar Glossary

Adjective An adjective is a word that can describe a noun or pronoun. It tells what kind, how many, or which one.

The <u>new</u> shoes are <u>comfortable</u>.

Adverb An adverb is a word that can describe a verb, an adjective, or another adverb. It tells how, when, where, or how much.

The chorus sang <u>softly</u> and <u>sweetly</u>.

Article An article is a special adjective. *A* and *an* are called **indefinite articles** because they refer to any of a group of people, places, things, or ideas. *The* is called a **definite article**, because it identifies a particular person, place, thing, or idea.

Comparative Adjective A comparative adjective is a form of an adjective that can compare two or more things. To compare two persons or things, form the comparative by adding *-er* to some adjectives. To compare more than two persons or things, you use the superlative form by adding *-est* to some adjectives.

Mount Shasta is <u>high</u>, but Mount Kenya is <u>higher</u>.

Pico Duarte and Mount Kazbek are <u>high</u>, but Mount Everest is the <u>highest</u> mountain on Earth.

For some other adjectives, add the word *more* or *less* to form the comparative. Add the word *most* or *least* to form the superlative.

I think that baseball is the <u>most interesting</u> sport to watch and football is the <u>least interesting</u> sport.

Complete Predicate The complete predicate is all the words in a sentence that tell what the subject is or does.

Chen <u>came home early</u>.

Complete Subject The complete subject is all the words in a sentence that tell what or whom the sentence is about.

<u>Ms. Patel's fourth grade class</u> is in the library.

Compound Predicate A compound predicate occurs when a sentence contains more than one equally important predicate, or verb phrase. The coordinating conjunctions *and, but,* or *or* can be used to join a compound predicate.

We <u>bought and wrapped gifts</u>.

Compound Sentence A compound sentence is formed by joining two or more sentences with a coordinating conjunction such as *and, but,* or *or.* In a compound sentence, a comma comes before the conjunction that joins the sentences.

Grammar Glossary

It had not rained for weeks, and the grass had turned brown.

Compound Subject A compound subject occurs when a sentence contains more than one equally important subject. The coordinating conjunctions *and, but,* or *or* can be used to join a compound subject.

Malik and Tamika are twins.

Compound Word A compound word is two or more words put together to make a new word.

airplane	footprint
daylight	underground

Conjunction A conjunction is a word that is used to join words or word groups. Coordinating conjunctions such as *and, but,* and *or* can be used to make compound sentences, subjects, and predicates.

Contraction A contraction is a short form of two words. An apostrophe takes the place of letters that are left out.

Isn't is a contraction for is not.

Double Negatives Two **negative words** cannot be used in the same sentence.

Some negative words: **no not nobody none no one nothing**

Correct: We have no time.
Correct: We do not have time.
Mistake: We do not have no time.

Exclamatory Sentence An exclamatory sentence shows excitement, surprise, or strong feeling. It ends with an exclamation mark.

What a beautiful day this is!

Homographs Homographs are words that have the same spelling but completely different meanings. *Pitcher* is a homograph because it can mean "a container that holds liquid" or "a baseball player who throws the ball to the batter."

Homophones Homophones sound the same but are spelled differently. *Sea* and *see* are homophones.

Imperative Sentence An imperative sentence gives a command or makes a strong request. It ends with a period or an exclamation mark.

Pick up your clothes.

Interrogative Sentence An interrogative sentence asks a question. It ends with a question mark.

Is this your pen?

Grammar Glossary

Irregular Verb An irregular verb is a verb that does not follow the rule of forming the past tense and the past participle by adding *-ed* or *-d* to the base form of the word.

base form: ring   past tense: rang
past participle: rung

Noun A noun is the name of a person, place, thing, or idea.

boy town table wish

Paragraph A paragraph is a group of sentences that tells about one main idea. It usually begins with a topic sentence that states the main idea. All other sentences in the paragraph tell more about, or support, the topic sentence. The first word in a paragraph is set in from the margin.

Plural Plural means "more than one." The plurals of most nouns are formed by adding *-s* or *-es* to the noun. Some plurals are formed by changing the spelling of the noun.

car cars   box boxes
woman women

Prefix A prefix is a meaningful unit of letters added to the beginning of a base word to form a new word.

re + play = replay

Pronoun A pronoun is a word that takes the place of a noun or a group of words acting as a noun.

Mr. Fong is my neighbor. He lives next door to me.

Proper Noun A proper noun is the name of a person, place, or thing. Capitalize the first letter of each important word in a proper noun.

Betsy Ross   Arkansas
Golden Gate Bridge

Question A question, or interrogative sentence, asks about something. It is followed by a question mark.

Where is the computer room?

Quotation A quotation includes the words that someone says. Quotation marks are used before and after a quotation. Commas are used to set it off from the rest of the sentence. The first word in a quotation is capitalized.

Mr. Valdez said, "Please open your books to page three."

Sentence A sentence is a group of words that tells one complete thought. The first word of a sentence begins with a capital letter. A sentence may end with a period, a question mark, or an exclamation mark.

Grammar Glossary

Simple Predicate The simple predicate, or verb, is in the complete predicate of a sentence. It tells what the subject is or does.

The horse <u>jumped</u> the fence.

Simple Subject The simple subject is the main word in the complete subject of a sentence. It is what the sentence is about.

My best <u>friend</u> likes swimming.

Statement A statement is a declarative sentence that tells something. It ends with a period.

It is going to rain today.

Subject/Verb Agreement The form of verbs changes depending on the number of people or things doing the action. This is called subject/verb agreement. If one person or thing is doing the action, the verb is **singular**. If more than one person or thing is doing the action the verb is **plural.**

The girl <u>swims</u>. The girls <u>swim</u>.

Suffix A suffix is a letter or letters added to the end of a word to change its meaning or part of speech.

help + <u>ful</u> = helpful

Verb A verb is a word that expresses action or state of being. The simple predicate in a sentence is a verb. The principal parts of verbs are the forms that show present, past, or future tense.

laugh laughed will laugh
seem seemed will seem

How to Use the Spelling Thesaurus

Thesaurus Entry

Have you ever looked for just the right word to make a sentence more interesting or exciting? You could find that word in a thesaurus. A **thesaurus** is a collection of synonyms and antonyms. It can help you with your writing. Read this sentence:

As the people *roar*, the winning runners *roar* with excitement.

The sentence would be better if the word *roar* wasn't used twice. You need another word that means the same or almost the same as *roar*. You can find one in your **Spelling Thesaurus**.

Read the thesaurus entry below. There are four synonyms for *roar*. You can use one of those synonyms to rewrite the sentence like this:

As the people *roar*, the winning runners *yell* with excitement.

Look at this entry for **roar**.

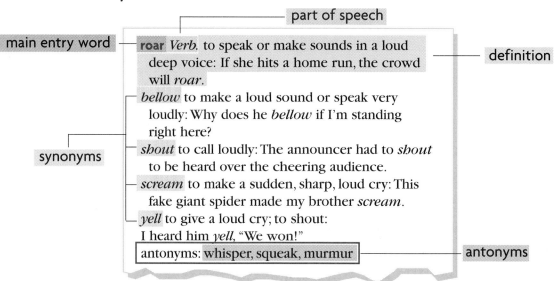

part of speech

main entry word →

roar *Verb.* to speak or make sounds in a loud deep voice: If she hits a home run, the crowd will *roar*.

definition

bellow to make a loud sound or speak very loudly: Why does he *bellow* if I'm standing right here?

synonyms

shout to call loudly: The announcer had to *shout* to be heard over the cheering audience.

scream to make a sudden, sharp, loud cry: This fake giant spider made my brother *scream*.

yell to give a loud cry; to shout: I heard him *yell*, "We won!"

antonyms: whisper, squeak, murmur

antonyms

A few **Spelling Thesaurus** entries have so many synonyms that you'll find a special box full of synonyms instead of sentences. The box also has some antonyms.

laugh

Verb. to show a happy feeling by making a sound.

chuckle	roar
giggle	shriek
guffaw	snicker
howl	snort

antonyms: mope, sob, moan, groan

Thesaurus Index

The index can help you find what is in your **Spelling Thesaurus**. The index is a listing of every word in the **Spelling Thesaurus**, including every synonym and every antonym. All the words are in alphabetical order.

Each **entry word** is listed in red:
> **roar** *Verb*

To find this entry word, look in the **Spelling Thesaurus** under **R.**

Each *synonym* is listed in italic print. Next to the synonym is the synonym's entry word.
> *yell* **roar** *Verb*

To find the meaning of the word *yell,* look up the thesaurus entry for **roar.**

Each antonym is listed in black print. Next to the antonym is its entry word.
> whisper **roar** *Verb*

To find this word, look up the thesaurus entry for **roar.**

Shades of Meaning

Take a moment to look through your **Spelling Thesaurus**. You'll find something interesting about synonyms. While some synonym pairs have exactly the same meaning, others don't. For example, two synonyms of **rough** are *bumpy* and *jagged. Bumpy* means "covered with lumps." *Jagged* means "with sharp or broken edges." You might describe a rough road as *bumpy,* but you wouldn't describe it as *jagged.* The definitions and sample sentences with each word will help you figure out whether the synonyms have slightly different meanings.

Try This: Replace each underlined word with a more exact word. Use your **Spelling Thesaurus** to help you. Then write your new sentence.

1. A small truck traveled down the path.

2. The sudden blasts of thunder scare the children.

3. In this story, a queen sends her sons on errands to other kingdoms.

4. Lee held her baby sister in a loving and gentle way.

5. The people in the audience honor the winning runners.

Spelling Thesaurus

Spelling Thesaurus Index

A

accept **believe** *Verb*
admire **honor** *Verb*
adore **love** *Verb*
against **near** *Preposition*
agree *Verb*
agreeable **pleasant** *Adjective*
aid **harm** *Verb*
aimed **meant** *Verb*
alarm **scare** *Verb*
all **nothing** *Noun*
allow *Verb*
always *Adverb*
angry **furious** *Adjective*
annoy *Verb*
answer **reply** *Verb*
anything **nothing** *Noun*
appear **disappear** *Verb*
appoint **employ** *Verb*
approach **reach** *Verb*
approve **agree** *Verb*
approve **allow** *Verb*
arrive **reach** *Verb*
ask **reply** *Verb*
attractive **beautiful** *Adjective*
awful *Adjective*
awful **terrible** *Adjective*

B

battle *Noun*
be convinced **believe** *Verb*

be sure **guess** *Verb*
beautiful *Adjective*
beginning **final** *Adjective*
believe *Verb*
bellow **roar** *Verb*
bent *Adjective*
beside **near** *Preposition*
bland **mild** *Adjective*
blaring **quiet** *Adjective*
blaze **glare** *Noun*
boo **honor** *Verb*
booming **quiet** *Adjective*
bored **curious** *Adjective*
boring **exciting** *Adjective*
bother **annoy** *Verb*
bother **worry** *Verb*
bracing **exciting** *Adjective*
bravery **fear** *Noun*
breathtaking **exciting** *Adjective*
brightness **shadows** *Noun*
built *Verb*
bumpy **rough** *Adjective*
bundle **package** *Noun*
burrow **cave** *Noun*

C

caller **visitor** *Noun*
calm **furious** *Adjective*
calm **mild** *Adjective*
calm **scare** *Verb*
calm **worry** *Verb*
careful *Adjective*
careless **careful** *Adjective*

Thesaurus Index

carnival *Noun*
category **nature** *Noun*
cautious **careful** *Adjective*
cave *Noun*
cavern **cave** *Noun*
cheer **honor** *Verb*
chuckle **laugh** *Verb*
circus **carnival** *Noun*
clean **oily** *Adjective*
clear **oily** *Adjective*
close **near** *Preposition*
closed **open** *Adjective*
closing **final** *Adjective*
coarse **rough** *Adjective*
comfort **worry** *Verb*
competitive **jealous** *Adjective*
completely **quite** *Adverb*
concealed **secret** *Adjective*
concern **worry** *Verb*
concluding **final** *Adjective*
conflict **battle** *Noun*
consent **agree** *Verb*
constructed **built** *Verb*
continually **always** *Adverb*
cord **yarn** *Noun*
courage **fear** *Noun*
courtesy **favor** *Noun*
covered **open** *Adjective*
covered **secret** *Adjective*
crisp **oily** *Adjective*
cruise **voyage** *Noun*
cure *Verb*
curious *Adjective*
curved **bent** *Adjective*

dagger **knife** *Noun*
damage **harm** *Verb*
damages **patches** *Verb*
damp **moist** *Adjective*
danger *Noun*
darkness **shadows** *Noun*
darns **patches** *Verb*
defeat **overcome** *Verb*
delicate **weak** *Adjective*
delight **enjoyment** *noun*
delight **worry** *Verb*
delightful **pleasant** *Adjective*
demolished **built** *Verb*
depart **reach** *Verb*
depend *Verb*
deserved **unfair** *Adjective*
designed **meant** *Verb*
despise **love** *Verb*
detailed **careful** *Adjective*
different **equal** *Adjective*
different **usual** *Adjective*
dimness **shadows** *Noun*
disagree **agree** *Verb*
disagreeable **pleasant** *Adjective*
disappear *Verb*
disappoint *Verb*
discharge **employ** *Verb*
disguised **secret** *Adjective*
dishonor **honor** *Verb*
dislike **love** *Verb*
dismiss **employ** *Verb*
dissatisfaction **enjoyment** *Noun*
dissatisfy **disappoint** *Verb*

Thesaurus Index

distant from **near** *Preposition*
distress **worry** *Verb*
distrust **depend** *Verb*
distrustful **loyal** *Adjective*
disturb **annoy** *Verb*
dive *Verb*
doubt **believe** *Verb*
doubt **depend** *Verb*
drag **haul** *Verb*
dreadful **awful** *Adjective*
dry **moist** *Adjective*
dry **oily** *Adjective*
dry **slippery** *Adjective*
dull **exciting** *Adjective*

easy **tough** *Adjective*
emerge **dive** *Verb*
employ *Verb*
emptiness **matter** *Noun*
enclose **insert** *Verb*
engage **employ** *Verb*
enjoy **love** *Verb*
enjoyable **pleasant** *Adjective*
enjoyable **terrible** *Adjective*
enjoyment *Noun*
enraged **furious** *Adjective*
enter **insert** *Verb*
entirely **quite** *Adverb*
envious **jealous** *Adjective*
equal *Adjective*
equal **unfair** *Adjective*
erect **bent** *Adjective*
errands *Noun*
esteem **honor** *Verb*
estimate **guess** *Verb*

evaporate **disappear** *Verb*
even **equal** *Adjective*
even **rough** *Adjective*
evenhanded **unfair** *Adjective*
everyday **usual** *Adjective*
everything **nothing** *Noun*
exciting *Adjective*
exhausted **weary** *Adjective*
expected **sudden** *Adjective*
exquisite **beautiful** *Adjective*
extreme **mild** *Adjective*

fable **tale** *Noun*
fade **disappear** *Verb*
fail **overcome** *Verb*
fair **beautiful** *Adjective*
fair **carnival** *Noun*
fair **unfair** *Adjective*
faithless **loyal** *Adjective*
false **loyal** *Adjective*
familiar **unknown** *Adjective*
fantastic **terrible** *Adjective*
far from **near** *Preposition*
fascinating **exciting** *Adjective*
fast **quickly** *Adverb*
faultless **perfect** *Adjective*
faulty **perfect** *Adjective*
favor *Noun*
fear *Noun*
fearlessness **fear** *Noun*
feeble **weak** *Adjective*
fickle **loyal** *Adjective*
fierce **mild** *Adjective*
final *Adjective*
fine **rough** *Adjective*

Thesaurus Index

fire **employ** *Verb*
first **final** *Adjective*
flare **glare** *Noun*
flash **glare** *Noun*
flat **exciting** *Adjective*
flawed **perfect** *Adjective*
flawless **perfect** *Adjective*
flimsy **weak** *Adjective*
follow **understand** *Verb*
forever **always** *Adverb*
frail **weak** *Adjective*
fresh **weary** *Adjective*
fright **fear** *Noun*
frighten **scare** *Verb*
frown *Verb*
furious *Adjective*

garbage *Noun*
gentle *Adjective*
giggle **laugh** *Verb*
glare *Noun*
glare **frown** *Verb*
glassy **slippery** *Adjective*
go **reach** *Verb*
goal **purpose** *Noun*
good-looking **beautiful** *Adjective*
gorgeous **beautiful** *Adjective*
graceful **beautiful** *Adjective*
grasp **understand** *Verb*
greasy **oily** *Adjective*
grin **frown** *Verb*
groan **laugh** *Verb*
guess *Verb*
guest **visitor** *Noun*
guffaw **laugh** *Verb*

handsome **beautiful** *Adjective*
happiness **enjoyment** *Noun*
happy **furious** *Adjective*
hard **gentle** *Adjective*
hard **tough** *Adjective*
harm *Verb*
harm **cure** *Verb*
harsh **gentle** *Adjective*
harsh **mild** *Adjective*
hate **love** *Verb*
haul *Verb*
hazard **danger** *Noun*
heal **cure** *Verb*
heal **harm** *Verb*
healthy **weak** *Adjective*
hear **listen** *Verb*
heed **listen** *Verb*
help **harm** *Verb*
hidden **secret** *Adjective*
hire **employ** *Verb*
holidays **vacation** *Noun*
honor *Verb*
horrible **terrible** *Adjective*
howl **laugh** *Verb*
hurt **cure** *Verb*
hurt **harm** *Verb*
hushed **quiet** *Adjective*

icy **slippery** *Adjective*
ideal **beautiful** *Adjective*
ideal **perfect** *Adjective*

ignore **listen** *Verb*
imperfect **perfect** *Adjective*
important *Adjective*
impress **disappoint** *Verb*
initial **final** *Adjective*
injure **cure** *Verb*
injure **harm** *Verb*
inquire **reply** *Verb*
insert *Verb*
insignificant **important** *Adjective*
intended **meant** *Verb*
intention **purpose** *Noun*
interested **curious** *Adjective*
interesting **exciting** *Adjective*
issue **question** *Noun*

jagged **rough** *Adjective*
jealous *Adjective*
jot **note** *Verb*
journey **voyage** *Noun*
joyful **furious** *Adjective*
just **unfair** *Adjective*

kind **nature** *Noun*
kindness **favor** *Noun*
knife *Noun*
know **guess** *Verb*
know **understand** *Verb*
known **secret** *Adjective*
known **unknown** *Adjective*

land **reach** *Verb*
last **final** *Adjective*
laugh *Verb*
laugh **frown** *Verb*
learn **understand** *Verb*
leave **reach** *Verb*
legend **tale** *Noun*
let **allow** *Verb*
let alone **annoy** *Verb*
let down **disappoint** *Verb*
let go **employ** *Verb*
light **shadows** *Noun*
listen *Verb*
lively **weary** *Adjective*
loathe **love** *Verb*
locked **open** *Adjective*
lose **overcome** *Verb*
loud **quiet** *Adjective*
love *Verb*
lovely **beautiful** *Adjective*
loyal *Adjective*
lying *Verb*

made **built** *Verb*
major **important** *Adjective*
make ill **cure** *Verb*
marred **perfect** *Adjective*
masked **secret** *Adjective*
mass **matter** *Noun*
matching **equal** *Adjective*
material **matter** *Noun*

Thesaurus Index

matter *Noun*
meant *Verb*
menace **danger** *Noun*
mends **patches** *Verb*
mild *Adjective*
minor **important** *Adjective*
miss **overlook** *Verb*
missions **errands** *Noun*
moan **laugh** *Verb*
mock **honor** *Verb*
moist *Adjective*
money **wealth** *Noun*
mope **laugh** *Verb*
moving **exciting** *Adjective*
muffled **quiet** *Adjective*
murmur **roar** *Verb*
muscular **weak** *Adjective*
must **ought** *Verb*
mustn't **ought** *Verb*
muted **quiet** *Adjective*
mysterious **secret** *Adjective*
mysterious **unknown** *Adjective*

nature *Noun*
near *Preposition*
neglect **overlook** *Verb*
never **always** *Adverb*
noiseless **quiet** *Adjective*
noisy **quiet** *Adjective*
none **nothing** *Noun*
nonskid **slippery** *Adjective*
note *Verb*
nothing *Noun*
nothing **matter** *Noun*
notice **overlook** *Verb*

offer *Verb*
oily *Adjective*
open *Adjective*
open **secret** *Adjective*
ordinary **usual** *Adjective*
ought *Verb*
outdo **overcome** *Verb*
outstanding **usual** *Adjective*
overcome *Verb*
overlook *Verb*

package *Noun*
painless **tough** *Adjective*
parcel **package** *Noun*
parched **moist** *Adjective*
partly **quite** *Adverb*
patches *Verb*
path *Noun*
pay attention to **overlook** *Verb*
peaceful **furious** *Adjective*
perfect *Adjective*
planned **meant** *Verb*
pleasant *Adjective*
pleasant **awful** *Adjective*
pleasant **terrible** *Adjective*
please **annoy** *Verb*
please **disappoint** *Verb*
please **worry** *Verb*
pleasing **beautiful** *Adjective*
pleasure **enjoyment** *Noun*
plunge **dive** *Verb*

Thesaurus Index

poison **cure** *Verb*
poverty **wealth** *Noun*
powerful **weak** *Adjective*
praise **honor** *Verb*
predicted **sudden** *Adjective*
prepared **ready** *Adjective*
pretty **beautiful** *Adjective*
problem **question** *Noun*
problem **trouble** *Noun*
prohibit **allow** *Verb*
prolonged **sudden** *Adjective*
property **wealth** *Noun*
propose **offer** *Verb*
protect **harm** *Verb*
prying **curious** *Adjective*
pull **haul** *Verb*
punctures **patches** *Verb*
purpose *Noun*

question *Noun*
quick **sudden** *Adjective*
quickly *Adverb*
quiet *Adjective*
quite *Adverb*

radiant **beautiful** *Adjective*
rapidly **quickly** *Adverb*
rarely **always** *Adverb*
reach *Verb*
ready *Adjective*
reappear **disappear** *Verb*

reason **purpose** *Noun*
reassure **scare** *Verb*
reassure **worry** *Verb*
recess **vacation** *Noun*
reclining **lying** *Verb*
recognizable **unknown** *Adjective*
record **note** *Verb*
refuse **agree** *Verb*
refuse **garbage** *Noun*
regular **usual** *Adjective*
reject **agree** *Verb*
reject **believe** *Verb*
rely **depend** *Verb*
remain **disappear** *Verb*
remove **insert** *Verb*
request **reply** *Verb*
repairs **patches** *Verb*
reply *Verb*
respect **annoy** *Verb*
respond **reply** *Verb*
restrict **allow** *Verb*
retort **reply** *Verb*
revealed **secret** *Adjective*
riches **wealth** *Noun*
right **unfair** *Adjective*
ripe **ready** *Adjective*
rips **patches** *Verb*
risk **danger** *Noun*
road **path** *Noun*
roar *Verb*
roar **laugh** *Verb*
rope **yarn** *Noun*
rotate **whirl** *Verb*
rough *Adjective*
rough **gentle** *Adjective*
rough **mild** *Adjective*
rough **slippery** *Adjective*
rousing **exciting** *Adjective*
route **path** *Noun*
rubbish **garbage** *Noun*

Thesaurus Index

safety **danger** *Noun*
satisfy **disappoint** *Verb*
scalpel **knife** *Noun*
scare *Verb*
scare **fear** *Noun*
scowl **frown** *Verb*
scream **roar** *Verb*
scribble **note** *Verb*
secret *Adjective*
secure **slippery** *Adjective*
seldom **always** *Adverb*
sensational **exciting** *Adjective*
shade **shadows** *Noun*
shadows *Noun*
shaky **weak** *Adjective*
should **ought** *Verb*
shouldn't **ought** *Verb*
shout **laugh** *Verb*
shout **roar** *Verb*
shriek **laugh** *Verb*
shut **open** *Adjective*
sickly **weak** *Adjective*
significant **important** *Adjective*
silent **quiet** *Adjective*
silky **rough** *Adjective*
similar **equal** *Adjective*
simple **tough** *Adjective*
sitting **lying** *Verb*
skip **overlook** *Verb*
sleepy **weary** *Adjective*
slick **slippery** *Adjective*
slightly **quite** *Adverb*
slimy **oily** *Adjective*
slippery *Adjective*
sloppy **careful** *Adjective*

slowly **quickly** *Adverb*
sluggishly **quickly** *Adverb*
smile **frown** *Verb*
smooth **rough** *Adjective*
smooth **slippery** *Adjective*
snicker **laugh** *Verb*
snort **laugh** *Verb*
soar **dive** *Verb*
sob **laugh** *Verb*
soft **gentle** *Adjective*
solid **weak** *Adjective*
something **nothing** *Noun*
somewhat **quite** *Adverb*
soothing **mild** *Adjective*
sort **nature** *Noun*
soundless **quiet** *Adjective*
speechless **quiet** *Adjective*
speedily **quickly** *Adverb*
spicy **mild** *Adjective*
spin **whirl** *Verb*
splendid **beautiful** *Adjective*
spot **overlook** *Verb*
sprawling **lying** *Verb*
squeak **roar** *Verb*
standing **lying** *Verb*
startle **scare** *Verb*
startling **sudden** *Adjective*
still **quiet** *Adjective*
stirring **exciting** *Adjective*
story **tale** *Noun*
straight **bent** *Adjective*
strange **unknown** *Adjective*
street **path** *Noun*
strengthened **weary** *Adjective*
string **yarn** *Noun*
strong **mild** *Adjective*
strong **weak** *Adjective*
struggle **battle** *Noun*
sturdy **weak** *Adjective*

Thesaurus Index

substance **matter** *Noun*
sudden *Adjective*
suggest **offer** *Verb*
suppose **guess** *Verb*
surface **dive** *Verb*
surpass **overcome** *Verb*
surrender **overcome** *Verb*
swoop **dive** *Verb*

take out **insert** *Verb*
tale *Noun*
tasks **errands** *Noun*
tears **patches** *Verb*
tender **gentle** *Adjective*
terrible *Adjective*
terrible **awful** *Adjective*
terrify **scare** *Verb*
terror **fear** *Noun*
thorough **careful** *Adjective*
thread **yarn** *Noun*
thrilling **exciting** *Adjective*
tired **weary** *Adjective*
topic **question** *Noun*
tore down **built** *Verb*
tough *Adjective*
tour **voyage** *Noun*
trail **path** *Noun*
trash **garbage** *Noun*
treat **cure** *Verb*
trip **voyage** *Noun*
trivial **important** *Adjective*
trouble *Noun*
troublesome **tough** *Adjective*
true **loyal** *Adjective*
trust **depend** *Verb*

trusty **loyal** *Adjective*
tug **haul** *Verb*
tumbledown **weak** *Adjective*
twine **yarn** *Noun*
twisted **bent** *Adjective*

unbearable **terrible** *Adjective*
unclosed **open** *Adjective*
uncommon **usual** *Adjective*
uncovered **open** *Adjective*
undercover **secret** *Adjective*
understand *Verb*
unenjoyable **pleasant** *Adjective*
unequal **equal** *Adjective*
unequal **unfair** *Adjective*
unexpected **sudden** *Adjective*
unexpected **usual** *Adjective*
unfair *Adjective*
unfamiliar **unknown** *Adjective*
unhappiness **enjoyment** *Noun*
unhurriedly **quickly** *Adverb*
unimportant **important** *Adjective*
uninterested **curious** *Adjective*
unjust **unfair** *Adjective*
unknown *Adjective*
unknown **secret** *Adjective*
unpleasant **pleasant** *Adjective*
unpredicted **sudden** *Adjective*
unprepared **ready** *Adjective*
unripe **ready** *Adjective*
unspeaking **quiet** *Adjective*
unsteady **weak** *Adjective*
unusual **usual** *Adjective*
uphill **tough** *Adjective*
usual *Adjective*

Thesaurus Index

vacation *Noun*
vanish **disappear** *Verb*
variety **nature** *Noun*
veiled **secret** *Adjective*
visitor *Noun*
voyage *Noun*

weak *Adjective*
wealth *Noun*
weary *Adjective*
wet **moist** *Adjective*
whirl *Verb*
whisper **roar** *Verb*
whispery **quiet** *Adjective*
wholly **quite** *Adverb*

wild **mild** *Adjective*
withheld **secret** *Adjective*
wonderful **awful** *Adjective*
wonderful **terrible** *Adjective*
worn-out **weary** *Adjective*
worry *Verb*
worry **trouble** *Noun*
wrecked **built** *Verb*
wrong **unfair** *Adjective*

yarn *Noun*
yell **roar** *Verb*

zero **nothing** *Noun*

Thesaurus Index

Spelling Thesaurus

agree
Verb. to say one is willing:
I *agree* to clean my room every Saturday.
consent to say yes:
I *consent* to your plan.
approve to agree to officially:
The committee will *approve* the use of music in the cafeteria.

antonyms: refuse, reject, disagree

allow
Verb. to permit:
She will *allow* him to watch TV after his homework is done.
let to give permission:
I will *let* you go later.
approve to officially agree to something:
Will your teacher *approve* the idea?

antonyms: prohibit, restrict

always
Adverb. as long as possible:
I will remember their kindness *always*.
forever for all time:
Ned will be my friend *forever*.
continually without stop:
My tooth aches *continually*.

antonyms: never, rarely, seldom

annoy
Verb. to irritate:
Too much noise will *annoy* me.
bother to pester:
Don't *bother* me when I'm reading.
disturb to distract:
Talking in the library will *disturb* others.

antonyms: please, let alone, respect

awful
Adjective. very bad:
It was an *awful* day for a picnic.
dreadful very frightening:
The *dreadful* storm caused a lot of damage.
terrible unpleasant, possibly painful:
Shawna has a *terrible* headache.

antonyms: pleasant, wonderful

battle
Noun. a fierce contest between people or groups:
The football game was a real *battle*.
struggle a contest of power or skill:
The *struggle* between the teams ended in a tie.
conflict a strong disagreement:
The two sides are in a bitter *conflict* over the issue.

Spelling Thesaurus

beautiful

Adjective. very nice to look at.

attractive	*ideal*
exquisite	*lovely*
fair	*pleasing*
good-looking	*pretty*
gorgeous	*radiant*
graceful	*splendid*
handsome	

believe

Verb. to think something is true:
Do you *believe* he is telling
the truth?
accept to take as truth:
He hoped she would *accept* his
version of the events.
be convinced to be persuaded:
Lu needs to *be convinced* that the
plan is good.

antonyms: doubt, reject

bent

Adjective. changed in shape:
The *bent* nail won't hold the
picture.
twisted bent or turned out of shape:
A *twisted* straw is hard to
drink with.
curved having no straight parts:
You need a *curved* needle to fix the
rip in the chair.

antonym: straight

built

*Verb, past tense and past participle
of* **build**. put together parts and
material:
They *built* the tree house yesterday.
made built or prepared:
Andrea *made* a salad.
constructed put up:
The school was *constructed* in 1912.

antonyms: tore down, wrecked,
demolished

careful

Adjective. done with close attention:
She made a *careful* check of the
electric wires.
thorough leaving nothing out; careful
and complete:
Please do a *thorough* job of cleaning
the desk.
detailed dealing with all the little
parts of something:
Roger made a *detailed* drawing of
the rabbit.
cautious using close care:
Sally was *cautious* when she walked
across the narrow bridge.

antonyms: careless, sloppy

carnival

Noun. a festival that has games,
rides, and shows: She won a teddy
bear at the *carnival.*

Spelling Thesaurus

circus a show with trained animals, acrobats, and clowns:
We saw animals at the *circus*.

fair an outdoor show with entertainment:
Jody rode the rollercoaster at the *fair*.

cave

Noun. a natural hollow space in the ground or in the side of a mountain:
Bears sleep in a *cave* for most of the winter.

cavern a large cave, often underground:
We explored a *cavern* deep in the ground.

burrow a hole in the ground made by an animal for shelter:
The rabbits lived in a *burrow*.

cure

Verb. to bring back health:
Rest will help *cure* that strained back.

heal to make better:
A doctor's job is to *heal* the sick.

treat to take care of an illness or injury:
A doctor should *treat* a high fever.

antonyms: make ill, harm, hurt, injure, poison

curious

Adjective. eager to learn about something:
I am *curious* about new inventions.

interested wanting to find out about something:
Miguel is *interested* in the habits

of whales.

prying looking or inquiring too closely:
I have been told that *prying* into someone's personal life can be impolite.

antonyms: bored, uninterested

danger

Noun. a chance of harm or injury:
Fire is a *danger* to forests.

risk a chance of loss or harm:
Firefighters often place their lives at *risk*.

hazard something that can cause injury:
Bad weather can be a traffic *hazard*.

menace a person or thing that is a threat:
Careless drivers are a *menace*.

antonym: safety

depend

Verb. to count on:
I can *depend* on my sister.

rely to trust in:
I will *rely* on you to be on time.

trust to have confidence in:
You can *trust* me to walk the dog twice a day.

antonyms: distrust, doubt

disappear

Verb. to go out of sight:

The jet will soon *disappear* into the clouds.

vanish to go out of sight or existence: When you use this cleaner, stains will *vanish*.

fade to become fainter and disappear: We heard the fire engines' sirens *fade* into the distance.

evaporate to fade away or end: Your homerun caused the other team's hopes for a win to *evaporate*.

> antonyms: appear, reappear, remain

disappoint

Verb. to fail to live up to a wish or hope: Rainy weather at the game on Saturday will *disappoint* the soccer team.

let down not to do as expected by others: By not showing up for the game, Shirley *let down* the team.

dissatisfy to fail to meet a need or wish: You *dissatisfy* me when you break a promise.

> antonyms: impress, please, satisfy

dive

Verb. to make a sudden downward movement: One by one, the swimmers *dive* into the pool.

plunge to fall suddenly: Did you see the kite *plunge* to the ground?

swoop to rush down suddenly:

Look at the hawk *swoop* down on the rabbit.

> antonyms: emerge, surface, soar

employ

Verb. to pay someone to do a job: Our neighbor will *employ* Rita to rake the leaves.

hire to give a job to: If you *hire* me, I'll do a good job.

engage to hire: I will *engage* a secretary to take notes at the meeting.

appoint to name for a job or an office: The President can *appoint* certain judges.

> antonyms: fire, dismiss, let go, discharge

enjoyment

Noun. a happy or pleased feeling: Baseball gives me much *enjoyment*.

pleasure a satisfied or pleased feeling: *Pleasure* can come from a job well done.

delight joy: It is a *delight* to listen to good music.

happiness gladness: Matthew got much *happiness* from the surprise party.

> antonyms: dissatisfaction, unhappiness

Spelling Thesaurus

equal

Adjective. the same in size, amount, or value:
Five pennies are *equal* to one nickel.
even the same:
At the end of the fifth inning, the score in the game was *even*.
matching the same, for example in size, color, or shape:
The sisters wore *matching* hats.
similar almost the same:
The two cars are *similar* but not exactly alike.

> antonyms: unequal, different

errands

Noun, plural of **errand**. things that a person is sent to do:
Monday I will run some *errands* at the store for my mom.
tasks jobs that must be done:
Luis gave Ned some *tasks* to do downtown.
missions special jobs or tasks:
The president sent people to several countries on *missions* of peace.

exciting

Adjective. causing stirred-up, strong feelings.

bracing	*rousing*
breathtaking	*sensational*
fascinating	*stirring*
interesting	*thrilling*
moving	

antonyms: dull, boring, flat

favor

Noun. a generous or kind act:
As a *favor,* she lent me a book.
courtesy an act of good manners:
Lou did me the *courtesy* of letting me use his umbrella.
kindness a kind or thoughtful act:
As a *kindness* to me, please turn your radio down.

fear

Noun. a feeling that trouble or danger is near:
He has a *fear* of heights.
fright a sudden, strong feeling of danger:
Surprising me like that gave me a real *fright*.
scare a sudden panic:
We jumped out and gave them a *scare*.
terror a great feeling of danger:
The *terror* in the movie was caused by dinosaurs.

> antonyms: fearlessness, courage, bravery

final

Adjective. coming at the end:
I read the *final* chapter of the book.
last at the end, after all the others:
The *last* runner reached the finish line.

concluding bringing a thing or series to an end:

He made the *concluding* speech of the play, and the curtain fell.

closing bringing something to an end:

After the chorus sang its *closing* song, the program ended.

> antonyms: first, beginning, initial

frown

Verb. to express anger or sadness with a look on the face:

Mom will *frown* when she sees the mess our dog made.

glare to give an angry look:

A messy room will make him *glare* in anger.

scowl to look at in a displeased way:

The barking dog caused Lucy to *scowl*.

> antonyms: smile, laugh, grin

furious

Adjective. extremely mad:

Losing her wallet made Bess *furious*.

angry feeling or showing anger:

The *angry* child stamped her feet and screamed.

enraged very angry:

The bear becomes *enraged* when anyone gets close to her cub.

> antonyms: happy, joyful, peaceful, calm

garbage

Noun. unwanted things that are thrown out:

Much of the *garbage* in our house comes from the packaging around food.

trash unwanted things that are thrown out:

Bottles should be recycled and not thrown away as *trash*.

rubbish useless material that is or should be thrown away:

He threw away the torn, crumpled papers and other *rubbish*.

refuse things that are thrown out:

The *refuse* will be taken out to the curb in the morning.

gentle

Adjective. mild and kind; not rough:

Babies need *gentle* handling.

soft smooth to the touch; not hard or sharp:

A *soft* breeze is blowing across the field.

tender delicate; kind or loving:

When I am sick, I need *tender* care.

> antonyms: harsh, hard, rough

glare

Noun. a strong, unpleasant light:

He shaded his eyes against the spotlight's *glare*.

blaze a strong light:

Spelling Thesaurus

The *blaze* of the sun made us want to walk on the shady side of the street.

flash a sudden, short burst of light:
I saw a *flash* of lightning near the hills.

flare a sudden bright light:
We saw the *flare* of fireworks in the night sky.

guess

Verb. to form an opinion without enough information:
I *guess* there are six hundred marbles in that jar.

estimate to form an opinion of the value or cost of something:
I *estimate* it will cost $50.00 to repair the bike.

suppose to believe that something is possible but not certain:
I *suppose* Jean will lend you her scarf.

> antonyms: know, be sure

harm

Verb. to cause someone or something injury or problems:
You can *harm* a plant by not giving it water.

hurt to give pain to:
If you fight you will *hurt* each other.

damage to harm or make less valuable:
Carelessness can cause *damage* to property.

injure to hurt:
Rose wears a helmet so she will not *injure* herself when she rides her bike.

> antonyms: help, aid, protect, heal

haul *Verb.* to move a heavy object:
The oxen will *haul* the cart.

pull to grab and move toward oneself:
The wheels on a wagon make it easy to *pull* even if it is loaded with groceries.

drag to move something along slowly:
Drag the couch over here near the fireplace.

tug to pull on something with great energy:
If you *tug* hard, the stuck door will open.

honor *Verb.* to treat with great respect:
We have a holiday to *honor* our war veterans.

praise to speak well of someone or something:
Speakers will *praise* the winner of the medal.

esteem to think highly of:
We *esteem* teachers for their knowledge.

admire to feel great respect for:
I *admire* the tired runner for finishing the race.

cheer to give a shout of praise:
We *cheer* our heroes to show them our respect.

antonyms: dishonor, boo, mock

important

Adjective. having great value or meaning:
Education is very *important.*

significant having special value or meaning:
July 4th is a *significant* day in American history.

major chief or more important:
The *major* reason I jog is to relax.

antonyms: unimportant, trivial, insignificant, minor

insert

Verb. to put something into:
Insert your card into the slot.

enter to put in or on:
Ms. Cheng will *enter* our names on the list for the award.

enclose to put something in along with something else:
He will *enclose* a check in the envelope with his letter.

antonyms: remove, take out

jealous

Adjective. wanting what someone else has:
Don't be *jealous* of a friend's popularity.

envious feeling jealousy:
He felt *envious* once he saw John's new bike.

competitive always trying to compete with or get the better of other people:
Lee is so *competitive* that he can't even stand it when people get ahead of him on the lunch line.

knife

Noun. a cutting tool with a blade attached to a handle:
Be careful not to cut yourself when using a *knife.*

scalpel a small, straight knife with a thin blade:
A doctor uses a *scalpel* to operate.

dagger a small weapon that looks like a knife:
The characters in the story I am reading found a *dagger* in the cave they were exploring.

laugh
Verb. to show a happy feeling by making a sound.

chuckle	*roar*
giggle	*shriek*
guffaw	*snicker*
howl	*snort*

antonyms: mope, sob, moan, groan

listen
Verb. to try to hear; pay attention:
Listen when the teacher is speaking.
hear to receive sound through the ears:
Do you *hear* what I'm saying?
heed to pay careful attention to; listen or mind:
I will *heed* my parent's advice and wear a sweater to the ball game.

antonym: ignore

love
Verb. to have a strong, warm feeling for:
I *love* my pets very much.
adore to love greatly:
The children *adore* their grandparents.
enjoy to get joy or pleasure from; be happy with:
I *enjoy* the company of my sisters.

antonyms: dislike, hate, loathe, despise

loyal
Adjective. faithful to a person, cause, or ideal:
Washington's soldiers were *loyal* to him.
true faithful:
Jerry proved he was a *true* friend when he protected Dave from some bullies.
trusty capable of being trusted or relied on:
My *trusty* watch never failed me.

antonyms: distrustful, fickle, false, faithless

lying
Verb, present participle of **lie.**
stretching out:
It is easier to fall asleep *lying* down than sitting up.
reclining leaning back; lying down:
Jake is *reclining* on the sofa and reading a book.
sprawling lying or sitting with the body stretched out in an awkward or careless manner:
My dog spent the morning *sprawling* on the rug with his eyes closed.

antonyms: standing, sitting

Spelling Thesaurus

matter

Noun. anything that has weight and takes up space:
Matter can be a solid, a liquid, or a gas.

material what something is made of:
This window is made from an unbreakable *material.*

substance a material that has certain qualities:
Ink is a *substance* that can make a stain.

mass a shapeless body of matter:
A *mass* of mud flowed down the mountainside.

antonyms: emptiness, nothing

meant

Verb, past tense and past participle of mean. had in mind:
I *meant* to write that letter today.

intended set about with a purpose:
Reba *intended* to become a scientist.

planned thought out ahead of time:
Dr. Reyes *planned* to see six patients that morning.

designed made for a special use or purpose:
That seat was *designed* for a small child.

aimed tried to reach a goal:
I *aimed* to be the best writer I could be.

mild

Adjective. not extreme:
She prefers food with a *mild* taste, but he likes spicy dishes.

soothing able to ease irritation:
The cream was *soothing* on his chapped skin.

bland without any harsh or extreme qualities:
Bland foods include rice and cottage cheese.

calm quiet:
The ocean is *calm*, and the wind is still.

antonyms: rough, wild, fierce, harsh, strong, extreme, spicy

moist

Adjective. containing some water:
The ground still feels *moist* after yesterday's rain.

damp a little wet:
Use a *damp* sponge to wipe up spills.

wet containing or covered with water:
The car's hood was *wet* with rain.

antonyms: dry, parched

nature

Noun. of a specific type:
I like books of a scientific *nature.*

category a class into which like things can be grouped:

Spelling Thesaurus

Swimming belongs in the *category* of water sports.

sort a type or category:
That's not the *sort* of sweater that I like to wear.

kind a type or category:
What *kind* of fruit do you like best?

variety a different kind or form:
Have you tried the new *variety* of cheese?

near

Preposition. a short distance from:
The library is *near* the museum.

close to not far from:
I live *close to* school.

beside right next to:
Roger usually stands *beside* Paco in the student chorus.

against touching:
Ugo leaned the folding chair *against* the wall.

> antonyms: far from, distant from

note

Verb. to put something in writing:
Graciela will *note* the address in her phone book.

jot to write something quickly or in few words:
I took a minute to *jot* down my idea for the story.

record to write something down so as to keep an accurate memory of it:
Choose one group member to *record* your discussion.

scribble to write quickly and often messily: I can't read your writing when you *scribble*.

nothing

Noun. not anything:
Ten minus ten leaves *nothing*.

zero nothing:
If none of your answers on the test are correct, your score will be *zero*.

none no one or not one:
Six people started the puzzle, but *none* finished it.

> antonyms: something, anything, everything, all

offer

Verb. to present for acceptance or rejection:
If you are hungry, I can *offer* you a peanut butter sandwich.

suggest to mention as a possibility:
I *suggest* we go to the movies today.

propose to put forward a plan:
We *propose* to write an outline before we write the report.

oily

Adjective. Covered or soaked with oil:
The puddle had an *oily* film on it.

greasy coated with grease, oil, or other fat:
Engine parts are often *greasy*, so handle them carefully.

slimy covered or coated with a thin, sticky film:
People think that snakes are *slimy*,

but their scales are dry and smooth.

antonyms: clear, dry, crisp, clean

open

Adjective. not having its lid, door, or other covering closed:
It was easy to see the toys in the *open* toy chest.
uncovered not having the lid or cover on:
Steam rose from the *uncovered* soup pot cooking on the stove.
unclosed not having its door or other covering shut:
An *unclosed* box will allow dust to get inside.

antonyms: closed, shut, covered, locked

ought

Helping Verb. to have a duty or to be expected to:
Prentiss *ought* to help Connie wash the dishes.
should another word expressing duty:
I *should* do my homework before I play.
must another word expressing duty, but stronger than *ought* or *should:*
To ride this bus, you *must* pay with exact change.

antonyms: shouldn't, mustn't

overcome

Verb. to beat:
Can our players *overcome* a more skillful team?
defeat to win against or beat:

This year, our city's swimmers will *defeat* everyone else.
outdo to do better than:
I hope to *outdo* the other runners in the race.
surpass to do better than:
I can *surpass* the grades I got last year.

antonyms: fail, surrender, lose

overlook

Verb. to fail to see:
Don't *overlook* the article I told you about.
neglect to fail to do:
Don't *neglect* to study your notes.
miss to fail to notice, find, or catch:
I didn't *miss* any errors in punctuation.
skip to pass by or leave out:
Did you *skip* the third question by accident?

antonyms: notice, spot, pay attention to

package

Noun. one or more objects that are wrapped or boxed:
I received a large *package* on my birthday.
parcel something wrapped up; bundle or package:
I received two *parcels* on my birthday.

parcel one or more objects that are wrapped up, usually to be mailed:
I sent him a *parcel* of candy and fruit.

bundle a group of things wrapped or tied together for ease in carrying:
Gerry carried the *bundle* of laundry to the cleaners.

patches

Verb, present tense of **patch.** sews a piece of cloth over a hole or a tear:
Ariana *patches* the jeans.

mends fixes:
Hal *mends* the rip in his shirt.

darns repairs clothing by sewing up a hole or a tear:
Gil *darns* the hole in his sock so he doesn't have to throw the pair away.

repairs fixes:
Jan *repairs* the broken lamp.

antonyms: rips, punctures, tears, damages

path

Noun. a trail or way made for walking:
We walked up the *path* that leads to the river.

trail a way, usually narrow, made for walking:
The hikers traveled single file along the *trail.*

route a traveled way:
The map showed an old trade *route* through Asia.

road a way made for walking or for vehicles:
The unpaved *road* gave cars a bumpy ride.

street a way in a city or town that is usually paved, and is often bordered by sidewalks:
Wait for the green light before crossing the *street.*

perfect

Adjective. without flaw or error in its appearance or nature:
A *perfect* math test is one with no mistakes.

faultless without error—often describing performance or behavior:
The gymnast performed a *faultless* routine with no mistakes.

flawless without imperfections such as marks or bumps:
The marble's smooth surface was *flawless.*

ideal exactly what is hoped for or needed:
Blue is the *ideal* color for these walls.

antonyms: imperfect, faulty, flawed, marred

pleasant

Adjective. giving a good feeling:
The mountain views make this walk *pleasant.*

enjoyable easy to find satisfying:
Swimming on a warm day is *enjoyable.*

agreeable likable:
She has an *agreeable* personality.

Spelling Thesaurus

delightful highly pleasing:
An icy glass of water is *delightful* on a hot, humid day.

> antonyms: unpleasant, unenjoyable, disagreeable

purpose

Noun. why something is done:
The book's *purpose* is to inform us.
reason why something happens or is done—more of an explanation than an aim:
What is your *reason* for being late?
intention aim:
Our *intention* is to wash all the windows.
goal aim: Winning is Thea's *goal*.

question

Noun. a matter to be talked over:
We discussed the *question* of sports clubs.
problem a matter needing to be solved:
The meeting will deal with the *problem* of noise.
issue a matter to be thought about, not necessarily a problem:
Recycling is an *issue* that many people have opinions about.
topic a subject or matter to be examined:
What would make a good *topic* for a speech to parents?

quickly

Adverb. at a high speed or in a short time:
I went *quickly* to my mother and told her what happened.
rapidly with great speed:
The marbles rolled away *rapidly*.
speedily quickly:
The waiter went *speedily* from table to table.
fast at high speed or in a short time:
The fan cooled the room *fast*.

> antonyms: slowly, sluggishly, unhurriedly

quiet

Adjective. making little or no noise.

hushed	*soundless*
muffled	*speechless*
muted	*still*
noiseless	*unspeaking*
silent	*whispery*

antonyms: noisy, loud, blaring, booming

quite

Adverb. completely, fully:
I have not *quite* finished writing.
completely in total, all:
The barrel is *completely* full.
entirely completely, all:
It will be *entirely* your fault if you are late.
wholly completely, in total:
The company is *wholly* owned by one family.

> antonyms: partly, somewhat, slightly

Spelling Thesaurus

reach

Verb. to come to:
We will *reach* the hotel by sunset.
arrive to get to or come to:
When you *arrive* at the museum, wait for me in the front hall.
land to come to the ground or to shore:
The plane should *land* at the airport soon.
approach to come near:
The ships slow down as they *approach* the dock.

antonyms: leave, go, depart

ready

Adjective. Set for use or action:
The soup is heated up and *ready* to eat.
prepared made ready:
The gym has been decorated and *prepared* for the dance.
ripe fully grown, in a condition to be eaten:
We'll eat these *ripe* pears for lunch.

antonyms: unprepared, unripe

reply

Verb. to answer in words or writing:
Did you *reply* to her letter?
answer to say or write something in return:
Will you *answer* his question right away?
respond to say or write something in return:
Think about how you will *respond* to the question.
retort to give a quick, witty, or sharp answer:
If you ask her that, she will probably *retort* jokingly.

antonyms: ask, inquire, request

roar

Verb. to speak or make sounds in a loud, deep voice:
If she hits a home run, the crowd will *roar*.
bellow to make a loud sound or speak very loudly:
Why does he *bellow* if I'm standing right here?
shout to call loudly:
The announcer had to *shout* to be heard over the cheering audience.
scream to make a sudden, sharp, loud cry:
This fake giant spider made my brother *scream*.
yell to give a loud cry, or to speak loudly:
I heard him *yell*, "We won!"

antonyms: whisper, squeak, murmur

rough

Adjective. not smooth:
Greg used sandpaper on the *rough* wood.
coarse made of large grains or threads instead of fine, smooth ones:
Burlap is a *coarse* cloth, while satin is a fine one.

bumpy covered with lumps:
 The clay pot had a *bumpy* surface.
jagged with sharp or broken edges:
 That *jagged* piece of glass could cut
 your hand.

> antonyms: smooth, fine, even, silky

scare

Verb. to make afraid:
Sudden movements can *scare*
the dog.
frighten to make afraid:
 That movie didn't *frighten* me—
 much!
alarm to disturb or make afraid:
 The prediction of tornadoes should
 alarm people living in that area.
startle to frighten or take by surprise,
 usually not seriously:
 Did that boom *startle* you?
terrify to frighten greatly:
 A lion's roar can *terrify* zebras.

> antonyms: calm, reassure

secret

Adjective. kept from others or
shared with only a few.

concealed	*mysterious*
covered	*undercover*
disguised	*unknown*
hidden	*veiled*
masked	*withheld*

antonyms: open, revealed, known

shadows

Noun, plural of **shadow**. dark areas
made when rays of light are blocked
by a person, animal, or thing:
 You will feel cooler if you walk in
 the *shadows* cast by the buildings.
shade a place sheltered from the sun:
 Sit in the *shade* of this tree.
dimness an area of very little light:
 In the *dimness*, the table was hard
 to see.
darkness an area with little or
no light:
 I heard footsteps, but in the
 darkness, I saw no one.

> antonyms: light, brightness

slippery

Adjective. having a surface so
smooth that it can cause one to
slide or fall:
 Walk carefully on that *slippery* ice.
smooth having an even or polished
surface:
 Smooth ice is best for skating.
slick smooth, usually because of a film
 like ice or oil:
 Spilled oil made the floor *slick*.
glassy with a surface like glass:
 The ice storm made the road *glassy*.
icy covered with ice:
 Icy roads can be dangerous to
 drive on.

> antonyms: dry, rough, secure,
> nonskid

sudden

Adjective. happening quickly and
without warning:

Spelling Thesaurus

The *sudden* bang from the car's engine made me jump.

startling surprising, happening without warning:
The outcome of the elections was *startling* to all of us.

unexpected coming without warning, but not necessarily sudden:
An *unexpected* storm flooded the streets.

unpredicted not guessed or expected ahead of time:
The team's win had *unpredicted* results.

quick fast:
The *quick* movement of the cat's paw surprised the squirrel.

antonyms: prolonged, predicted, expected

tale

Noun. a story:
Have you heard the *tale* of the fisherman and his wife?

story an account of something that happens:
I wrote a *story* about a mysterious horse.

fable a story that teaches a lesson:
In that *fable,* the steady tortoise beats the fast hare.

legend an old story that may not be entirely true:
Do you know the *legend* of Robin Hood?

terrible

Adjective. very bad or unpleasant:
We had *terrible* weather on our vacation.

horrible very bad, ugly, or unpleasant:
The garbage gave off a *horrible* smell.

unbearable difficult or impossible to stand:
The piercing sound was *unbearable* to listen to.

awful very bad:
Those colors look *awful* together.

antonyms: fantastic, wonderful, enjoyable, pleasant

tough

Adjective. difficult:
Cleaning this floor is a *tough* job.

hard not easy:
Our teacher gave us a *hard* math problem for extra credit.

troublesome causing trouble or difficulty:
Getting puppies to behave can be a *troublesome* job.

uphill against difficulties, as if going up a hill:
Training a cat can be an *uphill* task.

antonyms: easy, simple, painless

trouble

Noun. worry or difficulty:
He had *trouble* learning the computer program.

problem difficulty:
I have a *problem* doing this dance step.

worry an uneasy or fearful feeling:
My *worry* is that it just won't work.

understand
Verb. to get the meaning of:
Did you *understand* the math?
grasp to see or get the meaning of:
Can you *grasp* the sense of
this poem?
follow to pay attention to and
understand:
His story was hard to *follow*.
know to understand clearly or be
sure of:
I *know* how to add and subtract
numbers.
learn to get to know:
To *learn* sewing, watch someone
who knows how.

unfair
Adjective. not fair, right, or just:
The election was *unfair* because
some votes were not counted.
unjust not right, not deserved:
It is *unjust* to punish us all for what
one person did.
wrong not right, not to be allowed:
Letting someone get away with
cheating is *wrong*.
unequal not well matched; unfair:
When the older children played the
younger children in football, it was
an *unequal* contest.

antonyms: fair, just, deserved,
right, equal, evenhanded

unknown
Adjective. not known, not heard
of or seen before now:
That man is *unknown* to me.
unfamiliar not heard of or
seen before:
An *unfamiliar* voice was speaking.
strange not known before now:
A *strange* girl is sitting in Pete's
old seat.
mysterious puzzling or hard
to explain:
My mother investigated a *mysterious*
scratching noise and found a lost
kitten outside our door.

antonyms: known, familiar,
recognizable

usual
Adjective. done or used by habit:
We took the *usual* route to
Grandma's house.
regular usual, routine:
This is not my *regular* desk.
ordinary common or normal:
It was an *ordinary* box with no
decoration.
everyday not special:
We used our *everyday* dishes even
though it was a party.

antonyms: unusual, uncommon,
outstanding, different, unexpected

Spelling Thesaurus

vacation

Noun. time off away from school or work:
Are you going away during your *vacation?*

holidays time off away from school or work:
He spent his summer *holidays* in Canada.

recess a time when school or work stops:
Spring *recess* begins next week.

visitor

Noun. a person who visits:
That woman is a *visitor* to our class for the day.

guest someone who has been invited to visit:
We are having a *guest* to dinner tonight.

caller someone who comes to your home for business or friendship:
The *caller* rang the doorbell.

voyage

Noun. a long trip:
The family went on a *voyage* to Mexico.

journey a trip, usually long:
The *journey* took him through India.

cruise a trip by water:
The ocean *cruise* took three days.

trip travel that can be long or short:
Let's take a *trip* to the shore.

tour a trip with several stops, perhaps to look at the sights:

A *tour* of the West might include a stop at the Grand Canyon.

weak

Adjective. not having strength.

usually said of people or animals:	usually said of things:
delicate	*flimsy*
feeble	*shaky*
frail	*tumbledown*
sickly	*unsteady*

antonyms: strong, powerful, healthy, muscular, sturdy, solid

wealth

Noun. a great amount of money or valuable things:
People with great *wealth* can often buy things to make their lives more comfortable.

riches a great amount of money or valuable things:
The museum displayed the *riches* from the king's palaces.

money coins and bills in general, or wealth:
His family always had *money.*

property land, buildings, or other materials that are owned:
In his will, he left some of his *property* to charity.

antonym: poverty

Spelling Thesaurus

weary

Adjective. having little or no energy:
They felt *weary* after the long walk.

tired drained of energy:
After a hard day's work, I am too *tired* to stay up late.

exhausted very tired, completely drained of energy:
Jane was *exhausted* after painting the house all day.

worn-out very tired:
Chasing after a young child all day left me *worn-out.*

sleepy needing to go to sleep:
I start feeling *sleepy* around 9:00 P.M.

> antonyms: strengthened, lively, fresh

whirl

Verb. to turn quickly in a circle or around a central point:
The dancers *whirl* so fast that their faces are a blur.

spin to turn quickly in a circle or around a central point:
A pinwheel's blades *spin* when I blow on them.

rotate to turn, slowly or quickly, around a central point:
The wheels of a car *rotate* on axles, making the car move.

worry

Verb. to cause to feel uneasy:
The motor's scraping noises *worry* me.

distress to cause to feel anxious or upset:

Newspaper reports can *distress* us.

concern to cause to feel interested, often in an uneasy way:
Even a low fever can *concern* a parent.

bother to cause to feel annoyed:
A dripping faucet can really *bother* me.

> antonyms: calm, comfort, reassure, please, delight

yarn

Noun. a continuous strand of wool or other fiber, used to knit or weave:
He knitted the *yarn* into a vest.

string a thin strand of fibers used for tying:
Use *string* to attach the discs to the mobile.

twine a stronger, thicker string:
He tied the boxes together with *twine.*

cord a continuous strand that can be made of fiber but doesn't have to be:
The lamp has an electric *cord* and a plug.

rope a thick, strong cord:
The boat was attached to the dock with a *rope.*

thread a very thin strand of fiber used in sewing:
I used red *thread* to sew on that button.

Spelling Thesaurus

A **dictionary** helps you use a word correctly. You will see **guide words** at the top of each page. The guide word on the left shows the first word on that page. The one on the right shows the last word on that page.

A **definition** tells what the entry word means. If there is more than one meaning, each meaning will be numbered.

The word you look up is a **main entry** word. All entry words are in alphabetical order.

A **respelling** shows you how to pronounce the word. Look at the pronunciation key on each right-hand page in this Dictionary, or look at the table of Common Spelling Patterns on page 159.

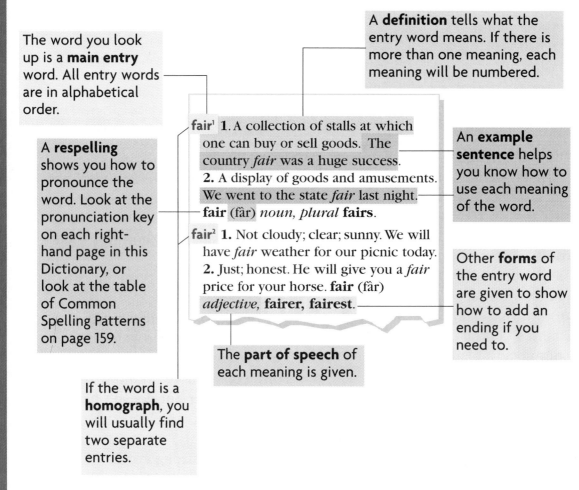

fair¹ **1.** A collection of stalls at which one can buy or sell goods. The country *fair* was a huge success.
2. A display of goods and amusements. We went to the state *fair* last night.
fair (fâr) *noun, plural* **fairs**.

fair² **1.** Not cloudy; clear; sunny. We will have *fair* weather for our picnic today.
2. Just; honest. He will give you a *fair* price for your horse. **fair** (fâr) *adjective,* **fairer, fairest**.

An **example sentence** helps you know how to use each meaning of the word.

Other **forms** of the entry word are given to show how to add an ending if you need to.

The **part of speech** of each meaning is given.

If the word is a **homograph**, you will usually find two separate entries.

Spelling Dictionary

able **1.** Knowing how. I am *able* to use the word processor. **2.** Having the power or skill to do something. Ms. Rice is *able* to lift 200 pounds. **a•ble** (ā′bəl) *adjective,* **abler, ablest.**

accept **1.** To receive something that is offered. I *accept* the gift. **2.** To receive as true. She couldn't *accept* the idea. **ac•cept** (ak sept′) *verb,* **accepted, accepting.**

across To or on the other side. She's gone *across* in a sailboat. *Adverb.*
—To or on the other side of. Let's race *across* the street. *Preposition.* **a•cross** (ə krôs′) *adverb; preposition.*

act **1.** Something that is done. Saving the cat was an *act* of kindness. **2.** Part of a play. The curtain fell at the end of the first *act. Noun.*
—**1.** To perform a part. Would you like to *act* in the play? **2.** To behave in a certain way. I wish he would *act* his age. *Verb.* **act** (akt) *noun, plural* **acts**; *verb* **acted, acting.**

action **1.** The process of doing something. The *action* of throwing a ball is easy. **2.** A deed. Helping a blind person across a street is a kind *action.* **ac•tion** (ak′shən) *noun, plural* **actions.**

address **1.** A place where a person or business receives mail. **2.** Directions on a letter that tell where it is to be delivered. **3.** *Computers: E-mail address.* A series of symbols describing a location on a computer network where communications can be sent and received. *Noun.*
—**1.** To write delivery directions on a letter or package. **2.** To make a speech. The principal will *address* the assembly. *Verb.* **ad•dress** (ə dres′ *or* ad′res) *noun, plural* **addresses**; *verb* **addressed, addressing.**

afternoon The time of the day between noon and evening. It is always quiet here in the

afternoon. **af•ter•noon** (af′tər nün′) *noun, plural* **afternoons.**

again Once more. We hope to see you *again.* **a•gain** (ə gen′) *adverb.*

against **1.** In disagreement with. Mom is *against* the idea. **2.** Competing with. The game is *against* a good team. **3.** In contact with. Lean your bicycle *against* the wall. **a•gainst** (ə genst′) *preposition.*

agree **1.** To be willing to do something. I *agree* to clean my room. **2.** To get along well. My sisters always *agree.* **a•gree** (ə grē′) verb, **agreed, agreeing.**

ahead **1.** In front. Go *ahead* of us. **2.** In the future. Let's think *ahead* to next year. **a•head** (ə hed′) *adverb.*

airplane A machine with wings that flies. An *airplane* is heavier than air, and is driven by propellers or jet engines. **air•plane** (âr′plān′) *noun, plural* **airplanes.**

airplane

airport A place where airplanes can take off and land. An *airport* has buildings for sheltering and repairing airplanes and for receiving passengers and freight. **air•port** (âr′pôrt′) *noun, plural* **airports.**

alike Much the same. The twins look *alike.* **a•like** (ə līk′) *adjective.*

at; āpe, fär, câre; end; mē, it, īce; pîerce; hot, ōld: sông, fôrk; oil; out; up; ūse; rüle; pull; tûrn; chin; sing; shop; thin; this; hw in white; zh in treasure. The symbol ə stands for the unstressed vowel sound in about, taken, pencil, lemon, and circus.

allow To give permission to or for. The store doesn't *allow* bare feet. **al•low** (ə lou′) *verb*, **allowed, allowing**.

aloud Loud enough for others to hear. Please read your story *aloud*. **a•loud** (ə loud′) *adverb*.

alphabet The ordered set of letters that make up a language. There are twenty-six letters in the English *alphabet*. **al•pha•bet** (al′fə bet′) *noun*; **alphabetical** *adjective*; **alphabetically** *adverb*.

already By or before a time. The party was *already* over when they arrived. **al•read•y** (ôl red′ē) *adverb*.

although Even if. *Although* she is short, she is a good basketball player. **al•though** (ôl thō′) *conjunction*.

always **1.** All the time; continuously. There is *always* snow and ice at the North Pole. **2.** Every time; at all times. No matter when I schedule our meetings, you are *always* late. **al•ways** (ôl′wāz *or* ôl′wēz) *adverb*.

among **1.** In the middle of. We walked *among* the flowers. **2.** With shares for each of. We divided the food *among* the children. **a•mong** (ə mung′) *preposition*.

annoy To bother or disturb. That loud music is beginning to *annoy* me. **an•noy** (ə noi′) *verb*; **annoyer**, *noun*; **annoyingly**, *adverb*.

annual **1.** Measured by the year. The average *annual* rainfall is fifteen inches. **2.** Happening or returning once a year. Thanksgiving is an *annual* holiday in November. **an•nu•al** (an′ū əl) *adjective*.

anyone Any person. Is *anyone* at home? **an•y•one** (en′ē wun′) *pronoun*.

anyway No matter what. It's supposed to rain, but we're going hiking *anyway*. **an•y•way** (en′ē wā′) *adverb*.

anywhere In, at, or to any place. We can eat *anywhere* you'd like. **an•y•where** (en′ē hwâr′ *or* en′ē wâr′) *adverb*.

apart **1.** Into more than one piece. The man pulled the chair *apart*. **2.** At a distance. Josh is standing *apart* from everyone in the crowd. **a•part** (ə pärt′) *adverb*.

appointment **1.** The naming of someone to a position. Ms. Brown accepted the *appointment* as the mayor's assistant. **2.** An agreement to meet at a certain time. I have an *appointment* with the doctor at twelve o'clock. **ap•point•ment** (ə point′mənt) *noun, plural* **appointments**.

April The fourth month of the year. **A•pril** (ā′prəl) *noun*.

argue To discuss a matter and to disagree. They always *argue* about which show to watch. **ar•gue** (är′gū) *verb*, **argued, arguing**.

army **1.** A large group of soldiers organized to defend a nation on land. The *army* was sent to aid the villagers. **2.** A large group. An *army* of ants came to our picnic. **ar•my** (är′mē) *noun, plural* **armies**.

art **1.** Works made by painters, writers, and musicians. We saw some great *art* at the museum. **2.** The study of such works. My sister studies *art*. **art** (ärt) *noun, plural* **arts**.

artery **1.** One of the blood vessels carrying blood away from the heart. **2.** A main road or channel. There is a major *artery* between the two cities. **ar•ter•y** (ärt′tə rē) *noun, plural* **arteries**.

article **1.** Composition written for a newspaper, magazine, or book. Did you see my *article* in the school newspaper? **2.** A particular thing or object. Several *articles* were stolen from the house. **ar•ti•cle** (är′ti kəl) *noun, plural* **articles**.

artist **1.** Person who is skilled in painting, music, literature, or any other form of art. **2.** Person whose work shows talent or skill. That dancer is a great *artist*. **art•ist** (är′tist) *noun, plural* **artists**.

asleep Not awake. **a•sleep** (ə slēp′) *adjective*.

asteroid One of thousands of small planets in between Jupiter and Mars that revolve around the sun. **as•ter•oid** (as′tə roid′) *noun, plural* **asteroids**.

atmosphere **1.** The layer of gas around the earth. Outer space lies beyond the earth's *atmosphere*. **2.** The layer of gases that surrounds any heavenly body. Scientists do not think people could live in the *atmosphere* of Mars. **at•mos•phere** (at′məs fîr′) *noun, plural* **atmospheres**.

attic A room or space in a house just below the roof. We keep our old furniture in the *attic*. **at•tic** (at′ik) *noun*.

attitude **1.** A way of carrying oneself. His *attitude* is always pleasant. **2.** A state of mind. What is your *attitude* toward the conflict? **at•ti•tude** (at′i tüd′ *or* at′i tūd′) *noun, plural* **attitudes**.

August The eighth month of the year. **Au•gust** (ô′gəst) *noun*.

author A person who has written a book, story, play, article or poem. The *author* of the book is Mark Twain. **au•thor** (ô′thər) *noun, plural* **authors**.

autumn The season of the year coming between summer and winter; fall. All of the leaves from this tree fell during *autumn*. **au•tumn** (ô′təm) *noun, plural* **autumns**.

avenue **1.** A way to reach a goal or place. Going to school is a good *avenue* to take if I want to become a doctor. **2.** A street. The *avenue* intersected with the expressway. **av•e•nue** (av′ə nū′) *noun*.

avoid To stay away from. I must *avoid* poison ivy. **a•void** (ə void′) *verb*.

awake To stop being asleep. He will *awake* when he hears the alarm clock. *Verb.*
—Not asleep. Is John *awake* yet? *Adjective.* **a•wake** (ə wāk′) *verb*, **awoke** or **awaked**, **awaking;** *adjective*.

awful Very bad. It was an *awful* day for a picnic. **aw•ful** (ô′fəl) *adjective*.

backyard Space at the rear of a house. Chad built a sand castle in his *backyard*. **back•yard** (bak′yärd′) *noun*.

balance **1.** The condition in which opposite sides or parts of something are the same in weight, amount, or force. The two children kept the seesaw in *balance*. **2.** A steady, secure position. I lost my *balance* on the ice. *Noun.*
—To put or keep in a steady position. I can *balance* a book on my head. *Verb.* **bal•ance** (bal′əns) *noun, plural* **balances;** *verb* **balanced, balancing**.

balance

bandage A piece of material used to cover a wound. I used a *bandage* to cover the cut on my finger. *Noun.*
—To cover a wound with a piece of material. The nurse will *bandage* my finger. *Verb.* **band•age** (ban′dij) *noun, plural* **bandages;** *verb* **bandaged, bandaging**.

barber Someone who makes a living cutting hair. The *barber* charges five dollars for a haircut. **bar•ber** (bär′bər) *noun*.

bare **1.** Without cover. His *bare* legs were badly sunburned. **2.** Empty. Our refrigerator is *bare*. **bare** (bâr) *adjective*, **barer, barest**.

barley The grain of a plant that is like grass. *Barley* is used to feed animals. **bar•ley** (bär′lē) *noun, plural* **barleys**.

barnyard The land or area near or around a barn. The *barnyard* was full of animals. **barn•yard** (bärn′yärd′) *noun, plural* **barnyards**.

basket A container that is woven. We put our lunch in a picnic *basket*. **bas•ket** (bas′kit) *noun, plural* **baskets**.

bathroom A room with a bathtub or shower, washbowl, and toilet. The *bathroom* was out of order. **bath•room** (bath′rüm′ *or* bath′rùm′) *noun*.

at; āpe, fär, câre; end; mē, it, īce; pîerce; hot, ōld; sông, fôrk; oil; out; up; ūse; rüle; pùll; tûrn; chin; sing; shop; thin; <u>th</u>is; hw in white; zh in treasure. The symbol ə stands for the unstressed vowel sound in about, taken, pencil, lemon, and circus.

Spelling Dictionary

bathtub A tub in which to bathe. The *bathtub* had soap suds in it. **bath•tub** (bath′tub′) *noun, plural* **bathtubs**.

battery A device that produces a flow of electricity. We need a new *battery* in the car. **bat•ter•y** (bat′ə rē) *noun, plural* **batteries**.

battle A fierce contest between two people or groups of people. The basketball game should be a real *battle. Noun.*
—To fight or struggle. We had to *battle* a storm. *Verb.* **bat•tle** (bat′əl) *noun, plural* **battles;** *verb,* **battled, battling.**

bazaar **1.** A market made up of rows of small shops or stalls. We bought some antiques at the *bazaar.* **2.** A sale of different things for a special purpose. We baked carrot cake for the church *bazaar.* **ba•zaar** (bə zär′) *noun, plural* **bazaars.**

bean A green or yellow vegetable having seeds in a pod. Jack planted a *bean* in the ground. **bean** (bēn) *noun, plural* **beans.**

beard Hair that grows on a man's face. My father has a grey *beard.* **beard** (bîrd) *noun, plural* **beards.**

beast An animal. My dog Sheba is a friendly *beast.* **beast** (bēst) *noun.*

beat Musical or poetic stress. The music has a fast *beat. Noun.*
—**1.** To hit again and again. We will take the dirty rug outside and *beat* it. **2.** To defeat. The other fourth grade team might *beat* us. *Verb.* **beat** (bēt) *noun, plural* **beats;** *verb,* **beaten** *or* **beat.**

beautiful Very nice to look at. My sister is a *beautiful* woman. **beau•ti•ful** (bū′tə fəl) *adjective.*

became past tense of **become.** Came to be. She *became* president of the class. **be•came** (bi kām′) *verb.*

bedroom A room used for sleeping. I went upstairs to my *bedroom.* **bed•room** (bed′rŭm′ *or* bed′rùm′) *noun, plural* **bedrooms.**

bedspread A cover for a bed. I put the *bedspread* on the bed. **bed•spread** (bed′spred′) *noun, plural* **bedspreads.**

beet A plant with a thick root used as a vegetable. The *beet* is a very healthful food to eat. **beet** (bēt) *noun.*

behave **1.** To act correctly. I will *behave* at the wedding tomorrow morning. **2.** To do things in a certain way; act. You *behaved* bravely after you hurt your knee. **be•have** (bi hāv′) *verb,* **behaved, behaving.**

believe To think something is real or true. Do you *believe* the truth? **be•lieve** (bi lēv′) *verb;* **believable,** *adjective;* **believably,** *adverb;* **believer,** *noun.*

below Lower than. We ducked *below* the fence. **be•low** (bi lō′) *preposition.*

belt **1.** A strap or band worn around the waist. My pants were too loose, so I put on a *belt.* **2.** A band of flexible material running around wheels and used for moving or carrying something. The *belt* and pulley were strong enough to hoist the piano up to the third floor. **belt** (belt) *noun.*

belt

bent **1.** Curved or crooked. The pipe was *bent. Adjective.* **2.** Past tense of **bend.** Caused a change of shape. The strong man *bent* the steel pipe. *Verb.* **bent** (bent) *verb; adjective.*

berry A small, juicy fruit. The *berry* tasted good with whipped cream. **ber•ry** (ber′ē) *noun, plural* **berries.**

beside By the side of. We sat *beside* each other at the concert. **be•side** (bi sīd′) *preposition.*

birth **1.** The act of coming into life. The *birth* of my sister sparked a huge celebration. **2.** The start of something; beginning. The *birth* of the women's movement took place in 1848. **birth** (bûrth) *noun.*

blade **1.** A very narrow leaf, especially of grass. The lawnmower could cut the thinnest *blade* of grass. **2.** The cutting part of a tool or weapon. The *blade* of the knife was very sharp. **blade** (blād) *noun, plural* **blades.**

blank A space to be filled in. Write your name on the first *blank. Noun.*

—Without marks or writing. Please take out a *blank* sheet of paper. *Adjective*. **blank** (blangk) *noun; adjective*.

blanket **1.** A cover for a bed. I have a warm *blanket* on my bed. **blan•ket** (blang′kit) *noun, plural* **blankets**.

blizzard A heavy snowstorm with very strong winds. During the *blizzard* the city received fifteen inches of snow. **bliz•zard** (bliz′ərd) *noun, plural* **blizzards**.

block **1.** Something hard and solid with flat edges. Please hand me that *block* of wood. **2.** An area in a town or city with four streets around it. I have several friends who live on my *block*. *Noun*.
—To get in the way of something; obstruct. The fallen tree had begun to *block* traffic. *Verb*. **block** (blok) *noun, plural* **blocks; *verb*, **blocked, blocking**.

bloom **1.** A flower or group of flowers. The vase held one white *bloom*. **2.** The time or state of flowering. The lilac tree is in *bloom*. *Noun*.
—To produce or open into flowers. The fruit trees will *bloom* early this year. *Verb*. **bloom** (blüm) *noun, plural* **blooms; *verb*.

board A long piece of sawed wood. I nailed down the loose *board*. *Noun*.
—To get on. She'll *board* the ship tomorrow. *Verb*. **board** (bôrd) *noun, plural* **boards; *verb* **boarded, boarding**.

body **1.** The complete shape of a person. My uncle has a tall *body*. **2.** The main part. Describe your vacation in the *body* of the letter. **bod•y** (bod′ē) *noun, plural* **bodies**.

boiling point The temperature at which a liquid begins to boil. **boil•ing point** (boi′ling point) *noun*.

bomb A hollow case filled with explosives to be used as a weapon. When the car backfired it sounded like a *bomb*. *Noun*.
—To drop bombs on. The airplanes will *bomb* the ice glaciers tomorrow. *Verb*. **bomb** (bom) *noun, plural* **bombs; *verb*.

boot A covering for the foot and lower leg to keep them dry. My *boot* has a hole in the bottom. **boot** (büt) *noun*.

bounce **1.** To make something go up and down. How long can you *bounce* the ball? **2.** To jump. Do not *bounce* on the bed. **bounce** (bouns) *verb*, **bounced, bouncing**.

bowl[1] **1.** A rounded dish that holds things. Please pour some milk into the *bowl*. **2.** Something shaped like a bowl. A football stadium is sometimes called a *bowl*. **bowl** (bōl) *noun, plural* **bowls**.

bowl[2] A wooden ball used in a game. *Noun*.
—**1.** To play the game of bowling. **2.** To roll a ball in bowling. *Verb*. **bowl** (bōl) *noun, plural* **bowls; *verb*, **bowled, bowling**.

box[1] A container made of wood or stiff paper. The *box* was filled with old clothes. **box** (boks) *noun, plural* **boxes**.

box[2] To fight wearing large gloves on the hands. The two athletes will *box* at the gym today. **box** (boks) *verb*, **boxed, boxing**.

boy A very young man. **boy** (boi) *noun, plural* **boys**.

branch **1.** A part of a tree or bush that grows out from the trunk. **2.** Something that goes out of or into a main part, like the branch of a tree. The main railroad line has many *branches*. The Missouri and Ohio rivers are *branches* of the Mississippi River. *Noun*.
—To divide into branches. Our cat got stuck in a place where the tree *branched*. *Verb*. **branch** (branch) *noun, plural* **branches; *verb*, **branched, branching**.

bread A food made of flour and baked into loaves. *Noun*.
—To cover with bread crumbs before cooking. We will *bread* the fish. *Verb*. **bread** (bred) *noun, plural* **breads; *verb*.

breakfast The morning meal. **break•fast** (brek′fəst) *noun, plural* **breakfasts**.

breath Air that goes into and out of the lungs. **breath** (breth) *noun*.

at; āpe, fär, câre; end; mē, it, īce; pîerce; hot, ōld; sông, fôrk; oil; out; up; ūse; rüle; pull; tûrn; chin; sing; shop; thin; this**; hw in white; zh in treasure. The symbol ə stands for the unstressed vowel sound in about, taken, pencil, lemon, and circus.**

brick A building material made from clay molded into blocks and baked until hard. Carlos bought a house made of *brick*. **brick** (brik) *noun, plural* **bricks**.

bridge A structure built for passing from one side to the other. The *bridge* went over the river. *Noun*.
—To go across. I will *bridge* the gap with a board. *Verb.* **bridge** (brij) *noun, plural* **bridges**; *verb* **bridged, bridging**.

broil To cook something under a direct flame. We're going to *broil* hamburgers tonight. **broil** (broil) *verb* **broiled, broiling**.

broom A long stick with a brush on it, used for sweeping. **broom** (brüm) *noun, plural* **brooms**.

brought Past tense and past participle of **bring.** Came with or carried from another place. I *brought* my own thermos along with me. **brought** (brôt) *verb*.

brush A tool made with bristles, used for sweeping, smoothing, cleaning, or painting. The *brush* was filthy. *Noun*
—**1.** To clean or paint with a brush. Please *brush* the crumbs off the table. **2.** To touch lightly. I felt a branch *brush* my arm. *Verb.* **brush** (brush) *noun, plural* **brushes**; *verb,* **brushed, brushing**.

bucket A round container with a handle, used for holding liquids. The *bucket* overflowed with water. **buck•et** (buk′it) *noun, plural* **buckets**.

built Past tense and past participle of **build**. Made by putting together parts or materials. They *built* the house by themselves. **built** (bilt) *verb*.

bull The adult male of cattle, whales, elephants, or certain other large animals. The bullfighter grabbed the *bull* by the horns. **bull** (bùl) *noun, plural* **bulls**.

bulldozer A heavy tractor with a blade, used for pushing or moving earth, rocks, or concrete. They used a *bulldozer* to clear the land. **bull•doz•er** (bùl′dō′zər) *noun, plural* **bulldozers**.

buoy **1.** A floating object that is anchored. A buoy is used to direct ships through difficult areas. The captain steered the ship left of the red *buoy*. **2.** A life preserver. **bu•oy** (bü′ē or boi) *noun, plural* **buoys**.

bureau **1.** A chest of drawers. He took a flannel shirt out of his *bureau*. **2.** A department of government. Which *bureau* does he work for? **bu•reau** (byùr′ō) *noun, plural* **bureaus**.

burn To hurt or damage by fire. If you light the match, you might *burn* your hand. **burn** (bûrn) *verb*, **burned** or **burnt**.

burst **1.** To break into pieces under pressure. The balloon *burst* when it was squeezed. **2.** To act suddenly. She *burst* into song. **burst** (bûrst) *verb* **burst, bursting**.

bury To place in the ground and cover up. Our dog likes to *bury* his bones. **bur•y** (ber′ē) *verb*, **buried, burying**.

bus A large truck or car with seats for many passengers. We ride to work on the city *bus*. **bus** (bus) *noun, plural* **buses** or **busses**.

butcher Someone who cuts and sells meat. The *butcher* cut the meat. **butch•er** (bùch′ər) *noun, plural* **butchers**.

button A small, round object fastened on clothes to hold them together. *Noun*.
—To fasten with buttons. *Verb.* **but•ton** (but′ən) *noun, plural* **buttons**; *verb*.

cabbage A vegetable with thick leaves that grow in a head. I love steamed *cabbage*. **cab•bage** (kab′ij) *noun, plural* **cabbages**.

cabbage

calendar **1.** A written record showing the months, weeks, and days of the year. **2.** A list of coming events. The fall play is a big event on the *calendar*. **cal•en•dar** (kal′ən dər) *noun, plural* **calendars**.

Spelling Dictionary

calf[1] A baby cow. The *calf* was born a few hours ago. **calf** (kaf) *noun, plural* **calves**.

calf[2] The back of the leg between the knee and the ankle. My *calf* was aching from the long walk. **calf** (kaf) *noun, plural* **calves**.

cane 1. A plant stem. The sugar *cane* was very sweet. 2. A stick for walking. **cane** (kān) *noun*.

cape[1] A sleeveless piece of clothing. A *cape* is worn loosely over the shoulders. **cape** (kāp) *noun, plural* **capes**.

cape[2] A piece of land that sticks out from the coastline into a sea or lake. **cape** (kāp) *noun, plural* **capes**.

capital A city or town where the government of a country or state is located. Austin is the *capital* of Texas. **cap•i•tal** (kap′i təl) *noun, plural* **capitals**.

captain A person who is a leader of a group or in charge of a ship. Who is *captain* of the volleyball team? **cap•tain** (kap′tən) *noun, plural* **captains**.

capture 1. To take something by force. Can we *capture* the fort in a day? 2. To catch and hold a person, animal, or thing. We can *capture* the fox in a net. **cap•ture** (kap′chər) *verb*, **captured, capturing**.

card A rectangular piece of plastic used in place of cash; a credit card. **card** (kärd) *noun, plural* **cards**.

cardboard A heavy, stiff paper used to make boxes and posters. **card•board** (kärd′bôrd′) *noun*.

care 1. To like or be fond of. My parents *care* about you very much. 2. To look after. Judy must *care* for her mother while she recuperates. **care** (kâr) *verb*, **cared, caring**.

careful Using care. Be *careful* when you're on the ladder. **care•ful** (kâr′fəl) *adjective*.

carnival An area set up with games, rides, shows, or exhibits. The *carnival* was full of people. **car•ni•val** (kär′nə vel) *noun*.

carpet A heavy woven material used to cover floors. This *carpet* was handmade in Morocco. **car•pet** (kär′pit) *noun, plural* **carpets**.

cart 1. A wagon with two wheels, usually pulled by horses or oxen. The donkey pulled the *cart* up the hill. 2. A small, wheeled vehicle pushed by hand. *Noun.* —To carry in a cart. I will *cart* the vegetables to the store. *Verb.* **cart** (kärt) *noun, plural* **carts**; *verb* **carted, carting**.

castle A large building or group of buildings protected by thick walls. **cas•tle** (kas′əl) *noun, plural* **castles**.

caution Close care; watchfulness. Use *caution*, and be sure the campfire is completely out. **cau•tion** (kô′shən) *noun, plural* **cautions**.

cave A natural hollow or hole in the ground or in the side of a mountain. **cave** (kāv) *noun, plural* **caves**.

cavity 1. A softened place on a tooth caused by decay. The dentist said I had one *cavity*. 2. A hollow place; hole. There was a small mouse hiding in a *cavity* in the wall. **cav•i•ty** (kav′i tē) *noun, plural* **cavities**.

celebrate To observe or honor a special day or event. I will *celebrate* my birthday tomorrow. **cel•e•brate** (sel′ə brāt′) *verb*, **celebrating, celebrated**.

cellar A room or space under a building. We stored vegetables in the *cellar*. **cel•lar** (sel′ər) *noun, plural* **cellars**.

century A period of 100 years. From 1650 to 1750 is one *century*. **cen•tu•ry** (sen′chə rē) *noun, plural* **centuries**.

cereal Food made from grains. I eat *cereal* for breakfast. **ce•re•al** (sîr′ē əl) *noun, plural* **cereals**.

ceremony A formal act or set of acts done on a special occasion. Did you watch the opening *ceremony* of the Olympics? **cer•e•mo•ny** (ser′ə mō′nē) *noun, plural* **ceremonies**.

certain 1. Having no doubt. Are you *certain* you want a skateboard? 2. Known but not

at; **āpe**, **fär**, **câre**; **end**; **mē**, **it**, **īce**; **pîerce**; **hot**, **ōld**: **sông**, **fôrk**; **oil**; **out**; **up**; **ūse**; **rüle**; **püll**; **tûrn**; **chin**; **sing**; **shop**; **thin**; **this**; **hw** in **white**; **zh** in treasure. The symbol ə stands for the unstressed vowel sound in about, taken, pencil, lemon, and circus.

named. I am looking for a *certain* cup. **cer•tain** (sûr′tən) *adjective*.

champion A person or thing that is the winner of first place in a contest. **cham•pi•on** (cham′pē ən) *noun, plural* **champions**.

chance **1.** Probability of something happening. There is a big *chance* that I might win the game. **2.** A risk. **chance** (chans) *noun, plural* **chances**.

charter A written document giving and explaining certain rights and obligations. The insurance company was granted a *charter* by the state. **char•ter** (chär′tər) *noun, plural* **charters**.

checkup A complete examination of the body to find if it is healthy. I went to the doctor for a *checkup*. **check•up** (chek′up′) *noun, plural* **checkups**.

cheer **1.** A shout of praise or encouragement. Let's give him a rousing *cheer*. **2.** A happy feeling. Be of good *cheer*! *Noun*.
—**1.** To give a yell of support. Let's *cheer* for our team. **2.** To make happy. The clown will *cheer* up everybody. *Verb*. **cheer** (chîr) *noun, plural* **cheers**; *verb* **cheered, cheering**; *adjective* **cheerful**.

cherry **1.** A small, round, smooth-skinned fruit that is often a reddish color and grows on trees. **cher•ry** (cher′ē) *noun, plural* **cherries**.

cherry

chicken A common bird. **chick•en** (chik′ən) *noun, plural* **chickens**.

chief The leader of a group. The *chief* of police is elected in our town. *Noun*.
—Of greatest importance. Her *chief* duty is to manage the money. *Adjective*. **chief** (chēf) *noun, plural* **chiefs**; *adjective*.

choice **1.** A person or thing chosen. My first *choice* is the red bike. **2.** The power to choose. You have a *choice* of colors. *Noun*.
—Of very good quality; excellent. This is a *choice* watermelon. *Adjective*. **choice** (chois) *noun, plural* **choices**; *adjective*, **choicer, choicest; choiceness**.

choose To pick out. Danny will *choose* his favorite flower. **choose** (chüz) *verb*, **chose, chosen, choosing**.

chosen Past participle of **choose.** To have picked one from two or more things. **cho•sen** (chō′zən) *verb*.

circulation Movement around many places or from person to person. The government put new coins into *circulation*. **cir•cu•la•tion** (sûr kyə lā′shən) *noun*.

citizen **1.** A person who lives in a city or town. I am a *citizen* of Philadelphia. **2.** A person who is by birth or choice a member of a state or nation. I am a *citizen* of the United States of America. **cit•i•zen** (sit′ə zən) *noun, plural* **citizens**.

civil Having to do with a citizen or citizens. I am studying the *civil* life of Ancient Rome. **civ•il** (siv′əl) *adjective*.

clear **1.** To remove things from. Let's *clear* the dishes off the table. **2.** To free from blame. I want to *clear* my name. *Verb*.
—**1.** Free from clouds or haze. It looks as if it will be a *clear* day. **2.** With nothing in the way. The road is *clear* now. **3.** Easy to understand. It is *clear* to me that we should help. *Adjective*. **clear** (klîr) *verb; adjective*.

clown A funny person who does tricks at a circus, fair, or parade. The *clown* was blowing a whistle and clapping his hands. **clown** (kloun) *noun, plural* **clowns**; *adjective*, **clownish**.

clue Something that helps one solve a mystery or a puzzle. The footprint was an important *clue*. **clue** (klü) *noun, plural* **clues**.

coach One who trains or teaches singers, dancers, actors, or athletes. The *coach* worked with the football players today on drills. *Noun*.
—To train or teach singers, dancers, actors, or athletes. I *coached* the fourth grade baseball team. *Verb*. **coach** (kōch) *noun, plural* **coaches**; *verb* **coached, coaching**.

coil A loop or loops. *Noun*.
—To wind round and round. I will *coil* my

kite string around a stick. *Verb.* **coil** (koil) *noun, plural* **coils;** *verb* **coiled, coiling.**

collect **1.** To bring together. They will *collect* money for the hospital. **2.** To gather and keep. I *collect* stamps. *Verb.*
—To be paid for by the receiver. I will make a *collect* phone call. *Adjective.* **col•lect** (kə lekt′) *verb; adjective; noun* **collector.**

Columbus Day October 12, a holiday in many states to honor Christopher Columbus. **Columbus Day** (kə lum′bəs dā) *noun.*

comb A flat tool with teeth used to smooth hair or hold hair in place. I need a big *comb* because my hair is thick. *Noun.*
—To smooth or put in place with a comb. I will *comb* my hair in the car. *Verb.* **comb** (kōm) *noun, plural* **combs;** *verb.*

common **1.** Belonging to or shared by everyone. The lobby was a *common* space. **2.** Not out of the ordinary. Tractors are a *common* sight in farming towns. **com•mon** (kom′ən) *adjective.*

companion Friend; comrade. We three students were constant *companions.* **com•pan•ion** (kəm pan′yən) *noun, plural* **companions.**

company **1.** A guest. We are having *company* for dinner. **2.** People in business together. **com•pa•ny** (kum′pə nē) *noun, plural* **companies.**

compound Made up of two or more parts. Carbon dioxide is a *compound* gas. *Adjective.*
—A mixture or combination. Water is a *compound* of oxygen and hydrogen. *Noun.*
—To mix or combine. The chemist tried to *compound* a new formula. *Verb.* **com•pound** (kom′ pound; kəm pound′ *for verb*) *adjective; noun, plural* **compounds;** *verb,* **compounding, compounded.**

congress An assembly of people who make laws. The United States *Congress* is made up of the Senate and the House of Representatives. **con•gress** (kong′gris) *noun, plural* **congresses.**

continent One of the seven large areas of land on the earth. Europe is a *continent.*

con•ti•nent (kont′ə nənt) *noun, plural* **continents.**

cookbook A book of recipes. I looked in a *cookbook* to find a recipe for cupcakes. **cook•book** (kùk′bùk′) *noun, plural* **cookbooks.**

cookie A small, flat, sweet cake. I have a chocolate chip *cookie.* **cook•ie** (kùk′ē) *noun, plural* **cookies.**

cord A rope or string. I tied the box with *cord.* **cord** (kôrd) *noun, plural* **cords.**

costume Clothes worn in order to look like someone else. Do you have a *costume* for the party? **cos•tume** (kos′tüm *or* kos′tūm) *noun, plural* **costumes.**

cotton The soft, white fiber of certain plants. Some people prefer *cotton* shirts. **cot•ton** (kot′ən) *noun; adjective.*

cough The sound made by coughing. My uncle had a bad *cough* after coming in from the rain. *Noun.*
—To force air out of the lungs quickly and with a noise. *Verb.* **cough** (kôf) *noun, plural* **coughs;** *verb* **coughed, coughing.**

couldn't Shortened form of "could not." **could•n't** (kùd′ənt) *contraction.*

countryside The land outside cities and towns. We drove through the *countryside* on our way home. **coun•try•side** (kun′trē sīd′) *noun, plural* **countrysides.**

county A geographic area in local government. We live in Delaware *County.* **coun•ty** (koun′tē) *noun, plural* **counties.**

couple Two people or things paired together. Your parents are a nice *couple.* **cou•ple** (kup′əl) *noun, plural* **couples.**

cousin The child of one's aunt or uncle. My *cousin's* mother is my aunt. **cou•sin** (kuz′in) *noun, plural* **cousins.**

crack **1.** A sudden sharp noise. My bat made a loud *crack* when it hit the ball. **2.** A narrow

at; āpe, fär, câre; end; mē, it, īce; pîerce; hot, ōld; sông, fôrk; oil; out; up; ūse; rüle; pùll; tûrn; chin; sing; shop; thin; this; hw in white; zh in treasure. The symbol ə stands for the unstressed vowel sound in about, taken, pencil, lemon, and circus.

Spelling Dictionary

break or opening. There is a *crack* in the window. *Noun.*
—To break with a sharp sound. We can *crack* the nuts with a hammer. *Verb.* **crack** (krak) *noun, plural* **cracks;** *verb.*

crater A hollow area that looks like the inside of a bowl. **cra•ter** (krā′tər) *noun, plural* **craters**.

crayon A stick of colored wax material used for drawing. My little sister likes to draw with her red *crayon. Noun.*
—To make marks with a crayon. Did you *crayon* this sketch for me? *Verb.* **cray•on** (krā′on) *noun, plural* **crayons;** *verb.*

cream The yellow part of milk containing butterfat. My father takes a lot of *cream* in his coffee. **cream** (krēm) *noun.*

crews Groups of people who work together. The airplane's *crew* took very good care of the passengers. **crews** (krüz) *plural noun.*

crooked Not straight. The line was *crooked.* **crook•ed** (krük′id) *adjective.*

cross 1. An object made of one upright piece and one horizontal piece that intersect. *Noun.*
—**1.** To go from one side to another. Please *cross* the street at the light. **2.** To draw a line through. *Cross* out the wrong answer. *Verb.*
—Angry. Don't be *cross* with me. *Adjective.* **cross** (krôs) *noun; verb; adjective.*

crow A rather large, glossy black bird with a harsh cry. Unafraid, the *crow* sat on the scarecrow. *Noun.*
—To make the loud, sharp cry of a rooster or crow. The bird will *crow* at the rising of the sun. **crow** (krō) *noun, plural* **crows;** *verb* **crowed, crowing.**

crown A ceremonial hat worn by a king or a queen. **crown** (kroun) *noun, plural* **crowns**.

culture The arts, beliefs, and customs that make up a way of life. We are studying the *culture* of the Inuit. **cul•ture** (kul′chər) *noun, plural* **cultures**.

cumulus A high towering cloud that has a flat base. Is that puffy cloud *cumulus*? **cu•mu•lus** (kū′myə ləs) *noun.*

cure Something that brings back health to someone or something sick. The scientists are still looking for a *cure* for the common cold. *Noun.*
—To bring back to health. I believe that this medicine will *cure* me. *Verb.* **cure** (kyủr) *noun; verb,* **cured, curing**.

curious 1. Eager to know or learn. The kitten has a *curious* nature. **2.** Strange or unusual. His *curious* habits bother us. **cu•ri•ous** (kyủr′ē əs) *adjective; adverb,* **curiously**.

curl A lock of coiled hair. My mother has a long white *curl* over her eye. *Noun.*
—To form into curves or twists. My hair *curls* when I get it wet. *Verb.* **curl** (kûrl) *noun, plural* **curls;** *verb.*

curve A line that keeps bending in one direction. A *curve* has no straight parts or angles. *Noun.*
—To bend or move in a curved line. The road *curves* around the hill. *Verb.* **curve** (kûrv) *noun, plural* **curves;** *verb.*

cushion A pillow used to sit, lie, or rest on. I rested my head on a soft velvet *cushion.* **cush•ion** (kủsh′ən) *noun, plural* **cushions**.

dairy 1. A farm where milk is kept or made into cheese or butter. We visited the *dairy.* **dair•y** (dâr′ē) *noun, plural* **dairies**.

damage Loss or harm caused by injury to persons or property. The *damage* to the car was beyond repair. *Noun.*
—To cause harm to. I cannot *damage* this video tape because it is not mine. *Verb.* **dam•age** (dam′ij) *noun, plural* **damages;** *verb,* **damaged, damaging**.

danger 1. Chance of injury. The *danger* of the undertow is highest during noontide. **2.** A thing that may cause injury. High waves are a *danger* to swimmers. **dan•ger** (dān′jər) *noun, plural* **dangers**.

dare A challenge. We swam across the river on a *dare*. *Noun.*
—To have the courage to do or try something. Would you *dare* to climb that mountain? *Verb.* **dare** (dâr) *noun, plural* **dares;** *verb* **dared, daring**.

daughter A female child. **daugh•ter** (dô′tər) *noun, plural* **daughters**.

daylight 1. The light during the day. The *daylight* came in brightly through the window. **2.** The dawn; daybreak. We will leave at *daylight*. **day•light** (dā′līt′) *noun.*

dead 1. No longer living. My plant is *dead*. **2.** No longer working. The car battery is *dead*. **dead** (ded) *adjective.*

deaf Unable to hear. My grandfather is *deaf* in one ear. **deaf** (def) *adjective.*

deal¹ 1. An amount that is not specified. Do not go to a great *deal* of trouble. **2.** A bargain or agreement. We shook hands on our *deal*. **deal** (dēl) *noun, plural* **deals**.

deal² 1. To give out. Who will *deal* the cards? **2.** To engage in selling or buying. Does that store *deal* in trading cards? **deal** (dēl) *verb* **dealt, dealing**.

dear 1. Beloved or esteemed. She is a *dear* friend. **2.** High-priced. We paid *dearly* for the car. **dear** (dîr) *adjective; adverb* **dearly**.

December The twelfth month of the year. **De•cem•ber** (di sem′bər) *noun.*

decide To make a choice. Please *decide* for me. **de•cide** (di sīd′) *verb* **decided, deciding**.

declare To make something known. Mr. Jones *declared* that he would run for mayor. **de•clare** (di klâr′) *verb* **declared, declaring**.

deer A wild, hoofed animal, with antlers on the males. I saw a *deer* run across the road. **deer** (dîr) *noun, plural* **deer** or **deers**.

delight Great pleasure, joy. The play was a *delight*. *Noun.*

deer

—To please greatly. The singer *delighted* the audience. *Verb.* **de•light** (di līt′) *noun, plural* **delights;** *verb.*

depend 1. To count on. I can always *depend* on my big sister. **2.** To be decided by. The picnic will *depend* on the weather. **de•pend** (di pend′) *verb* **depended, depending**.

design A drawing or outline used to serve as a guide. This architect has worked on several *designs* before. *Noun.*
—To draw or outline a building or other structure. He *designs* cars for a living. *Verb.* **de•sign** (di zīn′) *noun, plural* **designs;** *verb* **designed, designing**.

dessert A food served at the end of a meal. After dinner, we had *dessert*. **des•sert** (di zûrt′) *noun, plural* **desserts**.

destroy To ruin completely. The wrecking ball will *destroy* the condemned building. **de•stroy** (di stroi′) *verb.*

dew Moisture in the form of tiny drops. Early in the morning the grass is covered with *dew*. **dew** (dü) *noun.*

didn't Shortened form of "did not." **did•n't** (did′ənt) *contraction.*

dis- 1. Not. *Disapprove* means to not approve. **2.** The opposite of. **dis** (dis) *prefix.*

disappear 1. To pass from view. The ship *disappeared* into the fog. **2.** To become lost. Where did the cat *disappear* to? **dis•ap•pear** (dis′ə pîr′) *verb.*

disappoint To fail to live up to a wish or hope. I hate to *disappoint* my coach but I can't play today. **dis•ap•point** (dis′ə point′) *verb.*

district An area that is a special part of another area. That store is in the city's business *district*. **district** (dis′trikt) *noun.*

dive Swoop; to plunge into water. I like to *dive* in the deepest end of the pool. *Verb.*

at; āpe, fär, câre; end; mē, ĭt, īce; pîerce; hot, ōld: sông, fôrk; oil; out; up; ūse; rüle; pùll; tûrn; chin; sing; shop; thin; <u>th</u>is; hw in white; zh in treasure. The symbol ə stands for the unstressed vowel sound in about, taken, pencil, lemon, and circus.

—A headfirst plunge into water. Marie made a good *dive* into the water. *Noun.* **dive** (dīv) *verb,* **dived** or **dove**, **diving**; *noun, plural* **dives**.

dock A platform where ships or boats are tied up. There are several boats at the *dock.* *Noun.*
—To move into a dock. Our ship will *dock* in Acapulco soon. *Verb.* **dock** (dok) *noun, plural* **docks**; *verb* **docked, docking**.

does A form of **do.** Carries out. Sy *does* what he is told. **does** (duz) *verb.*

dollar United States money worth 100 cents. Jenny gave me a *dollar* to spend. **dol•lar** (dol′ər) *noun, plural* **dollars**.

dollhouse A playhouse; a house for dolls. My sister owns a nineteeth century *dollhouse.* **doll•house** (dol′hous′) *noun.*

done Past participle of **do.** Completed; finished. I've *done* my best. **done** (dun) *verb.*

downstream Moving in the same direction as the current of a stream. *Downstream* river traffic is faster than upstream traffic. *Adjective.*
—**1.** Down a stream. The raft drifted *downstream.* **2.** At a point farther down the stream. The water becomes rough *downstream. Adverb.* **down•stream** (doun′strēm′) *adjective; adverb.*

downtown To or in the business center of a town. We went *downtown* to look for a birthday present. *Adverb.*
— Relating to the business center of a town. The *downtown* park is more crowded than the one outside of town. *Adjective.* **down•town** (doun′toun′) *adverb; adjective.*

dragon A fairy-tale monster, often having wings and breathing fire. The princess feared the *dragon.* **drag•on** (drag′ən) *noun, plural* **dragons**.

dragon

dream **1.** A series of thoughts and pictures occurring during sleep. I had a *dream* that I met Sitting Bull. **2.** A hope or ambition. It is his *dream* to learn to fly. *Noun.*
—**1.** To have pictures in one's mind during sleep. **2.** To imagine something as possible. He did not *dream* he might win. *Verb.* **dream** (drēm) *verb* **dreamed** or **dreamt**; *noun, plural* **dreams**.

drew Past tense of **draw.** Christine *drew* a rainbow on her note pad. **drew** (drü) *verb.*

drill¹ **1.** A tool for making holes in wood or metal. My mother is handy with a *drill.* **2.** A regularly practiced exercise for teaching or learning something. We have a fire *drill* once a month. **drill** (dril) *noun, plural* **drills**.

drill² **1.** To train by practice. Our teacher will *drill* us on our multiplication tables. **2.** To make a hole with a drill. **drill** (dril) *verb* **drilled, drilling**.

drought A very long period of time when there is very little rain. During the *drought,* we conserved water. **drought** (drout) *noun, plural* **droughts**.

drum **1.** A musical instrument played with a stick or the hand. The *drum* was made in West Africa. *Noun.*
—To beat on something in rhythm. Must you *drum* your fingers on the table? *Verb.* **drum** (drum) *noun, plural* **drums**; *verb.*

due **1.** Owed or owing. How much money is *due?* **2.** Expected. She is *due* home any minute. **due** (dü) *adjective.*

dumb Stupid. Please don't call him *dumb* because he isn't. **dumb** (dum) *Adjective.*

durable Able to last a long time in spite of much use or wear. My shoes are well-made, and *durable.* **du•ra•ble** (dùr′ə bəl or dyùr′ə bəl) *Adjective.*

during **1.** For the length of time of. **2.** At some point in the course of. We arrived *during* the intermission. **dur•ing** (dùr′ing) *preposition.*

dust **1.** Anything that is made into a fine powder. The bones of the mummy turned to *dust.* **2.** Tiny pieces of dirt so light they float in the air. *Noun.*

—**1.** To wipe away. *Dust* the furniture once a week. **2.** To cover or sprinkle. *Dust* the cookies with sugar. *Verb.* **dust** (dust) *noun; verb* **dusted, dusting**.

ear 1. The organ of the body by which people and animals hear. The rabbit turned its long *ears* toward the sound. **ear** (îr) *noun, plural* **ears**.

eardrum Part of the ear that sends sound waves to the hearing nerves. Earplugs keep out noise and protect your *eardrums*. **ear•drum** (îr′drum′) *noun, plural* **eardrums**.

Earth Day A day in April on which many events take place to get people to think about the environment. **Earth Day** (ûrth dā) *noun*.

earthquake A shaking of the earth caused by rock layers shifting underground. **earth•quake** (ûrth′kwāk) *noun, plural* **earthquakes**.

easel Tall stand or rack used to hold blackboards, signs, or paintings. **ea•sel** (ē′zəl) *noun, plural* **easels**.

either 1. One and the other; each of two. Trees are being planted on *either* side of the street. **2.** One or the other. You can use *either* book. *Adjective*.
—Also; likewise. The house was not large; it wasn't beautiful, *either. Adverb.* **ei•ther** (ē′thər *or* ī′thər) *adjective; adverb*.

Election Day The day, usually in November, when citizens vote for government officials. On *Election Day*, my dad took me with him to the polls. **E•lec•tion Day** (i lek′shən dā) *noun*.

element One of the materials from which all other materials are made. Oxygen is an *element.* **el•e•ment** (el′ə mənt) *noun, plural* **elements**.

elephant A huge, strong animal with a trunk and a gray hide. **el•e•phant** (el′ə fənt) *noun, plural* **elephants**.

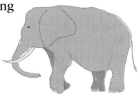
elephant

eleven One more than ten; 11. **e•lev•en** (i lev′ən) *noun, plural* **elevens;** *adjective*.

elf A small creature. An *elf* has magical powers in fairy tales. **elf** (elf) *noun, plural* **elves**.

else Other; instead. I'll give this to somebody *else. Adjective*.
—In a different way, place, or time. How *else* can we get there? *Adverb.* **else** (els) *adjective; adverb*.

employ To hire to do a job. I will *employ* six people this summer. **em•ploy** (em ploi′) *verb* **employed, employing**.

endanger 1. To put in a dangerous situation. The flood *endangered* many people. **2.** To threaten with becoming extinct. Pollution *endangers* many species of animals. **en•dan•ger** (en dān′jər) *verb*, **endangered, endangering**.

enemy 1. One who hates another. There is no reason for you to be my *enemy.* **2.** Anything that will harm. Snow is the *enemy* of drivers. **en•e•my** (en′ə mē) *noun, plural* **enemies**.

energy Strength or eagerness. Children are full of *energy.* **en•er•gy** (en′ər jē) *noun, plural* **energies**.

engine 1. A machine that uses energy to run other machines. The lawn mower needs a new *engine.* **2.** A machine that pulls a railroad train; locomotive. **en•gine** (en′jin) *noun, plural* **engines.**

engineer A person who designs airplanes, roads, or bridges. The city's *engineer* went

at; āpe, fär, câre; end; mē, it, īce; pîerce; hot, ōld; sông, fôrk; oil; out; up; ūse; rüle; pùll; tûrn; chin; sing; shop; thin; this; hw in white; zh in treasure. The symbol ə stands for the unstressed vowel sound in about, taken, pencil, lemon, and circus.

over the plans for a new road. **en•gi•neer** (en′jə nîr′) *noun, plural* **engineers**.

enjoyment Joy derived from something. Reading gives *enjoyment* to everyone. **en•joy•ment** (en joi′mənt) *noun, plural* **enjoyments**.

enough A sufficient amount. I have saved *enough* for now. *Noun.*
—As much as is needed. *Adjective.*
—To the needed amount. He fed the cat just *enough. Adverb.* **e•nough** (i nuf′) *noun; adjective; adverb.*

enter **1.** To go in or into. Let's *enter* the room together. **2.** To join. He will *enter* our class this year. **3.** *Computers.* To type information into a computer. I *entered* new names into the database. **en•ter** (en′tər) *verb.*

equal **1.** The same in size, amount, or number. Ten pennies are *equal* to one dime. **2.** Having the same opportunity. Everyone has an *equal* chance. **e•qual** (ē′kwəl) *adjective.*

equation A statement in mathematics that two quantities are equal. **e•qua•tion** (i kwā′zhən) *noun, plural* **equations**.

-er¹ A suffix that means someone or something who is or does. *Teacher* means a person who teaches.

-er² A *suffix* that means more. *Colder* means more cold than.

errand A short trip to do or get something. I went on an *errand* to buy potatoes. **er•rand** (er′ənd) *noun, plural* **errands**.

-est A *suffix* that means most. *Coldest* means the most cold.

evening The late afternoon and early nighttime. Do you have plans for this *evening? Noun.*
—Occurring during the late afternoon or early nighttime. *Adjective.* **eve•ning** (ēv′ning) *noun, plural* **evenings;** *adjective.*

ever **1.** At any time. Did you *ever* see such a storm? **2.** At all times. **ev•er** (ev′ər) *adverb.*

everybody Every person. *Everybody* will be there. **eve•ry•bod•y** (ev′rē bod′ē) *pronoun.*

everyone Each one. *Everyone* in this room is tired. **eve•ry•one** (ev′rē wun′) *pronoun.*

evil Bad, wicked, or harmful. He was punished for the *evil* act. **e•vil** (ē′vəl) *adjective,* **eviler** or **eviller; evilest** or **evillest**.

except Other than; but. I work every day *except* Sunday. *Preposition.*
—I would go, *except* I have work to do. *Conjunction.* **ex•cept** (ek sept′) *preposition; conjunction.*

exciting Stirring up feelings. The movie was *exciting.* **ex•cit•ing** (ek sī′ting) *adjective.*

fail **1.** To weaken. My strength began to *fail.* **2.** To disappoint. I will not *fail* my coach today in the game. **3.** To be unsuccessful. I can not *fail* this test because I am prepared. **fail** (fāl) *verb.*

fair¹ A collection of stalls at which one can buy or sell goods. The country *fair* was a huge success. **fair** (fâr) *noun, plural* **fairs**.

fair² **1.** Not cloudy; clear; sunny. We will have *fair* weather for our picnic today. **2.** Just; honest. He will give you a *fair* price for your horse. **fair** (fâr) *adjective* **fairer, fairest**.

family **1.** People related to one another. My *family* is very large. **2.** A group of related plants or animals. There are many breeds in the dog *family.* **fam•i•ly** (fam′ə lē) *noun, plural* **families**.

famous Very well-known. Lassie is a *famous* dog. **fa•mous** (fā′məs) *adjective.*

fan¹ **1.** An object or machine made to move air in order to cool something or someone. During the summer, we use a *fan. Noun.*
—To move air with a fan. I had to *fan* myself with a magazine. *Verb.* **fan** (fan) *noun, plural* **fans;** *verb.*

fan² One who supports or admires a person or team. I am a Philadelphia Flyers *fan.* **fan** (fan) *noun, plural* **fans**.

fanfare The attention of excited fans. The winning team received great *fanfare*. **fan•fare** (fan′fâr) *noun*.

fare Money paid to ride on public transportation. The bus *fare* is fifty cents for students. **fare** (fâr) *noun, plural* **fares**.

farmer A person who owns or works on a farm. The *farmer* plants corn. **farm•er** (fär′mər) *noun, plural* **farmers**.

farther A comparative of **far**. The boat drifted *farther* from the dock. **far•ther** (fär′thər) *adverb*.

Father's Day The second Sunday of June, when we celebrate male parents. **Fa•ther's Day** (fäth′ərz dā) *noun*.

favor An act of kindness. Can you do me a *favor* and pick up my mail? *Noun.*
—**1.** To show kindness to. *Favor* us with a song. **2.** To like something better than something else. I *favor* peaches over pears. *Verb.* **fa•vor** (fā′vər) *noun, plural* **favors;** *verb*.

fear A feeling that danger or trouble is near. I have a *fear* of spiders. *Noun.*
—To be afraid. I *fear* the dark. *Verb.* **fear** (fîr) *noun, plural* **fears;** *verb*.

feather One of the long, smooth outgrowths that covers a bird. The boy found a *feather* of a crow in his yard. **feath•er** (feth′ər) *noun*.

feather

February The second month of the year. **Feb•ru•ar•y** (feb′rü er′ē) *noun*.

fence A railing or wall made to keep things in or out. The house has a white picket fence around it. **fence** (fens) *noun*.

fern A green plant with feathery leaves and no flowers. The green *fern* usually is placed near the window for sunlight. **fern** (fûrn) *noun, plural* **ferns**

festival A time when people celebrate. The town has a yearly three-day *festival*. **fes•ti•val** (fes′tə vəl) *noun, plural* **festivals**.

few A small number. I would like a *few*. **few** (fū) *noun*.

fierce Angry. The lion had a *fierce* roar. **fierce** (fîrs) *adjective* **fiercer, fiercest**.

final Not to be changed. This is the *final* time he will alter the schedule. **2.** At the very end. The *final* call for lunch was given at 3 p.m. **final** (fī′nəl) *adjective*.

finger 1. One of the five separate parts at the end of the hand. **2.** Something that resembles a finger. We could see a *finger* of land. *Noun.*
—To handle. The salesclerk *fingered* the delicate fabric. *Verb.* **fin•ger** (fing′gər) *noun, plural* **fingers;** *verb*.

finish The end of something. Emily was tired at the *finish* of the race. *Noun.*
—To complete. When you *finish* the test, bring it to me. *Verb.* **fin•ish** (fin′ish) *noun, plural* **finishes,** *verb*.

firefighter A person whose work is to put out and prevent fires. **fire•fight•er** (fīr′fī′tər) *noun*.

fireplace An opening in a chimney to hold a fire. We have a *fireplace* in our house. **fire•place** (fīr′plās′) *noun, plural* **fireplaces**.

firm¹ A company of persons in business together. My sister works at one of the best law *firms* in Dallas. **firm** (fûrm) *noun, plural* **firms**.

firm² 1. Solidly fixed in place. The pole was made *firm* by the cement. **2.** Not to be changed. We made her a *firm* offer. **firm** (fûrm) *adjective*.

fist The clenched hand with fingers folded into the palm. The baby sucked on its *fist*. **fist** (fist) *noun, plural* **fists**.

fit¹ Attack of illness or emotion. Al shouted in a *fit* of anger. **fit** (fit) *noun*.

fit² 1. To be the same size as. Does the hat *fit* you? **2.** To arrange room for. We can *fit* you

at; āpe, fär, câre; end; mē, it, īce; pîerce; hot, ōld; sông, fôrk; oil; out; up; ūse; rūle; pùll; tûrn; chin; sing; shop; thin; this; hw in white; zh in treasure. The symbol ə stands for the unstressed vowel sound in about, taken, pencil, lemon, and circus.

Spelling Dictionary

in here. *Verb.*
—**1.** Good enough for; acceptable. This dress is *fit* for a queen. **2.** In good health; healthy. Exercise and eat right to stay *fit. Adjective.* **fit** (fit) *verb; adjective.*

Flag Day June 14th, the anniversary of the day when Congress adopted the Stars and Stripes as flag of the United States. **Flag Day** (flag dā) *noun.*

flock A large group. A *flock* of seagulls flew over the beach. *Noun.*
—To gather together in a crowd. Children *flock* around clowns. *Verb.* **flock** (flok) *noun, plural* **flocks;** *verb.*

flounder¹ To struggle or stumble about. The puppy floundered around the yard. **floun•der** (floun'dər) *verb.*

flounder² A flatfish that lives in saltwater. **floun•der** (floun'dər) *noun, plural* **flounders.**

flour Finely ground grain used to make bread. **flour** (flour) *noun.*

flow A smooth, nonstop movement. There was a constant *flow* of traffic *Noun.*
—To move in a stream. The river *flowed* to the sea. *Verb.* **flow** (flō) *noun, plural* **flows;** *verb.*

flute A musical instrument shaped like a tube, played by blowing over a hole at one end. **flute** (flüt) *noun, plural* **flutes.**

folk **1.** A group of people making up a nation or culture. I love the way country *folk* speak. **2.** Family or relatives. Ken visited his *folks* in Alaska last summer. **folk** (fōk) *noun, plural* **folks** *or* **folk.**

footprint A mark from a foot. The girls make *footprints* in the snow. **foot•print** (füt'print') *noun, plural* **footprints.**

forehead The part of the face above the eyebrows. **fore•head** (fôr'id *or* fôr'hed') *noun, plural* **foreheads.**

form **1.** The shape of something. The piece of clay had the *form* of an animal. **2.** A paper with blank spaces to fill in. A tax *form* can be difficult to complete. *Noun.*
—To give shape to. We will *form* the clay into a ball. **2.** To take a certain shape or

arrangement. Please *form* a line. *Verb.* **form** (fôrm) *noun, plural* **forms;** *verb.*

forty Four times ten; 40. The lollipop cost me *forty* cents. **for•ty** (fôr'tē) *Adjective.*

fountain **1.** A spring of water to drink from. **2.** Something that makes a stream of water. I'll meet you at the *fountain.* **foun•tain** (foun'tən) *noun, plural* **fountains.**

Fourth of July Independence Day in the United States. **Fourth of Ju•ly** (fôrth əv jü lī') *noun.*

fox Wild animal related to the wolf. **fox** (foks) *noun, plural* **foxes.**

freight **1.** Goods carried by truck or train. The truck was loaded with *freight.* **2.** A train that carries goods. The *freight* roared through the tunnel. **freight** (frāt) *noun, plural* **freights.**

Friday *Friday* is the sixth day of the week. **Fri•day** (frī'dā) *noun, plural* **Fridays.**

Word History

Friday comes from the Old English word meaning "Frigga's day." Frigga was the queen of the ancient English gods.

friend A person one likes. My best *friend* is Lori. **friend** (frend) *noun, plural* **friends.**

front The first or forward part. The engine is in the *front* of a train. **front** (frunt) *noun, plural* **fronts.**

frontier The far edge of a country where people are just beginning to settle. Space is the last *frontier.* **fron•tier** (frun tîr') *noun, plural* **frontiers.**

frost Tiny ice crystals. There was *frost* on his beard. *Noun.*
—To cover with icing. Please help me *frost* the cake. *Verb.* **frost** (frôst) *noun; verb.*

frost

frostbite Injury caused by exposure to extreme cold. We wore wool gloves to avoid *frostbite.* **frost•bite** (frôst'bīt') *noun.*

frown A wrinkling of the forehead. *Noun.* —**1.** To wrinkle the forehead in anger or displeasure. A *frown* came to my face when I saw the mess the cat made. **2.** To disapprove. Does your father *frown* on sleeping late? *Verb.* **frown** (froun) *noun, plural* **frowns**; *verb.*

fry To cook in a pan with the use of fat. **fry** (frī) *verb* **fried, frying**.

-ful **1.** Suffix, full of. *Hopeful* means full of hope. **2.** Suffix, able to or likely to. *Forgetful* means likely to forget. **-ful** (fəl) *suffix.*

fully Completely. She was *fully* satisfied with her meal. **full•y** (fùl′ē) *adverb.*

fungi Plural of fungus. A large group of living things including mushrooms, mildew, and molds. Look at the *fungi* growing on that tree. **fun•gi** (fun′jī) *noun.*

furious Full of rage. She was *furious* when she missed the train. **fur•i•ous** (fyùr′ē əs) *adjective.*

furniture Objects, tables, and beds, that are used in a room. I don't like a room cluttered with *furniture*. **fur•ni•ture** (fur′ni chər) *noun.*

further A comparative of **far**. We left without further delay. *Adjective.* —To help forward. I want to go to college to *further* my education. *Verb.* **fur•ther** (fûr′ thər) *adjective; verb.*

galaxy A very large group of stars. The Milky Way is a *galaxy* in the universe. **gal•ax•y** (gal′ək sē) *noun, plural* **galaxies**.

gallon A unit of measure for liquids. A gallon equals four quarts or about 3. 8 liters. **gal•lon** (gal′ən) *noun, plural* **gallons**.

garbage Scraps of food or other things to be thrown away. **gar•bage** (gär′bij) *noun.*

garden An area where plants, flowers, or vegetables are grown. The *garden* was planted by the students. *Noun.* —To work in a garden. My dad loves to *garden* during the summer. *Verb.* **gar•den** (gär′dən) *noun, plural* **gardens**; *verb.*

gear **1.** A wheel with teeth that fit into the teeth of another wheel. A little *gear* on the clock needs to be fixed. **2.** Equipment for a particular purpose. The fishing *gear* is new. **gear** (gîr) *noun, plural* **gears**.

geese Long-necked, web-footed birds related to ducks and swans. **geese** (gēs) *plural noun.*

general A high-ranking military officer. *Noun.* —**1.** Relating to all. There is a *general* interest in sports. *Adjective.* **gen•e•ral** (jen′ər əl) *noun, plural* **generals**; *adjective.*

gentle **1.** Not rough. His touch was very *gentle*. **2.** Mild and kindly. The old woman is *gentle* and sweet. **gen•tle** (jen′təl) *adjective* **gentler**; **gentlest**.

geologist A scientist who studies earthforms to find how the earth has changed throughout history. **ge•ol•o•gist** (jē ol′ə jist) *noun, plural* **geologists**.

germ A tiny mass of living material often able to cause disease. A *germ* can be spread when people cough or sneeze. **germ** (jûrm) *noun, plural* **germs**.

give **1.** To hand over. I will *give* Dave two tickets to the game. **2.** To offer. Please *give* me another chance. **give** (giv) *verb* **gave**; **given**; **giving**.

glance A quick movement of the eyes. I saw at a *glance* that you were happy. *Noun.* —To look at quickly. She will *glance* over the book tonight. *Verb.* **glance** (glans) *noun, plural* **glances**; *verb* **glanced**; **glancing**.

glare **1.** A bright light. The *glare* of the light hurt my eyes. **2.** An angry look. *Noun.* —**1.** To give off a strong bright light. The sunlight *glared* on the beach. **2.** To stare in

at; āpe, fär, câre; end; mē, it, īce; pîerce; hot, ōld; sông, fôrk; oil; out; up; ūse; rüle; pùll; tûrn; chin; sing; shop; thin; this; hw in white; zh in treasure. The symbol ə stands for the unstressed vowel sound in about, taken, pencil, lemon, and circus.

Spelling Dictionary

an angry way. *Verb.* **glare** (glâr) *noun,*
plural **glares;** *verb* **glared; glaring.**

glue A sticky substance used to fasten things
together. *Noun.*
—To stick things together with glue. *Glue*
that broken vase together. **glue** (glü) *noun,*
plural **glues;** *verb* **glued; gluing.**

goodness Kindness or generosity. I remember
her *goodness* during the time I was ill.
good•ness (güd'nis) *noun.*

gown **1.** A woman's dress. The evening *gown*
was blue. **2.** A loose robe. Each graduate
wore a long black *gown.* **gown** (goun)
noun, plural **gowns.**

grab To take quickly. Do not *grab* the food.
grab (grab) *verb* **grabbed; grabbing.**

gram A unit of mass in the metric system.
gram (gram) *noun, plural* **grams.**

grandfather The father of one's father or
mother. **grand•fa•ther** (grand'fä'<u>th</u>ər)
noun, plural **grandfathers.**

grandmother The mother of one's father or
mother. **grand•moth•er** (grand'mu<u>th</u>'ər)
noun, plural **grandmothers.**

graph A diagram used to show change. The
graph showed weather changes. **graph**
(graf) *noun, plural* **graphs.**

grave[1] Any place of burial. My dog has a *grave*
next to his favorite tree. **grave** (grāv) *noun,*
plural **graves.**

grave[2] Serious; very important. Hunger is a
grave problem in that part of the world.
grave (grāv) *adjective* **graver, gravest.**

greenhouse A room or building with walls
made of plastic or glass, used to contain
heat from the sun to grow plants.
green•house (grēn'hous') *noun,*
plural **greenhouses.**

groan A deep moan of pain or sadness.
The man let out a *groan* when he saw
that it was snowing. *Noun.*
—To moan in pain or sadness. She *groaned*
when she hurt her foot. *Verb.* **groan** (grōn)
noun, plural **groans;** *verb* **groaned,**
groaning.

grocery A store that sells food and household
things. The *grocery* was closed on Sunday.
gro•cer•y (grō'sə rē) *noun, plural*
groceries.

groundhog A small
animal that has a
plump body, short
legs, and a bushy tail.
ground•hog
(ground'hôg' *or*
ground'hog') *noun,*
plural **groundhogs.**

groundhog

Groundhog Day, February 2.
Ground•hog Day (ground'hôg' dā,
ground'hog' dā) *noun.*

growl A rumbling throaty sound. The dog
made a menacing *growl. Noun.*
—To make a low, throaty sound. The dog
growled at me. *Verb.* **growl** (groul) *noun,*
plural **growls;** *verb.*

guess An opinion formed without real
knowledge. My answer was a *guess. Noun.*
—To give an opinion without really
knowing. I *guess* it's that one. *Verb.* **guess**
(ges) *noun, plural* **guesses;** *verb.*

gum **1.** The part of the mouth in which the
roots of the teeth sit. **2.** A sticky substance.
There was a strong *gum* that we extracted
from the tree bark. **gum** (gum) *noun,*
plural **gums.**

H

hadn't Shortened form of had not. I *hadn't*
known he left. **had•n't** (had' ənt)
contraction.

hair A threadlike growth on the skin of
people and other mammals. My sister has
so much *hair* she can put it in a ponytail.
hair (hâr) *noun.*

halves Plural of **half.** Two equal parts made
from splitting something in half. Break the
chalk into two equal *halves. Noun.*
—Present tense form of **halve.** The chef
halves the mushrooms before cooking

Spelling Dictionary

them. *Verb.* **halves** (havz) *noun, plural* **halves**; *verb.*

handful An amount equal to what fits in a hand. You may have a *handful* of peanuts. **hand•ful** (hand′fŭl′) *noun, plural* **handfuls** or **handsful.**

hang 1. To fasten from above without support from below. We will *hang* the piñata from the ceiling. 2. To fasten to a wall. Can you *hang* this picture up? **hang** (hang) *verb* **hung, hanging.**

happen To take place. When will the party *happen*? **hap•pen** (hap′ən), *verb* **happened,** *verb* **happening.**

harbor A sheltered place along a coast where ships and boats anchor. **harbor** (här′bər) *noun, plural* **harbors.**

hardly 1. Just about. I *hardly* can read the sign. 2. Not often. It *hardly* ever snows in Florida. **hard•ly** (härd′lē) *adverb.*

hare A rabbit. **hare** (hâr) *noun, plural* **hare** or **hares.**

harm Hurt or damage. The *harm* to the animals was slight. *Noun.*
—To cause injury to. I will not *harm* a hair on your head. *Verb.* **harm** (härm) *noun, plural* **harms;** *verb* **harmed, harming.**

harmony A pleasing combination. The children sang in perfect *harmony.* **har•mo•ny** (här′mə nē) *noun, plural* **harmonies.**

harness The straps, bands, and other gear used to attach a work animal to a cart, plow, or wagon. They attached a huge *harness* made of wood and metal to the ox. *Noun.*
—To put a harness on. The farmer went to *harness* the horses. *Verb.* **har•ness** (här′nis) *verb.* **harnessed, harnessing;** *noun, plural* **harnesses.**

harsh 1. Rough or unpleasant to any of the senses. Ammonia has a *harsh* smell. 2. Unkind. Because she was angry, her voice was *harsh.* **harsh** (härsh) *adjective.*

haul To pull or move with force. It was hard to *haul* the heavy trunk up the stairs. *Verb*
—The act of hauling. Give the rope a *haul. Noun.* **haul** (hôl) *noun, plural* **hauls;** *verb.*

hawk A bird of prey. **hawk** (hôk) *noun, plural* **hawks.**

headache A pain felt inside the brain. The loud noise gave me a *headache.* **head•ache** (hed′āk) *noun, plural* **headaches.**

hear 1. To take sounds in by ear. I *hear* the dog bark. 2. To learn; to get news. I *hear* you got a new bike. **hear** (hîr) *verb.*

heavy 1. Having great weight. The grand piano is very *heavy.* 2. Great in amount or force. The traffic to the beach is always *heavy.* **heav•y** (hev′ē) *adjective* **heavier; heav•i•est.**

he'd Shortened form of "he had" or "he would." **he'd** (hēd) *contraction.*

heir A person who is to receive the money or property of a person after that person has died. The young prince was the *heir* to his father's throne. **heir** (âr) *noun, plural* **heirs.**

held Past tense and past participle of **hold** 1. Kept. I *held* my distance from the stray dog. 2. Supported. I *held* the dish in my hand. **held** (held) *verb.*

he'll Shortened form of "he will" or "he shall." **he'll** (hēl) *contraction.*

here 1. At or in this place. Turn *here.* 2. To or into this place. Come *here.* **here** (hîr) *adverb.*

here's Shortened form of "here is." *Here's* the place. **here's** (hîrz) *contraction.*

herself 1. Her *own* self. She insisted on coming *herself* 2. Her normal, usual self. She was *herself* again after a good sleep. **her•self** (hûr self′) *pronoun.*

he's Shortened form of "he is" or "he has." **he's** (hēz) *contraction.*

high Tall. The *high* brick building is the library. **high** (hī) *adjective.*

at; āpe, fär, câre; end; mē, it, īce; pîerce; hot, ōld: sông, fôrk; oil; out; up; ūse; rüle; pùll; tûrn; chin; sing; shop; thin; **th**is; hw in white; zh in treasure. The symbol ə stands for the unstressed vowel sound in about, taken, pencil, lemon, and circus.

history **1.** A record of important events and their causes. I am a lover of American *history*. **2.** Past events in general. This person has a *history* of good luck. **his•to•ry** *noun, plural* (his′tə rē) **histories**.

hoarse Having a rough or harsh, deep sound. My voice became *hoarse* from screaming during the game. **hoarse** (hôrs) *adjective*.

hobby An interest on which one spends leisure time. My *hobby* is collecting stamps. **hob•by** (hob′ē) *noun, plural* **hobbies**.

hold To keep. Will you *hold* this book for me? **hold** (hōld) *verb*.
—**on hold.** To be put on another telephone line until the person you need to talk to is ready to speak.

holiday A day on which most people do not work. Thanksgiving is a *holiday* for almost everyone. **hol•i•day** (hol′i dā′) *noun, plural* **holidays**.

hollow An empty space. There's a *hollow* in the log where frogs live. *Noun.*
—Not totally solid. *Adjective.* **hol•low** (hol′ō) *noun, plural* **hollows**; *adjective*.

homemade Made at home. I'll bring some *homemade* bread. **home•made** (hōm′mād′) *adjective*.

homestead A farm with its house and other buildings. We bought several animals and brought them back to the *homestead*. **homestead** (hōm′sted′) *noun, plural* **homesteads**.

homework Lessons to be done at home. I need a quiet place to do my *homework*. **home•work** (hōm′wûrk′) *noun*.

honor Outward respect. There was a dinner in *honor* of the retiring teacher. *Noun.*
—To treat with great respect. The United States has a holiday to *honor* Martin Luther King, Jr., on his birthday each year. *Verb.* **hon•or** (on′ər) *noun, plural* **honors**; *verb*.

hospital A place where the sick or injured are given medical care. The *hospital* is painted all white. **hos•pi•tal** (hos′pit′əl) *noun, plural* **hospitals**.

hour A unit of time equal to sixty minutes. Randy walked to school in a little less than an *hour*. **hour** (our) *noun, plural* **hours**.

however In whatever way. You can pay for the book *however* you like. *Adverb.*
—In spite of that; yet. He had a bad ankle; *however*, he continued to walk. *Conjunction.* **how•ev•er** (hou ev′ər)

how's Shortened form of "how is." *How's* your new car working out? **how's** (houz) *contraction*.

human A person. *Noun.*
—Of humans. *Adjective.* **hu•man** (hū′mən) *noun, plural* **humans**; *adjective*.

humidity Water vapor in the air; dampness. The high *humidity* that day made us feel warm and uncomfortable. **hu•mid•i•ty** (hū mid′i tē) *noun*.

humor The funny part of something. The *humor* in his finding was pleasant. *Noun.*
— To go along with. We'll have to *humor* him, or he'll leave. *Verb.* **hu•mor** (hū′mər) *noun, plural* **humors**; *verb*.

hung Past tense and past participle of **hang**. Held on to something. We *hung* onto the railing. **hung** (hung) *verb*.

I'd Shortened form of "I would"; "I had." **I'd** (īd) *contraction*.

idea A thing that exists in the mind. I have a good *idea*. **i•de•a** (ī dē′ə) *noun, plural* **ideas.**

I'll Shortened form of "I will"; "I shall." *I'll* be happy to walk with you. **I'll** (īl) *contraction*.

I'm Shortened form of "I am." **I'm** (īm) *contraction*.

important Having great value or meaning. This is an *important* meeting. **im•por•tant** (im pôr′tənt) *adjective*.

insert Something which is inserted. The catalog *insert* said there was a sale. *Noun.*
—To put something into something else.

Please *insert* the letter into the mail slot. *Verb.* **in•sert** (in sûrt′ *for verb*; in′sûrt′ *for noun*) *noun, plural* **inserts;** *verb.*

inside The part or area within. The *inside* of the cave was dark and wet. *Noun.*
—To or on the inner side. I am going *inside* because of the rain. *Adverb.*
—In, into, or on the inner side of. I looked *inside* the closet for my coat. *Preposition.* **in•side** (in sīd′, in′sīd′ or in′sīd′) *noun, plural* **insides;** *adverb; preposition.*

instead In place of. Michelle was going to go, but Jeff went *instead.* **in•stead** (in sted′) *adverb.*

iron **1.** A metal used in making building materials, tools, and machinery. *Iron* is used to make steel. **2.** An electrical hand tool used for pressing or smoothing cloth. The *iron* is hot so don't touch it. *Noun.*
—To smooth with an iron. I *iron* my clothes every day. *Verb.* **i•ron** (ī′ ərn) *noun, plural* **irons.**

it'll Shortened form of "it shall"; "it will." **it•'ll** (it′əl) *contraction.*

it's **1.** Shortened form of "it is." **2.** Shortened form of "it has." **it's** (its) *contraction.*

January The first month of the year. **Jan•u•ary** (jan′ū er′ē) *noun.*

jealous **1.** Fearful that a person one loves may love someone else. I'm not *jealous* of my older sister loving my younger sister. **2.** Wanting what someone else has. I am *jealous* because Terrance got a new guitar. **jeal•ous** (jel′əs) *adjective.*

joint A place where two bones come together. The elbow is a *joint* in the arm. *Noun.*
—Belonging to two or more persons. They have a *joint* savings account. *Adjective.* **joint** (joint) *noun, plural* **joints;** *adjective.*

joy Happiness. Our lives are filled with *joy.* **joy** (joi) *noun.*

July The seventh month of the year. **Ju•ly** (jù lī′) *noun.*

June The sixth month of the year. **June** (jün) *noun.*

jungle Land with very thick plant growth. The *jungle* was hot and steamy. **jun•gle** (jung′gəl) *noun, plural* **jungles.**

justice Fair or right treatment or action. The lawyer demanded *justice* for his innocent client. **jus•tice** (jus′tis) *noun.*

kitchen A room or area where food is cooked or prepared. Our father never permits us in the *kitchen* when he is cooking. **kitch•en** (kich′ən) *noun.*

knee The part of a leg that bends. David hurt his *knee* in the race. **knee** (nē) *noun, plural* **knees.**

knife A cutting instrument made of a thin, flat metal blade attached to a handle. That *knife* is good for slicing bread. **knife** (nīf) *noun, plural* **knives.**

knight A soldier in the Middle Ages. The King's *knight* protected him at all times. **knight** (nīt) *noun, plural* **knights.**

knight

knob **1.** A rounded lump. The *knob* is at the top end of the cane. **2.** A handle on a door or drawer. *Noun.* **knob** (nob) *noun, plural* **knobs.**

knowledge Understanding that is gained through experience or study. I have no *knowledge* of the Dutch language. **knowl•edge** (nol′ij) *noun.*

at; āpe, fär, câre; end; mē, it, īce; pîerce; hot, ōld; sông, fôrk; oil; out; up; ūse; rüle; pùll; tûrn; chin; sing; shop; thin; <u>th</u>is; hw in white; zh in treasure. The symbol ə stands for the unstressed vowel sound in about, taken, pencil, lemon, and circus.

Spelling Dictionary

knuckle A joint of a finger. To throw a slide ball, he bends a *knuckle* into the ball. **knuc•kle** (nuk'əl) *noun, plural* **knuckles**.

label **1.** A slip of paper or cloth that is attached to something to show what the item is made of. The *label* on the container fell off. **2.** A word used to describe persons or things. Don't try to put a *label* on her work. *Noun.*
—To mark with a label as, using a word or short phrase. His teachers *label* him as a hard worker. *Verb.* **la•bel** (lā'bəl) *noun, plural* **labels;** *verb* **labeled, labeling**.

Labor Day The first Monday in September; a legal holiday in the United States in honor of working people. **La•bor Day** (lā'bor dā) *noun.*

laid Past tense and past participle of **lay**. Put down. I *laid* the cloth over the table. **laid** (lād) *verb.*

laugh A show of happy feeling by smiling and making sounds. I heard a big *laugh* come from the room. *Noun.*
—**1.** To give a laugh. I can *laugh* really loud at times. **2.** To make fun. They shouldn't *laugh* at my plans for making money. *Verb.* **laugh** (laf) *noun, plural* **laughs;** *verb.*

law A rule made by a group of people for everyone who belongs to the group. The new *law* could save many lives. **law** (lô) *noun, plural* **laws**.

lazy **1.** Unwilling to work. My brother is big and *lazy*. **2.** Slow-moving. We took a boat ride down a *lazy* river. **la•zy** (lā'zē) *adjective* **lazier; laziest** *adjective.*

lead¹ The first position. With two minutes left, Pittsburgh took the *lead. Noun.*
—**1.** To guide, often by going first. I will *lead* the children through the woods. **2.** To live. He must *lead* a happy life. *Verb.* **lead** (lēd) *noun, plural* **leads;** *verb* **led**.

lead² A soft, heavy metal used in making pipes. *Lead* is used to make bullets. **lead** (led) *noun, plural* **lead**.

leaf **1.** One of the flat, green parts growing from a stem of a plant. Some leaves are made up of smaller parts called leaflets. **2.** A sheet of paper. The student tore a *leaf* out of the notebook. *Noun.*
—**1.** To grow leaves. Many trees *leaf* in the spring. **2.** To turn pages and glance at them quickly. I *leafed* through a magazine while waiting in the dentist's office. *Verb.* **leaf** (lēf) *noun, plural* **leaves;** *verb,* **leafed, leafing**.

lean¹ To bend from an upright position. I can *lean* on this crutch. **lean** (lēn) *verb.*

lean² Having little or no fat. My father is tall and *lean. Adjective.* **lean** (lēn) *adjective.*

leave **1.** To go away from. I must *leave* the dance at nine o'clock. **2.** To let someone or something stay behind. You can *leave* your bicycle at my house. *Verb.* **leave** (lēv) *verb* **left; leaving**.

lemon **1.** A small, yellow, egg-shaped fruit with a juicy center. The *lemon* fell from the tree. **2.** A bright yellow color. My new dress color is *lemon.* **lem•on** (lem'ən) *noun, plural* **lemons**.

-less Without. *Useless* means without use or no good. **-less** (ləs) *adjective suffix.*

lesson **1.** Something taught or learned in school. Today Mrs. Clarke began the fifth spelling *lesson.* **2.** Something learned from a story or experience. I had a *lesson* I'll never forget. **les•son** (les'ən) *noun, plural* **lessons**.

let's Shortened form of "let us." *Let's* go to the movies. **let's** (lets) *contraction.*

lettuce A plant with large green or reddish leaves. We need more *lettuce* to make the Caesar salad. **let•tuce** (let'is) *noun, plural* **lettuces**.

level A carpenter's tool that shows whether a surface is even. *Noun.*
—To make flat or even. Please *level* the shelf so it can hold the books. *Verb.*
—Flat and even. We looked for a *level* place in which to build. *Adjective.* **lev•el** (lev'əl) *noun; verb* **leveling, leveled;** *adjective.*

liberty The ability to act, speak or think the way one pleases. I do not have the *liberty* to leave work whenever I want to. **lib•er•ty** (lib′ər tē) *noun, plural* **liberties**.

lie[1] **1.** To be in, go into, or stay in a flat position. I will *lie* down after dinner. **2.** To spread out and cover something. The snow may *lie* in the fields for weeks. **lie** (lī) *verb,* **lay; lain; lying**.

lie[2] To tell something untrue. **lie** (lī) *verb,* **lied, lying, lie;** *noun* **li•ar**.

lift To position in a higher place. Can he *lift* such a heavy weight? **lift** (lift) *verb*.

limb **1.** A leg, arm, or wing. The bird had a broken *limb*. **2.** A branch of a tree. The big *limb* broke and it fell to the grass. **limb** (lim) *noun, plural* **limbs**.

limber Bending or moving easily; loose jointed and flexible. The *limber* running back squeezed past the defenders and over the goal line. **lim•ber** (lim′bər) *adjective*.

lion A large, meat-eating wildcat of Africa and Asia. **li•on** (lī′ən) *noun, plural* **lions**.

listen To pay attention in order to hear. **lis•ten** (lis′ən) *verb*.

loose **1.** Not fastened. My shoe lace was *loose*. **2.** Free. The canary was *loose* in the house. **loose** (lüs) *adjective* **looser; loosest**.

love A strong feeling of liking and caring. Give my *love* to Grandpa. *Noun.* —**1.** To show strong feeling for. I *love* my mother. **2.** To like something very much. I *love* to play in the snow. *Verb.* **love** (luv) *noun; verb,* **loved, loving**.

loyal Faithful to a person, cause, or ideal. Washington's soldiers were *loyal* to him. **loy•al** (loi′əl) *adjective*.

lumber[1] Logs that have been sawed into boards. The *lumber* we had outside had snow on it. **lum•ber** (lum′bər) *noun*.

lumber[2] To move heavily. The bear will *lumber* through the forest.

lumber

lum•ber (lum′bər) *verb*.

lunar Of or having to do with the moon. The *lunar* satellite collected information while orbiting the moon. **lu•nar** (lü′nər) *adjective*.

lunch A light meal eaten in the middle of the day. I had a turkey sandwich for *lunch*. **lunch** (lunch) *noun, plural* **lunches**.

-ly A suffix that means in a certain way. **-ly** (lē) *adverb suffix*.

lying[1] Present participle of **lie; lay; lain**. Stretching out. He was *lying* in a comfortable position. **ly•ing** (lī′ing) *verb*.

lying[2] Present participle of **lie; lied**. Telling something that is not true. He was *lying* when he told you that. **ly•ing** (lī′ing) *verb*.

mad Very angry. I was *mad* when I found that my new bicycle was scratched. **mad** (mad) *adjective* **madder; maddest;** *adverb* **madly**.

major **1.** Bigger or more important. Rain was the *major* reason why our game was cancelled. **2.** In music, referring to the presence of whole steps, or major intervals as opposed to half steps, or minor intervals. The song is played with *major* chords. **ma•jor** (mā′jər) *adjective*.

manufacture To make or process something, especially in quantity and with the use of machinery. That company's main purpose is to *manufacture* bicycles. **man•u•fac•ture** (man′yə fak′chər) *verb* **manufacturing, manufactured**.

marble **1.** A hard rock formed from limestone. The counter is made of expensive *marble*. **2.** A small ball made of glass. I lost my *marble* down the crack. **mar•ble** (mär′bəl) *noun, plural,* **marbles**.

at; āpe, fär, câre; end; mē, it, īce; pîerce; hot, ōld: sông, fôrk; oil; out; up; ūse; rüle; pull; tûrn; chin; sing; shop; thin; <u>th</u>is; hw in white; zh in treasure. The symbol ə stands for the unstressed vowel sound in about, taken, pencil, lemon, and circus.

Spelling Dictionary

March The third month of the year. **March** (märch) *noun.*

marshal **1.** An officer of a federal court with the duties of a sheriff. The *marshal* escorted the defendant into the courtroom. **2.** A person who arranges certain ceremonies. She was chosen to be *marshal* of this year's Thanksgiving Day parade. **mar•shal** (mär′shəl) *noun, plural* **marshals.**

Martin Luther King Day Holiday honoring Martin Luther King, Jr.'s, birthday on the third Monday in January. *Noun.* **Mar•tin Lu•ther King Day** (mär′tin lü′thər king dā) *noun.*

match **1.** Two persons or things that are alike or equal. **2.** A contest. We watched a boxing *match.* **3.** A small, thin strip of wood or cardboard tipped with a mixture that lights when scratched. The wind blew out the *match* and the fire went out. **match** (mach) *noun, plural* **matches.**

material What something is made of or used for. My winter coat is made of heavy *material.* **ma•te•ri•al** (mə tîr′ē əl) *noun, plural* **materials.**

matter **1.** Anything that takes up space and has weight. The universe is made up of *matter.* **2.** Something that is the subject of interest. The meeting was about a business *matter. Noun.*
—To be important. It does *matter* a great deal to me. *Verb.* **mat•ter** (mat′ər) *noun, plural* **matter;** *verb.*

May The fifth month of the year. **May** (mā) *noun.*

maybe Perhaps; possibly. *Maybe* Pattie will tell us a story. **may•be** (mā′bē) *adverb.*

May Day A day often celebrated in May as a spring festival or, in some countries, as Labor Day. **May Day** (mā dā) *noun.*

mayor The person who is the official head of a city or town government. My city has a new *mayor.* **may•or** (mā′ər) *noun, plural* **mayors.**

meant Past tense and past participle of mean. **1.** Intended or planned. I *meant* to get there on time. **2.** Designed for a special purpose. This part was *meant* for you to play. **meant** (ment) *verb.*

melody A series of musical notes that make up a tune. That song has a pleasing *melody.* **mel•o•dy** (mel′ə dē) *noun, plural* **melodies.**

Memorial Day A legal holiday celebrated in most of the United States on the last Monday in May, to honor those who died for their country. **Me•mo•ri•al Day** (mə môr′ē əl dā) *noun.*

-ment **1.** A suffix that means the act of. *Development* means the act of developing. **2.** A suffix that means the state of. *Contentment* means the state of being content. **ment** (mənt).

mess *A* confused or dirty state or condition. The top of my desk is a *mess. Noun.*
—To cause to be in a confused or untidy state. Please do not *mess* up my hair. *Verb.* **mess** (mes) *noun, plural* **messes;** *verb.*

meter¹ The basic unit of length in the metric system. A *meter* is equal to 39. 37 inches. **me•ter** (mē′tər) *noun, plural* **meters.**

meter² The regular rhythm of a poem or piece of music. Did you notice how the *meter* changed at that point in the symphony? **me•ter** (mē′tər) *noun.*

meter³ A device that measures or records. She checked the water *meter* to see how much water had been used. **me•ter** (mē′tər) *noun, plural* **meters.**

mice Plural form of **mouse.** Small animals with pointed snouts, small ears, and long, thin tails. We don't have any *mice* in our house. *noun, plural* **mice** (mīs).

midnight Twelve o'clock at night; the middle of the night. I go to sleep long before *midnight.* **mid•night** (mid′nīt′) *noun, plural* **midnights.**

migrate To move from one place to another. Many birds *migrate* south in the fall. **mi•grate** (mī′grāt) *verb* **migrating, migrated.**

mild **1.** Gentle. Nothing ever disturbs her *mild* disposition. **2.** Not strong. A *mild* wind blew through the trees. **mild** (mīld) *adjective;* **mild•ly,** *adverb.*

mirror A glass in which you can see yourself. Ricky never looks in the *mirror* when he combs his hair. **mir•ror** (mir′ər) *noun, plural* **mirrors**.

mitten A protective covering for the hand, with one section for the four fingers and one section for the thumb. **mit•ten** (mit′ən) *noun, plural* **mittens**.

mitten

mix To put two or more different things together. We *mixed* flour and water to make paste. *Verb.* —Something that is made by mixing. We bought a pancake *mix* at the store. *Noun.* **mix** (miks) *verb,* **mixed, mixing;** *noun, plural* **mixes**.

model 1. A pattern for work to be done. The *model* we copied from was defective. 2. A small copy of something. I made an airplane *model. Noun.* —1. Worthy of being imitated. I will *model* the proper way of greeting someone. 2. To show by wearing. She will *model* the clothes. *Verb.* **mod•el** (mod′əl) *noun, plural* **models;** *verb* **modeled** *or* **modelled; modeling**.

moist Just a little damp. The ground still feels *moist* after yesterday's rain. **moist** (moist) *adjective.*

moisture Slight wetness; water or other liquid in the air or on a surface. There was *moisture* on the kitchen window. **mois•ture** (mois′chər) *noun.*

Monday The second day of the week. **Mon•day** (mun′dē *or* mun′dā) *noun.*

monkey A mammal with long limbs and a long tail. **mon•key** (mung′kē) *noun, plural* **monkeys.**

monsoon A very strong wind that occurs in the Indian ocean and off Southeast Asia. The *monsoon* wrecked the beach and nearby roads. **mon•soon** (mon sün′) *noun, plural* **monsoons**.

moon 1. A heavenly body that revolves around the earth from west to east once every 29½ days. The *moon* seems to shine because it reflects light from the sun. 2. A satellite of any planet. Mars has two *moons.* **moon** (mün) *noun, plural* **moons**.

moose A large, heavy animal, related to the deer. The adult male has large antlers. **moose** (müs) *noun, plural* **moose**.

Mother's Day The second Sunday of May, when we celebrate our female parents. Did you get Mom a present for *Mother's Day?* **Moth•er's Day** (mu<u>th</u>′ərs dā) *noun.*

motor An engine that makes a machine work. The mechanic worked on our *motor. Noun.* —To travel by automobile. I'd like to *motor* around town. *Verb.* —Run by a motor. I wish I had a *motor* scooter. *Adjective.* **mo•tor** (mōt′ər) *noun, plural* **motors;** *verb; adjective.*

mourn To feel or show sorrow or grief. I *mourned* the death of my pet canary. **mourn** (môrn) *verb.*

mouth The part of the face with lips, tongue, and teeth, where food is taken in. Kelly smelled the food and then put it in her *mouth.* **mouth** (mouth) *noun, plural* **mouths**.

movie A motion picture. The *movie* was two hours long. **mov•ie** (mü′vē) *noun, plural* **movies**.

mustard A yellow powder or sauce used to flavor food. Do you like *mustard* on your hot dog? **mus•tard** (mus′tərd) *noun, plural* **mustards**.

mustn't Shortened form of "must not." You *mustn't* forget to thank people for gifts. **must•n't** (mus′ənt) *contraction.*

at; āpe, fär, câre; end; mē, it, īce; pîerce; hot, ōld; sông, fôrk; oil; out; up; ūse; rüle; pu̇ll; tûrn; chin; sing; shop; thin; <u>th</u>is; hw in white; zh in treasure. The symbol ə stands for the unstressed vowel sound in about, taken, pencil, lemon, and circus.

Spelling Dictionary

nature **1.** The world; all things except those made by human beings. The mountains and woods are parts of *nature*. **2.** The regular ways in which things are or act. It's in the vulture's *nature* to hunt for food. **3.** Sort or kind; variety. I like books of a scientific *nature*. **na•ture** (nā′cher) *noun, plural* **natures**.

near **1.** Close to in comparison. He walked along the *near* side of the street. **2.** Done or missed by only a slight margin. I was in a *near* accident on my bike. *Adjective.* —Just a short distance from in time or space. The ducks are *near* the pond. *Preposition.* **near** (nîr) *adjective; preposition.*

nearby A short distance away. We rushed the man to a *nearby* hospital. *Adjective.* —Not far off. There is a store *nearby*. *Adverb.* **near•by** (nîr bī′, nîr′bī) *adjective; adverb.*

neither Not this one or that one. *Neither* is home today. *Pronoun.* —Not either. *Neither* book told me what I wanted to know. *Adjective.* —Both not; also not. It was *neither* hot nor cold. *Conjunction.* **nei•ther** (nē′thər, nī′thər) *pronoun; adjective; conjunction.*

nervous Unable to relax; tense. Loud noises make me *nervous*. **ner•vous** (nûr′vəs) *adjective.*

-ness Suffix that means the state or quality of being. *Happiness* is the state of being happy.

newspaper A publication printed daily or weekly and containing news, articles, stories, and advertisements. I read the *newspaper* every day. **news•pa•per** (nüz′pā′pər *or* nūz′pā′pər) *noun.*

New Year's Day The first day of the year, January 1. **New Year's Day** (nü yirz dā *or* nū yirz dā) *noun.*

noble Impressive or magnificent and/or having high rank or title. Courage and honesty are *noble* qualities. **no•ble** (nō′bəl) *adjective.*

noise Any sound. The roaring *noise* was coming from the cellar. **noise** (noiz) *noun, plural* **noises**.

noisy Loud; making much noise. The children were very *noisy* today in the playground. **nois•y** (noi′zē) *adjective* **noisier; noisiest.**

note **1.** A short letter. I left my mother a *note* to tell her that I'll be late. **2.** Something written down to be remembered. I wrote myself a *note* to get eggs at the store. *Noun.* —To write down as something to be remembered. I will *note* it if he says it. **note** (nōt) *noun, plural* **notes;** *verb* **noted; noting.**

nothing Zero. Ten minus ten leaves *nothing*. *Noun.* —Not anything. *Pronoun.* **noth•ing** (nuth′ing) *noun; pronoun.*

noun A word used as the name of a person, place, thing, or idea. In the sentence, "The car drove," "car" is the noun. **noun** (noun) *noun, plural* **nouns**.

November The eleventh month of the year. **No•vem•ber** (nō vem′bər) *noun.*

number **1.** The total amount of things in a group; how many there are of something. The *number* of children in our family is three. **2.** A symbol or word that tells how many or which one. 2, 5, 77, and 396 are numbers. Their apartment *number* is 2D. *Noun.* **—1.** To find out the number of; count. The police officers *numbered* the crowd at about 1,000. **2.** To give a number or numbers to. The teacher told us to *number* the pages of our book reports before turning them in. *Verb.* **num•ber** (num′bər) *noun, plural* **numbers;** *verb,* **numbered, numbering.**

nurse One trained in caring for the sick. My mother is a registered *nurse*. **nurse** (nûrs) *noun, plural* **nurses**.

nursery A baby's bedroom or a place where young children are taken care of during the day. His parents began decorating the *nursery* for his new brother. **nurs•er•y** (nûr′sə rē) *noun, plural* **nurseries**.

oak A hardwood tree with nuts called acorns. We hung the swing from the *oak* tree. **oak** (ōk) *noun, plural* **oaks**.

oak

observe 1. To see or notice. We went to the zoo to *observe* the animals. 2. To follow, obey, or celebrate. The driver *observed* the speed limit. **ob•serve** (əb zûrv′) *verb,* **observing, observed**.

o'clock A word used with the hour to tell time. Alice wakes up at eight *o'clock* every morning. **o'•clock** (ə klok′) *adverb*.

October The tenth month of the year. **Oc•to•ber** (ok tō′bər) *noun*.

offer 1. To present for acceptance or rejection. Did you *offer* to do the work? 2. To suggest. Can you *offer* a better plan? *Verb*.
—An act of offering. We thank you for your *offer* of help. *Noun*. **of•fer** (ô′fər) *verb; noun, plural* **offers**.

office 1. A room or rooms in which to work. My *office* is full of books and papers. 2. A public job. She has a high *office* in government. **of•fice** (ôf′əs) *noun, plural* **offices**.

oily 1. Greasy. My face gets *oily* after I sweat. 2. Slippery. The wax made the floor *oily*. **oil•y** (oi′lē) *adjective* **oilier; oiliest**.

ointment A soft, oily substance that is put on the skin to heal, protect, or soften it. The doctor put an *ointment* on my sore shoulder. **oint•ment** (oint′mənt) *noun, plural* **ointments**.

open 1. Allowing movement in, out, or through. The bird flew in through the *open* window. 2. Not having its lid, door, or other covering closed. There is an *open* box of tissues on the shelf. *Adjective*.
—1. To make or become open. *Open* the envelope and read the letter. 2. To have an opening. The room *opens* onto a porch. 3. To spread out; unfold. The petals of the flower *opened*. *Verb*.
—Any space that is not closed in. The party was held in the *open*. *Noun*. **o•pen** (ō′pən) *adjective, verb,* **opened, opening;** *noun, plural* **opens**.

-or A suffix that means one who acts. An *actor* is a person who acts.

order 1. An arrangement of things, ideas, or people. She put the words in the right *order*. 2. Tidiness. I'm much happier when my room is in *order*. 3. A command. The captain gave an *order* to the soldiers. *Noun*.
—1. To give a command. Did she *order* you to come immediately? 2. To put in a special arrangement. She *ordered* her blouses by color. *Verb*. **or•der** (ôr′dər) *noun, plural* **orders;** *verb,* **ordered, ordering**.

organ 1. A musical instrument with a keyboard. I can play that song on my electronic *organ*. 2. A body part of a plant or animal that does a specific job. The heart is a very important *organ*. **or•gan** (ôr′gən) *noun, plural* **organs**.

ought To be expected. Frankie *ought* to help Connie with the dishes. **ought** (ôt) *verb*.

outdoors The world outside of a house or building. I love camping in the great *outdoors*! *Noun*.

at; āpe, fär, câre; end; mē, it, īce; pîerce; hot, ōld; sông, fôrk; oil; out; up; ūse; rüle; pùll; tûrn; chin; sing; shop; thin; <u>th</u>is; hw in white; zh in treasure. The symbol ə stands for the unstressed vowel sound in about, taken, pencil, lemon, and circus.

—In the open air. Children like to play *outdoors. Adverb.* **out•doors** (out′dôrz′) *noun; adverb.*

outside The part or area that is not within. The *outside* of the house needs painting. *Noun.*
—Of or being in the outer part. Put the plant on the *outside* ledge of the window. *Adjective.*
—On or to the outside. We played *outside* all day. *Adverb.*
—Beyond. They live just *outside* Dallas. *Preposition.* **out•side** (out′sīd′, out′sīd′, or out′sīd′) *noun, plural* **outsides;** *adjective; adverb; preposition.*

oven An enclosed space for warming, baking, or drying with heat. **ov•en** (uv′ən) *noun, plural* **ovens.**

overcome To get the better of, to conquer. The runner had to *overcome* his fatigue to win the race. **o•ver•come** (ō′vər kum′).

overlook **1.** To fail to see. Don't *overlook* the article I told you about. **2.** To give a view from a high place. The houses *overlook* the bay. **o•ver•look** (ō′vər lůk′) *verb.*

owl A night bird with a large head, bright eyes, and a hooked beak. **owl** (oul) *noun, plural* **owls.**

owner The one to whom something belongs. Larry is the *owner* of the winning horse. **own•er** (ō′nər) *noun, plural* **owners.**

pack **1.** A bundle tied up for carrying. I put the books in a *pack.* **2.** A group of related people or animals. The deer were attacked by a *pack* of wolves. *Noun.*
—**1.** To put together in a box, suitcase, or trunk. I will *pack* my clothes up and leave soon. **2.** To crowd together. Too many people tried to *pack* into the one small room. *Verb.* **pack** (pak) *noun, plural* **packs;** *verb.*

package **1.** A group of things that are wrapped. **2.** A box or case in which things

are wrapped. *Noun.*
—To put in a package. *Package* the food in these containers. *Verb.* **pack•age** (pak′ij) *noun, plural* **packages;** *verb.* **packaged, packaging.**

pail A container with a handle for holding liquids. The *pail* tilted and all the water spilled out. **pail** (pāl) *noun, plural* **pails.** ▲ Another word that sounds like this is **pale.**

pale **1.** Having a very light skin color. She looked *pale* after her long illness. **2.** Without much color. I would rather have *pale* walls than bright colors. *Adjective.*
—To turn pale. Their faces *paled* when they saw the scary picture. *Verb.* **pale** (pāl) *verb; adjective;* **paled; paling.**

parade A march or procession in honor of a person or event. Did you march in the Memorial Day *parade?* **pa•rade** (pə rād′) *noun, plural* **parades.**

parent **1.** A father or mother. The *parent* of the child is in the office. **2.** Any animal or plant that produces another. The *parent* of this puppy is a poodle. **par•ent** (pâr′ənt) *noun, plural,* **parents.**

pass **1.** To go or move by or beyond. We enjoy watching the cars *pass* our house.
2. To hand or throw something to another. *Pass* the ball to Ruth. **pass** (pas) *verb.*

past **1.** Time gone by. History is a study of the *past.* **2.** The verb form that shows a happening in the past.
—Gone by. In *past* years, we traveled a lot. *Adjective.*
—Beyond in time or space. Mrs. Fink is *past* seventy. *Preposition.* **past** (past) *noun, plural* **pasts;** *adjective; preposition.*

pasture **1.** A grassy field used for animals to graze. The shepherd is watching his *pasture.* **2.** Grass and other growing plants for animals to feed on. *Noun.*
—To put animals in a field to feed. *Verb.* **pas•ture** (pas′chər) *noun, plural* **pastures;** *verb* **pastured; pasturing.**

patch **1.** A piece of material used to mend a hole or tear. I put a yellow *patch* on my jeans. **2.** A covering worn over an injured eye. The captain wore a *patch* over his eye. **3.** A small piece of ground. There was a grassy *patch* left in the barren field. *Noun.* —**1.** To mend with a patch. I will *patch* the hole in my jeans. **2.** To piece together. I'll try to *patch* the broken lamp. *Verb.* **patch** (pach) *noun, plural* **patches;** *verb.*

path **1.** A trail for walking. We followed the *path* to the big house. **2.** The line along which something moves. The sun has a regular *path* through the sky. **path** (path) *noun, plural* **paths**.

peace **1.** Freedom from war. The nation is looking for *peace*. **2.** Freedom from worry or disagreement. I'm at *peace* with the world. **peace** (pēs) *noun*. ▲ Another word that sounds like this is **piece**.

peach A round, sweet fruit with fuzzy skin. **peach** (pēch) *noun, plural,* **peaches**.

pear A fruit that is round at the bottom and smaller at the stem. Please wash the *pear* if you take it straight from the tree. *Noun.* **pear** (pâr) *noun, plural* **pears**. ▲ Other words that sound like this are **pair** and **pare**.

peasant A person who works on a farm or owns a small farm. *Noun.* **peas•ant** (pez′ənt) *noun, plural* **peasants**.

peg A piece of wood, metal, or other material that can be fitted or driven into a surface. My coat is hanging on that *peg*. **peg** (peg) *noun, plural* **pegs**.

penny **1.** 1/100 of a dollar. *A penny* will not buy much nowadays. **pen•ny** (pen′ē) *noun, plural* **pennies**.

perfect To make flawless; complete. I will *perfect* this project by Friday. *Verb.* —**1.** Without fault; excellent. I have the *perfect* solution! **2.** Not missing anything; complete. The launch was a *perfect* success. *Adjective.* **per•fect** (pər fekt′ *for verb;* pûr′fikt *for adjective*) *verb, adjective.*

period **1.** A punctuation mark (.) that shows the end of a declarative sentence or of an abbreviation. Always end your sentences with a *period*. **2.** A length of time. For a brief *period* they were silent. **per•i•od** (pîr′ē əd) *noun, plural* **periods**.

person A human being. I can't imagine a nicer *person*. **per•son** (pûr′sən) *noun, plural* **persons**.

phone A telephone. The *phone* was ringing all day. *Noun.* —To call by telephone. I will *phone* your parents for you. *Verb.* **phone** (fōn) *noun, plural* **phones;** *verb* **phoned, phoning**.

phone

photograph A picture made by means of a camera. The *photograph* was old and yellowish. *Noun.* —To make a picture with a camera. I can *photograph* you myself for free! *Verb.* **pho•to•graph** (fō′tə graf′) *noun, plural* **photographs;** *verb* **photographed, photographing**.

phrase **1.** A group of words that expresses a thought but does not contain both a subject and a predicate. "Around the block" is an incomplete sentence or a *phrase*. **2.** A short expression. The marchers shouted the *phrase,* "Lower Taxes!" *Noun.* —To put carefully into words. How should we *phrase* our agreement in the contract? **phrase** (frāz) *noun, plural* **phrases,** *verb* **phrasing, phrased.**

picture **1.** An image produced by painting, drawing, or photography. Can I take your *picture*? **2.** A description in words. She

at; āpe, fär, câre; end; mē, it, īce; pîerce; hot, ōld: sông, fôrk; oil; out; up; ūse; rūle; pùll; tûrn; chin; sing; shop; thin; <u>th</u>is; hw in white; zh in treasure. The symbol ə stands for the unstressed vowel sound in about, taken, pencil, lemon, and circus.

described a good *picture* of the scene. *Noun.* To imagine. *Picture* me on the beach. *Verb.* **pic•ture** (pik′chər) *noun, plural* **pictures;** *verb,* **pictured; picturing.**

pile Many things stacked up. The *pile* was about to topple over. *Noun.*
—To place in a stack. Please *pile* the hay neatly in the corner. *Verb.* **pile** (pīl) *noun, plural* **piles;** *verb,* **piled, piling.**

pilgrim A person who travels to a sacred place for a religious reason. The Muslim *pilgrim* boarded a plane for Mecca. **pil•grim** (pil′grəm) *noun, plural* **pilgrims.**

pillow A bag filled with feathers or sponge rubber used to support a sleeping person's head. I have a big, fluffy *pillow.* **pil•low** (pil′ō) *noun, plural* **pillows.**

pine A cone-bearing evergreen tree. The woodsman planted a *pine* tree. *Noun.*
—To grow weak from sadness or longing. He will *pine* away if he doesn't see her again. *Verb.* **pine** (pīn) *noun, plural* **pines;** *verb.*

pine cone The cone produced by an evergreen tree. I found a *pine cone* that was about ten inches long. **pine cone** (pīn kōn) *noun, plural* **pine cones.**

pitch To throw or toss. *Pitch* the ball to the batter. *Verb.*
—A throw of the ball. The batter missed the first *pitch. Noun.* **pitch** (pich) *verb* **pitched, pitching;** *noun, plural* **pitches.**

pitcher **1.** A container used to hold and pour liquids. The *pitcher* of milk fell to the floor. **2.** A baseball player who throws the ball to the batter. The *pitcher* struck out three batters in a row! **pitch•er** (pich′ər) *noun, plural* **pitchers.**

plain A large area of flat or rolling country with few or no trees. We could see for miles across the *plain. Noun.*
—**1.** Without decoration. She is wearing a *plain* white blouse. **2.** Straight forward, direct. I will tell you the *plain* truth. *Adjective.* **plain** (plān) *noun, plural* **plains;** *adjective.*

plane **1.** An airplane. The *plane* took off from the runway. **2.** A flat surface. This highway has a *plane* surface. *Noun.*

—To make even or smooth. He will use a tool to *plane* the wood. *Verb.* **plane** (plān) *noun, plural* **planes;** *verb* **planed, planing.**

plank A flat, wide, long piece of wood. He put the *plank* across the two stepladders. **plank** (plangk) *noun, plural* **planks.**

plastic Any of a large group of materials that can be formed into objects such as bottles and containers. The bottle is made of *plastic. Noun.*
—**1.** Easily molded. Wax is a *plastic* material when it is heated. *Adjective.* **plas•tic** (plas′tik) *noun, plural* **plastics;** *adjective.*

plateau An area of flat land that is raised above the surrounding country. From that *plateau* we could see the entire valley. **pla•teau** (pla tō′) *noun, plural* **plateaus.**

playground A piece of land set aside for play. The school *playground* is small. **play•ground** (plā′ground′) *noun, plural* **playgrounds.**

pleasant Easy to get along with. She is a very *pleasant* person. **pleas•ant** (plez′ənt) *adjective.*

pocket An enclosed space with one opening, used for storage. I put the money in my *pocket. Noun.*
—To put into a pocket. She *pocketed* the change. *Verb.*
—Small enough to be carried in a pocket. He used his *pocket* calculator to solve the problem. *Adjective.* **pock•et** (pok′it) *noun, plural* **pockets;** *verb; adjective.*

point **1.** The sharp end of something. I broke the *point* of my pencil. **2.** The main idea. The *point* of the story is that many people are brave. *Noun.*
—**1.** To use one's finger to show where someone or something is. Please *point* to the judge's house. **2.** To turn something in a certain direction. Don't *point* the camera at me. *Verb.* **point** (point) *noun, plural* **points;** *verb* **pointed, pointing.**

pointed Having a point. The *pointed* pencil was sharp. **point•ed** (point′əd) *adjective.*

police The department of government that helps keep law and order. The *police*

guarded the party for us. *Noun.*
—**1.** To keep order in. Guards *policed* the streets. *Verb.* **po•lice** (pə lēs′) *noun; verb* **policed; policing**.

pollute To make dirty or impure. Some of the chemicals we use everyday *pollute* the air. **pol•lute** (pə lüt′) *verb* **polluting, polluted**.

possible Able to exist, happen, or be done. It is *possible* to finish the painting by tomorrow. **pos•si•ble** (pos′ə bəl) *adjective.*

post¹ **1.** A wooden or metal support for a fence. The *post* was torn from the ground by accident. **2.** Any wooden or metal support. The fence *post* was replaced the other day. *Noun.*
—To name to a job or station. We must *post* a guard tonight. *Verb.* **post** (pōst) *noun, plural* **posts;** *verb.*

post² To send by mail. Will you *post* this letter for me? **post** (pōst) *verb.*

pound A unit or weight that equals sixteen ounces (453 grams). I brought a *pound* of cheese. *Noun.*
—To strike in a hard and repeated manner. The carpenter will *pound* the nail with the hammer. *Verb.* **pound** (pound) *noun, plural* **pounds** or **pound;** *verb.*

powder Small bits of a dry material. There was some *powder* left in the cannon. *Noun.*
—To sprinkle with or apply powder. She always *powders* her face. *Verb.* **pow•der** (pou′dər) *noun, plural* **powders;** *verb.*

practice **1.** Something done regularly. It was her *practice* to get up early. **2.** The act of doing something in order to get better. Did you go to football *practice*? *Noun.*
—To do over and over again to improve. She will *practice* at the piano every day. *Verb.* **prac•tice** (prak′tis) *noun, plural* **practices;** *verb* **practiced; practicing**.

preservative A substance that keeps something from spoiling. The manufacturer used a *preservative* to keep the food from spoiling. **pre•ser•va•tive** (pri zûr′və tiv) *noun, plural* **preservatives**.

Presidents' Day A day in February set aside for honoring Abraham Lincoln and George Washington. **Pres•i•dents' Day** (prez′i dənts dā) *noun.*

press **1.** Newspapers, magazines, and the people who write them. The president's speech was described in the *press*. **2.** A printing machine. The *press* broke down. *Noun.*
—**1.** To push. Please do not *press* him any further. **2.** To flatten. I *press* my clothes with an iron. *Verb.* **press** (pres) *noun, plural* **presses;** *verb.*

problem **1.** A question to be thought about and answered. Mark studied the math *problem*. **2.** A troubling condition or fact. The *problem* with this bicycle is a flat tire. **prob•lem** (prob′ləm) *noun, plural* **problems**.

public The people in general. The *public* has the right to know the truth. *Noun.*
—**1.** Of the people. The *public* opinion was that he was innocent. **2.** For everyone. This is a *public* park. *Adjective.* **pub•lic** (pub′lik) *noun; adjective.*

puddle A small pool, usually of dirty water. I sloshed through the *puddle*. *Noun.*
—To form small pools of water. The rain will *puddle* in the corner if we don't patch up the roof. *Verb.* **pud•dle** (pud′əl) *noun, plural* **puddles;** *verb* **puddled, puddling**.

pulley A wheel with a groove around the outside to hold a rope, used to move or lift objects. There is a *pulley* at each end of the clothesline. **pul•ley** (pu̇l′ē) *noun, plural* **pulleys**.

pumpkin A large, round, orange fruit that grows on a vine. Can you carve a face on the *pumpkin* for us? **pump•kin** (pump′kin) *noun, plural* **pumpkins**.

pumpkin

at; āpe, fär, câre; end; mē, it, īce; pîerce; hot, ōld; sông, fôrk; oil; out; up; ūse; rüle; pu̇ll; tûrn; chin; sing; shop; thin; this; hw in white; zh in treasure. The symbol ə stands for the unstressed vowel sound in about, taken, pencil, lemon, and circus.

Spelling Dictionary (side tab)

punch¹ A beverage often made by combining several liquids. We made a big bowl of *punch* for the party. **punch** (punch) *noun*.

punch² To hit with the fist. That man can *punch* harder than you. **punch** (punch) *verb*.

pupil¹ A student. The teacher looked down and smiled at her *pupil*. **pu•pil** (pū′pəl) *noun*.

pupil² A round opening in the eye. The sunlight makes the *pupils* of my eyes smaller. **pu•pil** (pū′pəl) *noun, plural* **pupils**.

puppy A young dog. My dog is just a *puppy*. **pup•py** (pup′ē) *noun, plural* **puppies**.

pure **1**. Not mixed with anything. There was *pure* water in the pitcher **2**. Nothing but. It was *pure* luck. **pure** (pyùr) *adjective*.

purple A dark color made by mixing red and blue. Sharon's favorite color is *purple*. *Noun*.
—Having the dark color made by mixing red and blue. Those shiny *purple* plums look delicious! *Adjective*. **pur•ple** (pûr′pəl) *noun, plural* **purples**; *adjective*.

purple

purpose The reason for doing something. What *purpose* did you have in telling us that story? **pur•pose** (pûr′pəs) *noun, plural* **purposes**.

push To press against something with force. Be careful, or you will *push* her down the stairs. **push** (pùsh) *verb*.

quantity A number or amount. The recipe calls for a small *quantity* of milk. **quan•ti•ty** (kwon′ti tē) *noun, plural* **quantities**.

queen **1**. A female ruler. The *queen* visited the village today. **2**. The wife of a king. The king married my aunt, making her a *queen*. **queen** (kwēn) *noun, plural* **queens**.

question **1**. Something asked in order to find an answer. The *question* was too easy to get wrong. **2**. A matter to be talked over. Let's discuss the *question* of safety in the home. *Noun*.
—To ask in order to find an answer. The lawyer will *question* the defendant. *Verb*. **ques•tion** (kwes′chən) *noun, plural* **questions**; *verb*.

quick Done or happening in a short time; fast. She moved at a *quick* pace. **quick** (kwik) *adjective*.

quickly Fast. She moved *quickly*. **quick•ly** (kwik′lē) *adverb*.

quiet A state of no noise. The church was full of *quiet*. *Noun*.
—To make quiet. We'll try to *quiet* the children. *Verb*.
—Making little or no noise. The *quiet* mouse ran across the floor. *Adjective*. **qui•et** (kwī′ ət) *noun; verb; adjective*.

quilt A bed cover made of two layers of fabric filled with padding. My grandmother made me a *quilt* for my bed. *Noun*.
—To sew materials together to make a quilt or something like a quilt. My cousin likes to *quilt* for a hobby. *Verb*. **quilt** (kwilt) *noun, plural* **quilts**; *verb*.

quit **1**. To stop. I wish you would *quit* ringing the bell. **2**. To leave; to give up. He was very far behind the leader of the race but he still didn't *quit*. **quit** (kwit) *verb* **quit** or **quitted**.

quite Very much or completely. The sign made it *quite* clear what road we should take. **quite** (kwīt) *adverb*.

quiz A short or informal test. The *quiz* was very easy if you studied. **quiz** (kwiz) *noun, plural* **quizzes**.

quotient A number obtained by dividing one number into another. 49 divided by 7 yields a *quotient* of 7. **quo•tient** (kwō′shənt) *noun, plural* **quotients**.

race A contest to see who or what is the fastest. There were thousands of people running in the *race*. *Noun.*
—To be in or a part of a contest of speed. I'll *race* you to the house. *Verb.* **race** (rās) *noun, plural* **races;** *verb* **raced, racing.**

rail A bar of wood or metal used as a guard. The porch *rail* is broken. **rail** (rāl) *noun, plural* **rails.**

railroad A road of steel rails providing a track for trains. The *railroad* was under repair so we took the car. **rail•road** (rāl′rōd′) *noun, plural* **railroads.**

ranch A large farm with grazing land for raising horses, sheep, or cattle. My uncle owns a *ranch* in Texas. **ranch** (ranch) *noun, plural* **ranches.**

rather **1.** In preference; more willingly. I would *rather* go to the movies. **2.** More than a little. The tutor is *rather* late for our session. **rath•er** (rath′ər) *adverb.*

re- **1.** A prefix that means again. *Review* means to view again. **2.** A prefix that means back. *Replace* means to put back. (ri or rē)

reach **1.** The act of reaching. **2.** The distance one is able to reach. The can was out of *reach*. *Noun.*
—To stretch out. I can *reach* out and grab another. *Verb.* **reach** (rēch) *noun, plural* **reaches;** *verb.*

ready **1.** Prepared for use or action. Your order is *ready*. **2.** Willing. Are you *ready* to help? *Adjective.* **read•y** (red′ē) *adjective* **readier; readiest.**

rear[1] **1.** The back part. Move to the *rear* of the bus. **2.** The part of a military force that is farthest from the enemy. The troops in the *rear* were the last to fight. **rear** (rîr) *noun, plural* **rears.**

rear[2] **1.** To bring up; to raise. How many children did he *rear*? **2.** To rise up on the hind legs. When the gun goes off the horse will *rear*. **rear** (rîr) *verb.*

reason **1.** A cause or motive. Do you have a good *reason* for leaving? **2.** The ability to think clearly and logically. After he calmed down, he was willing to listen to *reason*. *Noun.*
—To try to persuade or influence someone. His mother tried to *reason* with him. *Verb.* **rea•son** (rē′zən) *noun, plural* **reasons;** *verb.*

recess Time during which work stops. The students had a *recess* between classes. *Noun.* To take a short break. The students took a *recess* in the yard. *Verb.* **re•cess** (rē′ses′, ri ses′) *noun, plural* **recesses;** *verb.*

repair **1.** The act of repairing. The car needed a *repair*. **2.** Condition after something has been repaired. The road is now in good *repair*. *Noun.*
—**1.** To put in good condition. Can you *repair* my radio? **2.** To make up for an injury or damage. How can we *repair* the harm done? *Verb.* **re•pair** (ri pâr′) *noun, plural* **repairs;** *verb.*

reply To answer in words or writing. I will *reply*, but first you must give me a chance to speak. **re•ply** (ri plī′) *verb.*

report **1.** A statement written or spoken about something. The *report* was typed and handed in to the professor. **2.** An official record. The court made a *report* of the hearings. *Noun.*
—**1.** To give a description. I will *report* it to you later. **2.** To present oneself. I must *report* for work. *Verb.* **re•port** (ri pôrt′) *noun, plural* **reports;** *verb.*

rescue The act of saving from danger. The *rescue* was simply amazing. *Noun.*
—To save or free from danger of some kind. Can you *rescue* my cat from the tree? *Verb.* **res•cue** (res′kū) *noun, plural* **rescue;** *verb* **rescued, rescuing.**

research A careful study or investigation in order to obtain facts. I did *research* at the library for my report. *Noun.*

at; āpe, fär, câre; end; mē, it, ice; pîerce; hot, ōld; sîng, fôrk; oil; out; up; ūse; rüle; pull; tûrn; chin; sing; shop; thin; this; hw in white; zh in treasure. The symbol ə stands for the unstressed vowel sound in about, taken, pencil, lemon, and circus.

—To make a careful study or investigation to obtain facts. Will you *research* this subject for me? *Verb.* **re•search** (ri sûrch′ *or* rē′sûrch′) *noun, plural* **researches;** *verb,* **researching, researched**.

rest **1.** Sleep. I must get some *rest* for tomorrow. **2.** A break or pause. I need a *rest* before continuing to type. **3.** What is left. You can have the *rest. Noun.*
—**1.** To lie down. My mom will *rest* before we go. **2.** To stop work or activity. Please *rest* awhile before going on. *Verb.* **rest** (rest) *noun, plural* **rests;** *verb.*

ribbon **1.** A strip of cloth used to decorate. She wore a yellow *ribbon* in her hair. **2.** An inked strip of cloth used in a typewriter or printer. I need to replace the *ribbon* in the printer. **rib•bon** (rib′ən) *noun, plural* **ribbons**.

ribbon

rid To do away with. Please get *rid* of the trash before you leave. **rid** (rid) *verb* **rid** *or* **ridded, ridding**.

roar A loud, deep sound or cry. The lion's *roar* was heard throughout the zoo. *Noun.*
—To make a loud, deep sound. Can you hear the lion *roar? Verb.* **roar** (rôr) *noun, plural* **roars;** *verb.*

roll **1.** A kind of bread or cake. I had a buttered *roll* with my soup. **2.** Anything rolled up. We need a *roll* of film. *Noun.*
—To move by turning over and over. Please help me *roll* out the carpet. *Verb* **roll** (rōl) *noun, plural* **rolls;** *verb.*

roof **1.** The top covering of a building. The *roof* was covered with snow. **2.** The top part of the mouth. The cotton candy stuck to the *roof* of my mouth. *Noun.*
—To cover with a roof. We will *roof* the

house tomorrow. *Verb.* **roof** (rüf *or* rùf) *noun, plural* **roofs;** *verb,* **roofed, roofing.**

rope A large cord made of smaller cords twisted together and used for tying things. We tied a *rope* around the box. **rope** (rōp) *noun, plural* **ropes.**

rose[1] **1.** A sweet-smelling flower with thorny stems. The *rose* was for her birthday. **2.** A pinkish-red color. **rose** (rōz) *noun, plural* **roses.**

rose[2] Past tense of **rise**; got up. We *rose* early this morning. **rose** (rōz) *verb.*

rough **1.** Not smooth. The seas were growing *rough.* **2.** Not having or showing gentleness. The *rough* game left several players bruised. **rough** (ruf) *adjective.*

royal Of or like a king and queen. The king and queen live in a *royal* palace. **roy•al** (roi′əl) *adjective.*

royalty A royal person or persons. Kings, queens, princes and princesses are *royalty.* **roy•al•ty** (roi′əl tē) *noun, plural* **royalties.**

ruler **1.** One who governs or rules. Queen Elizabeth II is the *ruler* of Great Britain. **2.** A strip of wood, plastic, or metal that is marked off by units of measure. I used my *ruler* to draw a straight line. **rul•er** (rü′lər) *noun, plural* **rulers.**

sack A paper container. We gave Martha a *sack* of old clothes. **sack** (sak) *noun, plural* **sacks.**

sale **1.** The act of selling. There was a garage *sale* yesterday. **2.** A selling of things at reduced prices. The *sale* at Kresslers is only for today. **3.** Money made. Did you make a good *sale* on your old bicycle? **sale** (sāl) *noun, plural* **sales.**

sandwich One or more slices of bread or a roll with a filling. Marian made a cheese *sandwich.* **sand•wich** (sand′wich) *noun, plural* **sandwiches.**

sat Past tense and past participle of **sit**. I *sat* at the table. **sat** (sat) *verb*.

Saturday The seventh day of the week. **Sat•ur•day** (sat′ər dē′ *or* sat′ər dā′) *noun, plural* **Saturdays**.

sauce A liquid topping for food. Dad made a good spaghetti *sauce*. **sauce** (sôs) *noun, plural* **sauces**.

scarce In short supply, difficult to find. Eagles are becoming *scarce* in America. **scarce** (skârs) *adjective*, **scarcer, scarcest**.

scare A feeling of fear. The noise gave me quite a *scare*. *Noun*.
—To make afraid. I *scare* my sister with funny faces. *Verb*. **scare** (skâr) *noun, plural* **scares**; *verb* **scared, scaring**.

scarf A long, wide strip of material worn around the neck or over the shoulders. My scarf keeps my neck warm. **scarf** (skärf) *noun, plural* **scarves** or **scarfs**.

scene **1**. The place in which the action of a story occurs. The *scene* takes place in an old warehouse. **2**. Part of an act in a play. This *scene* is where she tells him the news. **scene** (sēn) *noun, plural* **scenes**.

science **1**. Knowledge in which facts, laws, and causes are arrived at by tests and experiments. I take *science* in school. **2**. Knowledge in a specific field that is an object of study. Some people say that chess is a *science*. **sci•ence** (sī′əns) *noun, plural* **sciences**.

scout **1**. One sent ahead to get information. We needed a *scout* to go ahead. **2**. One sent to search for talent. He is a baseball *scout*. *Noun*.
—To go ahead in search of information. *Scout* ahead and see who's there. *Verb*. **scout** (skout) *noun, plural* **scouts**.

season **1**. One of the four parts of the year; spring, summer, fall, or winter. **2**. Any special part of the year. There is almost no rain during the dry *season* in parts of Africa. **sea•son** (sē′zən) *noun, plural* **seasons**.

secret Something kept from others or shared with only a few. *Noun*.
—Kept from the knowledge of others. They used a *secret* handshake. *Adjective*. **se•cret** (sē′krit) *noun, plural* **secrets**.

seem To appear to be; to look. The carpenters *seem* to know what they are doing. **seem** (sēm) *verb*.

self A person thought of as someone apart from everyone else. I know my own *self*. **self** (self) *noun, plural* **selves**.

September The ninth month of the year. **Sep•tem•ber** (sep tem′bər) *noun*.

sequence The order in which a series of things occur. The *sequence* of the photos shows the tree growing larger year to year. **se•quence** (sē′kwəns) *noun, plural* **sequences**.

serum The thin, clear liquid part of blood, which can be used to prevent diseases. They discovered a *serum* to prevent mumps. **se•rum** (sîr′əm) *noun, plural* **serums**.

session A specific period of time during which people meet to get something done. We attended a *session* of the Supreme Court. **ses•sion** (sesh′ən) *noun, plural* **sessions**.

settle **1**. To make a place home. They will *settle* in the West. **2**. To sink. The sand will *settle* at the bottom of the water. **set•tle** (set′əl) *verb* **settled, settling**.

several More than two but not many. There were *several* people standing outside. **sev•er•al** (sev′rəl, sev′ər əl) *adjective*.

shadow A dark area produced when a person, animal, or thing blocks rays of light. I saw Earth's *shadow* on the moon during the eclipse. **shad•ow** (shad′ō) *noun, plural* **shadows**.

share A part belonging to someone. She saved her *share* of the money. *Noun*.
—**1**. To divide in parts. I will cut my

at; āpe, fär, câre; end; mē, it, īce; pîerce; hot, ōld; sông, fôrk; oil; out; up; ūse; rüle; pùll; tûrn; chin; sing; shop; thin; <u>th</u>is; hw in white; zh in treasure. The symbol ə stands for the unstressed vowel sound in about, taken, pencil, lemon, and circus.

Spelling Dictionary

sandwich in half and *share* it with you. **2.** To use or experience something with others. I will *share* my life story with you. *Verb.* **share** (shâr) *noun, plural* **shares;** *verb* **shared, sharing.**

shark A fish that lives in the sea. A shark has gray scales, and a large mouth with sharp teeth. **shark** (shärk) *noun, plural* **sharks.**

she'd 1. Shortened form of "she had." *She'd* better do her homework. **2.** Shortened form of "she would." *She'd* come if she could. **she'd** (shēd) *contraction.*

shed¹ A small building. The *shed* was used as a storage space. **shed** (shed) *noun, plural* **sheds.**

shed² 1. To pour forth. Don't *shed* tears over your mistakes. **2.** To let drop or fall. Does your dog *shed* much hair? **shed** (shed) *verb* **shed, shedding.**

shelf A thin flat piece of wood or glass fastened to a wall or frame. The *shelf* was too high to reach. **shelf** (shelf) *noun, plural* **shelves.**

shell The outer covering of a seed, nut, egg, or animal. The *shell* of a turtle is its protection. *Noun.*
—To take away the covering. A squirrel knows how to *shell* nuts quickly. *Verb.* **shell** (shel) *noun, plural* **shells.**

she'll 1. Shortened form of "she will." *She'll* come tomorrow. **2.** Shortened form of "she shall." *She'll* take care of the dog. **she'll** (shēl) *contraction.*

should've Shortened form of "should have." To recommend that a situation would have been better if something else had been done. You *should've* stirred the ingredients more before baking the cake. **should•'ve** (shùd'əv) *contraction.*

shower 1. A brief fall of rain. It was a sunny day except for one brief *shower.* **2.** A bath in which water is sprayed on a person.
—To fall from overhead in a great number. Confetti *showered* down on the parade. **show•er** (shou'ər) *noun, plural* **showers;** *verb.* **showering, showered.**

silver 1. Shiny white metal. Mom's new ring is made of *silver.* **2.** A light gray color. Our team's colors are blue and *silver. Noun.*
—Made of silver. That *silver* bracelet is very pretty. *Adjective.* **sil•ver** (sil'vər).

simple 1. Made up of only one thing. Water is a *simple* liquid. **2.** Easy to understand and do. The test was *simple.* **sim•ple** (sim'pəl) *adjective* **simpler; simplest.**

sincerely 1. Not false; honest. **2.** A form of closing a letter. *Sincerely* yours, your friend. *Adverb.* **sin•cere•ly** (sin sîr'lē).

sink A basin or tub, usually connected to a water supply. *Noun.*
—**1.** To go under the surface. The boat will *sink* if we don't patch up the hole. **2.** To fall slowly. My boot began to *sink* in the mud. *Verb.* **sink** (singk) *noun, plural* **sinks;** *verb* **sank.**

sink

sir A title of respect addressed to men, used in place of a name. *Sir* Galahad was a knight. **sir** (sûr) *noun.*

siren A whistle with a loud, sharp sound. The fire *siren* went off in the middle of the night. *Noun.* **si•ren** (sī'rən) *noun, plural* **sirens.**

sketch A rough, quick drawing. The artist made several *sketches* of the picture. *Noun.*
—To make a sketch of. I *sketched* the barn for my art class. *Verb.* **sketch** (skech) *noun, plural* **sketches;** *verb,* **sketching, sketched.**

skirt A garment or part of a dress that hangs from the waist. She wore a red *skirt* and a white blouse. *Noun.*
—To go around or to avoid. This road will *skirt* the city. *Verb.* **skirt** (skûrt) *noun, plural* **skirts;** *verb.*

slippery 1. Having a surface so smooth as to cause one to slip or slide. Walk carefully on that *slippery* ice! **2.** Slipping or sliding away easily. When soap gets wet it becomes *slippery*. **slip•per•y** (slip′ə rē *or* slip′rē) *adjective* **slipperier, slipperiest**.

smash 1. To violently and suddenly break something into pieces. Be careful not to *smash* that cup! 2. To destroy or damage by violent means. Did the ball really *smash* a window? *Verb*. **smash** (smash) *verb*.

smoke The gas from burning materials, like tobacco, wood, or coal. *Smoke* came out the chimney. *Noun*.
—To give off smoke. If you use hickory wood for cooking, it will *smoke* and smell good. *Verb*. **smoke** (smōk) *noun, plural* **smokes;** *verb,* **smoked, smoking**.

smooth To make flat or level. The baker will *smooth* out the icing on the cake. *Verb*.
—1. Having an even surface. The *smooth* snow was perfect for skiing. 2. Gentle in movement. It was a *smooth* ride all the way. *Adjective*. **smooth** (smüth) *verb*.

smuggle To take in and out of a country illegally. The thief tried to *smuggle* the jewels out of the country. **smug•gle** (smug′əl) *verb*. **smuggling, smuggled**.

snap 1. A sudden closing. The *snap* came from over there near the tree. 2. Something that is easy. That test was a *snap*! *Noun*.
—1. To close the jaws suddenly. The dog will *snap* at the cat if you put it there. 2. To speak harshly. The angry man *snapped* at the bus driver. *Verb*. **snap** (snap) *noun, plural* **snaps;** *verb* **snapped, snapping**.

snow Soft, white crystals of ice that fall to earth as precipitation. Snow is formed when water vapor freezes in the air. **snow** (snō) *noun, plural* **snows**.

soccer Game played by two teams of eleven players each in which the players move the ball around with their feet. **soc•cer** (sok′ər) *noun*.

sock A cloth covering for the foot. My *sock* is damp. **sock** (sok) *noun, plural* **socks**.

somewhere In, at or to some place not known or named. He lives *somewhere* around here. **some•where** (sum′hwâr) *adverb*.

son A male child. **son** (sun) *noun, plural* **sons**.

song 1. A piece of music that has words. 2. The musical call of a bird, whale, or other animal. **song** (sông) *noun, plural* **songs**.

soreness The state of being painful. After running, she felt *soreness*. **sore•ness** (sôr′nis) *noun*.

sorry Feeling sadness, sympathy or regret. I am *sorry* to hear that you have been so sick. **sor•ry** (sor′ē) *adjective*, **sorrier, sorriest**.

southern In, toward or from the south. **south•ern** (suth′ərn) *adjective*.

soybean A seed rich in oil and protein used as food. Soybeans grow in pods. **soy•bean** (soi′bēn′) *noun, plural* **soybeans**.

spare 1. To leave unhurt or uninjured; show mercy to. They tried to *spare* my feelings by not telling me I was wrong. 2. To give or get along without. Can you *spare* a dollar? *verb*.
—More than is needed; extra. We have a *spare* tire in the trunk. *Adjective*.
—1. One or an amount of something that is extra. 2. The knocking down of all the pins in bowling with two rolls of the ball. I bowled eight *spares* in that game. *Noun*. **spare** (spâr) *verb*, **spared, sparing;** *adjective,* **sparer, sparest;** *noun, plural* **spares**.

spark 1. A small bit of burning or glowing material. *Sparks* fly off burning wood. 2. A flash of light. The small flash caused by electricity passing through the air. *Noun*.
—To send out sparks. The burning logs spark in the fireplace. *Verb*. **spark** (spärk) *noun, plural,* **sparks;** *verb,* **sparked, sparking**.

sparrow A common, small bird with brown, white and grey feathers. **spar•row** (spar′ō) *noun, plural* **sparrows**.

speak 1. To use or utter words; talk. The baby cannot *speak* yet. 2. To make known or express an idea, fact, or feeling. Did you *speak* to him about going fishing?

at; **āpe, fär, câre; end; mē, it, ice; pîerce; hot, ōld; sîng, fôrk; oil; out; up; ūse; rüle; pu̇ll; tûrn; chin; sing; shop; thin; this; hw** in **white; zh** in treasure. The symbol ə stands for the unstressed vowel sound in **a**bout, tak**e**n, penc**i**l, lem**o**n, and circ**u**s.

•**to speak out** or **to speak up. 1.** To speak loudly and clearly enough to be understood. *Speak up* so that we can hear you. **2.** To say what one really believes; be frank. The mayor *spoke out* against crime. **speak** (spēk) *verb,* **spoke, spoken, speaking.**

spear 1. A weapon with a sharp, pointed head attached to a long shaft. **2.** A long, thin stalk, blade, or sprout of a plant. Asparagus grows in *spears. Noun.*
—To stab with something sharp. *Verb.* **spear** (spîr) *noun, plural* **spears;** *verb,* **speared, spearing.**

spell[1] 1. To write or say the letters of a word in the right order. You *spell* "speak" s-p-e-a-k. **2.** To be the letters that form. D-o-g *spells* "dog."
•**to spell out.** To explain clearly and completely. The official *spelled out* the rules for sailing in the harbor to us. **spell** (spel) *verb,* **spelled** or **spelt, spelling.**

spell[2] A period of time. We had been going through a dry *spell* before it rained in June. **spell** (spel) *noun, plural,* **spells.**

spent Past tense of **spend.** Paid. You *spent* too much for your bike. *Verb.*
—Tired. I felt *spent* after a long day at work. *Adjective.* **spent** (spent) *verb; adjective.*

sphere 1. A round body like a ball. The earth is a *sphere.* **2.** An area of interest, knowledge, or activity. Chemistry is outside my *sphere* of knowledge. **sphere** (sfîr) *noun, plural,* **spheres.**

spiderweb A web a spider makes to catch bugs for food. I saw a fly caught in a *spiderweb.* **spi•der•web** (spī′dər web) *noun, plural* **spiderwebs.**

spiderweb

spill 1. To make or let something fall, run out, or flow. The child *spilled* milk on the tablecloth. **2.** To fall or flow out. Water *spilled* from the glass onto the floor. *Verb.*
—**1.** An act or instance of spilling or the amount spilled. The oil *spill* polluted the river. **2.** A tumble or fall. The rider was hurt in a *spill* from a horse. *Noun.* **spill** (spil) *verb,* **spilled** or **spilt, spilling;** *noun, plural* **spills.**

spirit 1. The part of a person that is thought to control what he or she thinks, feels, and does. **2.** Enthusiasm and pep. They danced with *spirit.* **3.** The real meaning or interest. The *spirit* of the law is not written in the law book. **spir•it** (spir′it) *noun, plural* **spirits.**

split To break apart or divide into parts. The jacket *split* at the seams. The search party *split* into two groups. *Verb.*
—**1.** A break or division in something. The heavy wind made a *split* in the sail. **2.** A movement in which a person's body slides to the floor with the legs spread out in opposite directions. *Noun.* **split** (split) *verb,* **split, splitting;** *noun, plural* **splits.**

sport A game in which a person or team competes physically with another. Baseball is my favorite *sport.* **sport** (spôrt) *noun, plural* **sports.**

spray 1. Water or other liquid in tiny drops. The *spray* from the ocean waves felt cool. **2.** A device used to produce a spray. We used a *spray* to keep the insects away from the flowers. *Noun.*
—To put on or send out in a spray. The workers *sprayed* paint on the wall. *Verb.* **spray** (sprā) *noun, plural* **sprays;** *verb,* **sprayed, spraying.**

spring 1. To move forward quickly. The dog had to *spring* out of the way to avoid the bicycle. **2.** To snap quickly. The door *sprang* shut behind me. *Verb.*
—**1.** A jump or leap. The acrobat made a beautiful *spring* from one trapeze to the next. **2.** An elastic device that can be stretched or bent and will return to its original shape when released. The bed has

metal *springs* inside it. **3.** A season of the year that comes between winter and summer. *Noun.* **spring** (spring) *verb,* **sprang** or **sprung, springing;** *noun, plural,* **springs.**

square 1. A figure having four sides that are all the same length and four right angles. **2.** Something having the shape of a square. A checkerboard has light and dark *squares. Noun.*

square

—**1.** Having four sides that are all the same length and four right angles. **2.** Shaped like a cube. The hat came in a *square* box. *Adjective.*
—To multiply a number by itself. Two *squared* equals four because 2 x 2 = 4. *Verb.* **square** (skwâr) *noun, plural* **squares;** *adjective,* **squarer, squarest;** *verb,* **squared, squaring.**

stadium A structure made up of rows of seats built around an open field. People sit in *stadiums* to watch sports contests. **sta•di•um** (stā′dē əm) *noun, plural* **stadiums.**

stair 1. stairs. A set of steps for going from one level or floor to another. **2.** A step in such a set. **stair** (stâr) *noun, plural* **stairs.**

stampede A sudden wild run of frightened animals. A *stampede* of animals came over the hills. *Noun.*
—To make a sudden, wild rush. The horses began to *stampede* when they heard the thunder. *Verb.* **stam•pede** (stam pēd′) *noun, plural* **stampedes.**

stare To look very hard or very long with the eyes wide open. We *stared* at the fancy watches in the store window. *Verb.*
—A long, fixed eyed look. *Noun.* **stare** (stâr) *verb,* **stared, staring;** *noun, plural* **stares.**

starve 1. To suffer from or die of hunger. **2.** To be very hungry. I'm *starving* for lunch. **starve** (stärv) *verb,* **starved, starving.**

station 1. A regular stopping place along a route. There are *stations* along railroad and bus routes where passengers can get on or off. **2.** A building or place used by a business. My cousin works at a gas *station. Noun.*
—To place at a post or position. We *stationed* ourselves by the door. *Verb.* **sta•tion** (stā′shən) *noun, plural* **stations;** *verb,* **stationed, stationing.**

statue A likeness of a person made out of stone or metal. There are many statues of great Americans around the city. **stat•ue** (stach′ü) *noun, plural* **statues.**

steady 1. Firm in movement or position; not shaky. Make sure the ladder is *steady.* **2.** Going at an even rate. We walked at a *steady* pace. *Adjective.*
—To make or become steady. I *steadied* myself on the end of the diving board. *Verb.* **stead•y** (sted′ē) *adjective,* **steadier, steadiest;** *verb,* **steadied, steadying.**

stew A dish made of pieces of meat or fish and vegetables cooked together in a liquid. We had beef *stew* for dinner. *Noun.*
—To cook food slowly in a liquid. The chef let the prunes *stew* on the stove. *Verb.* **stew** (stü or stū) *noun, plural* **stews;** *verb,* **stewed, stewing.**

stood Past tense and past participle of **stand.** We *stood* at the window. I've *stood* here for twenty minutes. **stood** (stůd) *verb.*

stool 1. A seat without back or arms. We sat on *stools* at the counter. **2.** A low bench used to rest the feet on. *Noun.* **stool** (stül) *noun, plural* **stools.**

stout 1. Thick and heavy; fat. The *stout* dog found it hard to climb our stairs. **2.** Having courage; brave. The soldier had a *stout* heart. **stout** (stout) *adjective,* **stouter, stoutest.**

stove An object made of metal, used for cooking or heating. Some stoves burn wood,

at; āpe, fär, câre; end; mē, it, ice; pîerce; hot, ōld; sîng, fôrk; oil; out; up; ūse; rüle; půll; tûrn; chin; sing; shop; thin; this; hw in white; zh in treasure. The symbol ə stands for the unstressed vowel sound in about, taken, pencil, lemon, and circus.

coal, or gas, and others work by electricity. **stove** (stōv) *noun, plural* **stoves**.

straddle To sit on something so you are half on one side and half on another. She *straddled* the horse. **strad•dle** (strad'əl) *Verb.*

straight **1.** Not bent, curved, or crooked. I used a ruler to draw a *straight* line. **2.** In proper order. Please keep your closet *straight. Adjective.*
—**1.** In a straight way. Stand up *straight.* **2.** Without delay; immediately. We went *straight* home from school. *Adverb.* **straight** (strāt) *adjective,* **straighter, straightest;** *adverb.* ▲ Another word that sounds like this is **strait**.

stranger **1.** Someone whom one does not know. A *stranger* rang our doorbell. **2.** A person from another place or country. **stran•ger** (strān'jər) *noun, plural* **strangers**.

strap A long strip of leather, cloth, or other material. It is used to hold things together or in place. This bag hangs by a *strap* from the shoulder. *Noun.*
—To fasten or hold with a strap. *Strap* your knapsack to your back for the hike. *Verb.* **strap** (strap) *noun, plural* **straps;** *verb,* **strapped, strapping**.

strategy A plan for achieving a goal. What is the team's *strategy* for winning the game? **strat•e•gy** (strat'i jē) *noun.*

street A public way in a town or city, often with sidewalks and buildings on both sides. **street** (strēt) *noun, plural* **streets**.

strengthen To make or become strong. We need to *strengthen* our defense to win this game. **streng•then** (strengk'thən *or* streng'thən) *verb.*

stressful Causing stress. Final exams can be very *stressful.* **stress•ful** (stres'fəl) *adjective.*

stretch **1.** To spread out one's arms, legs, or body to full length. I got up and *stretched.* **2.** To reach; extend. The elephant will *stretch* its trunk for the leaf. *Verb.*
—**1.** An unbroken space or area. The campers canoed along a *stretch* of the

river. **2.** The act of stretching. I can touch the ceiling with a *stretch* of my arms. *Noun.* **stretch** (strech) *verb,* **stretched, stretching;** *noun, plural* **stretches**.

strike **1.** To give a blow to; to hit. He *will strike* the gong with a stick. **2.** To make an impression on. His jokes *strike* me as funny. *Verb.*
—**1.** The stopping of work. The workers went on *strike* for higher pay. **2.** In baseball, a pitched ball that the batter swings at and misses or hits foul, or a pitched ball that passes through the strike zone. **strike** (strīk) *verb,* **struck, struck** or **stricken, striking;** *noun, plural* **strikes**.

stroke¹ **1.** The act of striking. That lumberjack can split a log with one *stroke* of an ax. **2.** An unexpected event. Winning that money was a *stroke* of good luck. **stroke** (strōk) *noun, plural* **strokes**.

stroke² To rub gently. I *stroke* the puppy. **stroke** (strōk) *verb,* **stroked, stroking**.

strong **1.** Having much power, force, or energy; full of strength. Are you *strong* enough to move the table? **2.** Able to resist; firm. The house has *strong* walls. **strong** (strông) *adjective,* **stronger, strongest**.

struck The past tense and a past participle of **strike**. You *struck* your head on the table when you fell. **struck** (struk) *verb.*

study **1.** To try to learn by reading about, thinking about, or looking carefully at something. We *study* the planets of the solar system. **2.** To look at closely; examine. I *study* the face in the picture to see if I knew the person. *Verb.*
—**1.** The act of studying. Many hours of *study* are needed to learn French well. **2.** A close look at something; examination. Make a careful *study* of the photograph to see if you know anyone in it. *Noun.* **stud•y** (stud'ē) *verb,* **studied, studying;** *noun, plural* **studies**.

stunt¹ To slow or hinder growth. Lack of light and water can *stunt* the growth of plants. **stunt** (stunt) *verb.*

stunt² An act that shows skill or strength. The acrobat performed a *stunt* on the high trapeze. **stunt** (stunt) *noun*.

style 1. A particular way of saying or doing something. That writer has a clear and simple *style*. **2.** Fashion. Models wear clothes in the latest *style*. **style** (stīl) *noun, plural* **styles**.

sudden 1. Happening without warning; not expected. A *sudden* storm caught me without an umbrella. **2.** Hasty; quick. A *sudden* decision may not be the best one. **sud•den** (sud′ən) *adjective*.

summer The season of the year that comes between spring and autumn. *Noun.*
—To spend the summer. The family will *summer* in the mountains. *Verb.* **sum•mer** (sum′ər) *noun, plural* **summers**; *verb,* **summered, summering**.

Sunday The first day of the week **Sun•day** (sun′dē *or* sun′dā) *noun, plural* **Sundays**.

sunshine The light that comes from the sun. **sun•shine** (sun′shīn′) *noun*.

sunshine

supply To provide with something needed or wanted. Rain *supplies* water. *Verb.*
—A quantity of something that is needed or ready for use. The teacher keeps a large supply of paper on hand. *Noun.* **sup•ply** (sə plī′) *verb,* **supplied, supplying**; *noun, plural* **supplies**.

sure 1. Having no doubt; confident. I am *sure* that you are right. **2.** Certain to be; dependable. Our team is a *sure* winner. *Adjective.*
—Surely; certainly. *Sure,* I'm going. *Adverb.* **sure** (shùr) *adjective,* **surer, surest**; *adverb*.

surgery An operation performed by a surgeon. The athlete needed *surgery* on his injured knee. **sur•ge•ry** (sûr′jə rē) *noun*.

survive To live through, to exist. Plants need water to *survive*. **sur•vive** (sər vīv′) *verb,* **survived, surviving**.

sweat 1. A salty fluid given off through the skin. *Sweat* helps to keep the body cool. **2.** Moisture formed in drops on a surface. *Sweat* formed on the glass of cold water. *Noun.*
—**1.** To give off sweat. The horse *sweated* in the hot sun. **2.** To gather moisture in drops from the surrounding air. The glass of cold lemonade *sweated* in the warm room. *Verb.* **sweat** (swet) *noun; verb,* **sweated, sweating**.

sweet 1. Having a taste like that of sugar or honey. This apple is *sweet* and juicy. **2.** Pleasing to the smell. A rose has a *sweet* odor. *Adjective.*
—Something that tastes sweet. That store sells cookies, candy, and other *sweets*. *Noun.* **sweet** (swēt) *adjective,* **sweeter, sweetest**; *noun, plural* **sweets**. ▲ Another word that sounds like this is **suite**.

swept Past tense and past participle of **sweep**. We *swept* the floor of the cabin. **swept** (swept) *verb*.

tail 1. A slender, flexible part of an animal's body that sticks out from the back end. Our dog wags its *tail* when it sees us coming home from school. **2.** The end or rear part of anything. The *tail* of a comet always points away from the sun. *Noun.*
—To follow closely and secretly. The secret agent *tailed* the spy. *Verb.* **tail** (tāl) *noun, plural* **tails**; *verb,* **tailed, tailing**. ▲ Another word that sounds like this is **tale**.

at; āpe, fär, câre; end; mē, it, ice; pîerce; hot, ōld; sîng, fôrk; oil; out; up; ūse; rüle; pùll; tûrn; chin; sing; shop; thin; this; hw in white; zh in treasure. The symbol ə stands for the unstressed vowel sound in about, taken, pencil, lemon, and circus.

tale **1.** A story. That was a good *tale* about life at sea! **2.** A story that is not true; falsehood. Stop telling *tales* and give us the truth. **tale** (tāl) *noun, plural* **tales**. ▲ Another word that sounds like this is **tail**.

tea **1.** A drink that is made by pouring boiling water over the dried leaves of a shrub that is grown in China, Japan, India and Africa. **2.** This shrub or its dried and crumbled leaves. **tea** (tē) *noun, plural* **teas**.

tear[1] **1.** To pull or become pulled apart by force. I will *tear* the envelope open. **2.** To make a hole or cut into by force; rip. I *tore* my shirt when I caught it on a nail. **3.** To move very quickly; rush. When the door is open, the dog *tears* out of the house. *Verb.* —A torn part or place. The tailor sewed the *tear* in my coat. *Noun* **tear** (târ) *verb,* **tore, torn, tearing;** *noun, plural* **tears**.

tear[2] **1.** A drop of clear, salty liquid that comes from the eye. *Tears* help keep the eye clean. **2. tears.** The act of crying. The baby fell and burst into *tears*. **tear** (tîr) *noun, plural* **tears**. ▲ Another word that sounds like this is **tier**.

telephone **1.** A system for sending sound or other information by wire or radio waves over a long distance. **2.** An instrument used to send sound or other information over a long distance. A telephone includes a part for speaking into and a part for listening. It can also be used to send messages between computers. *Noun.* —**1.** To talk with someone by telephone. I will *telephone* you tomorrow. **2.** To send by telephone. My cousin *telephoned* love and good wishes on my birthday. *Verb.* **tel•e•phone** (tel′ə fōn) *noun, plural* **telephones;** *verb,* **telephoned, telephoning**.

terrible **1.** Causing fear or terror; awful. The volcano erupted with a *terrible* roar. **2.** Very bad. We had *terrible* weather on our vacation. **ter•ri•ble** (ter′ə bəl) *adjective*.

Thanksgiving A holiday in the United States observed on the fourth Thursday in November to celebrate the anniversary of the first harvest feast held by Pilgrims and Native Americans in 1621. **Thanks•giv•ing** (thangks′giv′ing) *noun, plural* **Thanksgivings**.

there's Shortened form of "there is." *There's* some milk in the refrigerator. **there's** *contraction*.

they'd **1.** Shortened form of "they had." *They'd* better leave now, or they will be late for the show. **2.** Shortened form of "they would." *They'd* be too polite to leave without saying good-bye. **they'd** *contraction*.

thief A person who steals. The *thief* broke into the house and stole the television. **thief** (thēf) *noun, plural* **thieves**.

thirsty **1.** Feeling the need to drink something. The *thirsty* softball players drank lots of water. **2.** Lacking water or moisture. The plants became *thirsty* in the hot sun. **thirst•y** (thûrs′tē) *adjective,* **thirstier, thirstiest**.

thorough Leaving nothing out; careful and complete. I emptied all my shelves and drawers in a *thorough* search for the missing key. **thor•ough** (thûr′ō) *adjective*.

thoughtful **1.** Thinking or looking as if one is thinking. The reader looked up with a *thoughtful* expression. **2.** Showing careful thought. The student paused and then gave a *thoughtful* answer. **thought•ful** (thôt′fəl) *adjective*.

thread

thread **1.** A very thin cord that is used in sewing and in weaving cloth. **2.** Anything that is thin and long like a thread. *Threads* of paint dripped from the brush. *Noun.*

—**1.** To pass a thread through. Please *thread* this needle for me. **2.** To put on a thread; string. I *threaded* the beads and made a necklace. *Verb.* **thread** (thred) *noun, plural* **threads;** *verb,* **threaded, threading.**

threshold **1.** A piece of material that forms the bottom of a doorframe. He crossed the *threshold* and entered the room. **2.** A point of entering or beginning. The scientist was on the *threshold* of a discovery. **3.** The point below which something cannot be felt or does not produce a reaction. The athlete had a high *threshold* for pain. **thresh•old** (thresh′ōld) *noun, plural* **thresholds.**

threw Past tense of **throw.** I caught the ball and *threw* it back. Look up **throw** for more information. **threw** (thrü) *verb.* ▲ Another word that sounds like this is **through.**

thrill **1.** A sudden feeling of pleasure or excitement. Seeing the ocean for the first time gave me a great *thrill.* **2.** Something that gives a sudden feeling of pleasure or excitement. It was a *thrill* to see the famous athlete. *Noun.*
—To fill with pleasure or excitement. The home team's victory *thrilled* the crowd. *Verb.* **thrill** (thril) *noun, plural* **thrills;** *verb,* **thrilled, thrilling.**

throat **1.** The passage in the body between the mouth and the esophagus. Food and air pass through the throat. **2.** The front of the neck. My new dress is open at the *throat.* **throat** (thrōt) *noun, plural* **throats.**

throw To send up into or through the air. *Throw* me the rag that's on the table. *Verb.*
—The act of throwing; toss. The shortstop made the *throw* to third base. *Noun.* **throw** (thrō) *verb,* **threw, thrown, throwing;** *noun, plural* **throws.**

thumb The short, thick finger on the hand. The thumb makes it easier to pick things up and grip things. *Noun.*
—To turn and look through pages quickly. The patient *thumbed* through a magazine while waiting to see the dentist. *Verb.* **thumb** (thum) *noun, plural* **thumbs;** *verb,* **thumbed, thumbing.**

Thursday The fifth day of the week. **Thurs•day** (thûrz′dē *or* thûrz′dā) *noun.*

Word History

Thursday comes from the Old English word meaning "Thor's day." Thor was the ancient English god of thunder.

---

tied **1.** To have fastened or attached with string or rope. A red bow was *tied* onto the gift. **2.** To have evened the score. The Tigers and the Suns were *tied. Verb.* **tied** (tīd) *Verb.*

tiger A large animal that is a member of the cat family. Most tigers have an orange or yellow coat with black or brown stripes. Tigers live in Asia. **ti•ger** (tī′gər) *noun, plural* **tigers.**

tire[1] **1.** To make or become weak from too much work or use. The long walk *tired* us. **2.** To lose or cause to lose interest; bore or become bored. I *tired* of the dull game. **tire** (tīr) *verb,* **tired, tiring.**

tire[2] A band of rubber that fits around a wheel. Most *tires* are filled with air. **tire** (tīr) *noun, plural* **tires.**

toast Sliced bread that has been browned by heat. *Noun.*
—To brown by heating. We *toasted* marshmallows over the campfire. *Verb.* **toast** (tōst) *noun; verb,* **toasted, toasting.**

tomb A grave or building in which a dead body is placed. We saw the *tomb* of an ancient king. **tomb** (tüm) *noun, plural* **tombs.**

tomorrow **1.** The day after today. If today is Saturday, then *tomorrow* is Sunday. **2.** The future. I wonder if people will live in outer space in the world of *tomorrow. Noun.*
—On the day after today. We are going on a trip *tomorrow. Adverb.* **to•mor•row** (tə môr′ō *or* tə mor′ō) *noun; adverb.*

---

at; āpe, fär, câre; end; mē, it, ice; pîerce; hot, ōld: sîng, fôrk; oil; out; up; ūse; rüle; pùll; tûrn; chin; sing; shop; thin; this; hw in white; zh in treasure. The symbol ə stands for the unstressed vowel sound in about, taken, pencil, lemon, and circus.

Spelling Dictionary

tonight The night of this day. The rain should stop by *tonight. Noun.*
—On or during this night. I am going to go to sleep early *tonight. Adverb.* **to•night** (tə nīt′) *noun; adverb.*

topsoil The top part of the soil that has most of the foods that plants need to grow. **top•soil** (top′soil′) *noun.*

torn Past participle of **tear.** The sheet was *torn.* Look up **tear** for more information. **torn** (tôrn) *verb.*

total **1.** Being all there is; making up the whole; entire. I paid the *total* amount of the bill. **2.** Complete; utter. The experiment was a *total* failure. *Adjective.*
—The whole amount. The cost of repairs cost a *total* of seventy dollars. *Noun.*
—**1.** To find the sum of; add up. I *totaled* the long column of numbers. **2.** To amount to. The bill *totaled* ten dollars. *Verb.* **to•tal** (tō′təl) *adjective; noun, plural* **totals;** *verb,* **totaled, totaling.**

tough **1.** Not easy to break, cut, or damage; strong. Canvas is a *tough* cloth. **2.** Able to put up with difficulty, strain, or hardship. The pioneers had to be *tough.* **3.** Hard to deal with or do; demanding. Clearing the field for planting was a *tough* job. **tough** (tuf) *adjective,* **tougher, toughest.**

tour A trip or journey in which many places are visited or many things are seen. *Noun.*
—To travel in or through a place. *Verb.* **tour** (tùr) *noun, plural* **tours;** *verb,* **toured, touring.**

toward **1.** In the direction of. The puppy ran *toward* the house. **2.** In regard to; concerning; about. The nurse showed great kindness *toward* the patients. **to•ward** (tə wôrd′ *or* tôrd) *preposition.*

tower A tall, narrow building or structure. The castle had a *tower* at each corner. *Noun.*
—To rise high up in the air. The skyscraper *towered* above the city. *Verb.* **tow•er** (tou′ər) *noun, plural* **towers;** *verb,* **towered, towering.**

transparent Allowing light to pass through so that things can be seen on the other side. Most windows are *transparent. Adjective.*

trans•par•ent (trans pâr′ənt *or* trans par′ənt) *adjective.*

tray A flat open container with a low rim. Our waiter carried our food on a *tray.* **tray** (trā) *noun.*

treasure Money, jewels, or other things that are valuable. There was a bag of gold and many diamonds in the lost *treasure. Noun.* **treas•ure** (trezh′ər) *noun, plural* **treasures.**

tree A plant with a single main stem or trunk that is made up of solid, woody tissue. Trees have branches and leaves at a distance above the ground. *Noun.*
—To chase up a tree. The dog *treed* the squirrel. *Verb.* **tree** (trē) *noun, plural* **trees;** *verb,* **treed, treeing.**

trouble **1.** A difficult or dangerous situation. The people in the valley will be in serious *trouble* if the dam breaks. **2.** Extra work or effort. We all went to a lot of *trouble* to make this party a success. *Noun.*
—To disturb or make uncomfortable. Does your headache still *trouble* you? *Verb.* **trou•ble** (trub′əl) *noun, plural* **troubles;** *verb,* **troubled, troubling.**

trout A fish that lives in fresh water. Some trout have speckles on their bodies. **trout** (trout) *noun, plural* **trout** or **trouts.**

trust **1.** To believe to be true, honest, or reliable. I *trust* you to keep this secret. **2.** To feel sure; hope or expect confidently. I *trust* that you will enjoy this movie. *Verb.*
—A belief that someone or something is true, honest, or reliable; confidence. I have a complete *trust* in your ability. *Noun.* **trust** (trust) *verb,* **trusted, trusting;** *noun.*

truth Something that is true. They taught their children to tell the *truth.* **truth** (trüth) *noun, plural* **truths.**

Tuesday The third day of the week. **Tues•day** (tùz′dē *or* tüz′dā) *noun.*

Word History

Tuesday comes from the Old English word meaning "Tiw's day." Tiw was the pagan English god of war.

Spelling Dictionary

tug To give a pull on something. He began to *tug* on my sleeve. *Verb.*
—A hard pull. Suddenly I felt a *tug* on the fishing line. *Noun.* **tug** (tug) *Verb; noun.*

tune **1.** A series of musical tones that form a pleasing, easily remembered unit; melody. We hummed the *tune* when we couldn't remember the words. **2.** The right pitch or key. The old piano was out of *tune. Noun.*
—To adjust a musical instrument so that it plays notes of the right pitch. I learned how to *tune* my guitar. *Verb.* **tune** (tün *or* tūn) *noun, plural* **tunes;** *verb,* **tuned, tuning.**

turkey A large North American bird with a tail shaped like a fan. **tur•key** (tûr′kē) *noun, plural* **turkeys.**

turtle

turtle An animal with a low, wide body covered by a hard, rounded shell. **tur•tle** (tûr′təl) *noun, plural* **turtles.**

un- **1.** A *prefix* that means not. *Unable* means not able. **2.** A prefix that means the opposite of. *Unemployment* means the opposite of employment.

uncle **1.** The brother of one's mother or father. **2.** The husband of one's aunt. **un•cle** (ung′kəl) *noun, plural* **uncles.**

underground **1.** Below the earth's surface. The workers built an *underground* passage for the subway. **2.** Secret; hidden. The spies belonged to an *underground* organization. *Adjective.*
—A place below the earth's surface. *Noun.*
—Below the earth's surface. Moles live *underground. Adverb.* **un•der•ground** (un′dər ground′ *for adjective and adverb;*

un′dər ground′ *for noun*) *adjective; noun, plural* **undergrounds;** *adverb.*

understand **1.** To get the meaning of; comprehend. I didn't *understand* the teacher's question. **2.** To know well. My parents *understand* French because they lived for a time in France. **un•der•stand** (un′dər stand′) *verb,* **understood, understanding.**

underweight Having less than the normal or needed weight. **un•der•weight** (un′dər wāt′) *adjective.*

unfair Not fair or just. The champion athlete had an *unfair* advantage over the younger and less experienced athlete in the competition. **un•fair** (un fâr′) *adjective.*

unknown Not known; not familiar. That person's name is *unknown* to me. *Adjective.*
—A person or thing that is unknown. *Noun.* **un•known** (un nōn′) *adjective; noun, plural* **unknowns.**

until **1.** Up to the time of. Wait *until* eight o'clock before you call me. **2.** Before. Tickets for the play are not available *until* Wednesday. *Preposition.*
—Up to the time when. Wait here *until* I get back. **2.** Before. We can't leave *until* we finish our chores. *Conjunction.* **un•til** (ən til′ *or* un til′) *preposition; conjunction.*

upstairs **1.** Up the stairs. I ran *upstairs* to get my jacket. **2.** On or to an upper floor. My parents are *upstairs. Adverb.*
—On an upper floor. We live in the *upstairs* apartment. *Adjective.*
—An upper floor or floors. The *upstairs* of our house is not finished being painted. *Noun.* **up•stairs** (up′stârz′) *adverb; adjective; noun.* ▲ The noun "upstairs" is used with a singular verb.

used That has been used by someone else; not new. I intend to buy a *used* car. **used** (ūzd) *adjective.*

at; āpe, fär, câre; end; mē, it, īce; pîerce; hot, ōld; sông, fôrk; oil; out; up; ūse; rüle; pùll; tûrn; chin; sing; shop; thin; <u>th</u>is; hw in white; zh in treasure. The symbol ə stands for the unstressed vowel sound in about, taken, pencil, lemon, and circus.

usual **1.** Regular. He ate his *usual* dessert. **2.** Common or expected; customary. Hot weather is *usual* for July and August. **u•su•al** (ū′zhü əl) *adjective*.

vacation A period of rest or freedom from school, business, or other activity. Summer *vacation* begins next week. Our family took a *vacation* to the shore. *Noun.* —To take or spend a vacation. We *vacationed* in Canada. *Verb.* **va•ca•tion** (vā kā′shən) *noun, plural* **vacations;** *verb,* **vacationed, vacationing**.

Valentine's Day The day, February 14, that is celebrated by the sending of Valentines. **Val•en•tine's Day** (val′ən tīnz dā) *noun*.

Valentine's Day

vessel A ship or large boat. Every sea *vessel* was docked by the time the storm hit the island. **ves•sel** (ves′əl) *noun*.

Veterans Day A holiday to honor all those who have served in the armed forces, celebrated on November 11. **Vet•er•ans Day**. (vet′ər ənz dā) *noun*.

visitor A person who visits; guest. We have to clean up our room because we are having *visitors* this afternoon. **vis•i•tor** (viz′i tər) *noun, plural* **visitors**.

voiceprint A diagram that shows the sound pattern of a person's voice as a series of markings. Each person's *voiceprint* is different. **voice•print** (vois′print′) *noun*.

voyage **1.** A journey by water or through space. The ship's *voyage* across the Atlantic took two weeks. **2.** A long journey. *Noun.* —To journey by water or through space. Astronauts *voyaged* to the moon in 1969. *Verb.* **voy•age** (voi′ij) *noun, plural* **voyages;** *verb,* **voyaged, voyaging**.

wagon **1.** A vehicle that has four wheels. It is used for carrying heavy loads. *Wagons* are usually drawn by a horse or horses. **2.** A low vehicle with four wheels that is pulled by a long handle. **wag•on** (wag′ən) *noun, plural* **wagons**.

wait **1.** To stay in a place until someone comes or something happens. *Wait* until it stops raining before you leave. **2.** To be put off or delayed. That job of cleaning the garage can *wait* for a week. *Verb.* —The act of waiting or the amount of time spent waiting. There will be a two-hour *wait* until the next plane arrives. *Noun.* **wait** (wāt) *verb,* **waited, waiting;** *noun, plural* **waits**. ▲ Another word that sounds like this is **weight.**

warehouse A building where merchandise is stored. Our new sofa is being delivered from a *warehouse*. **ware•house** (wâr′hous′) *noun*.

warfare Armed fighting between countries or groups; war. **war•fare** (wôr′fâr′) *noun*.

Washington's Birthday A holiday that used to be celebrated on February 22, but that is now observed on the third Monday in February. It is also called **Presidents' Day**. **Wash•ing•ton's Birth•day** (wash′ing tənz bûrth′dā) *noun*.

weak **1.** Likely to fall or give way. The legs of the old chair are *weak*. **2.** Not having strength, force or power. **weak** (wēk) *adjective,* **weaker, weakest**. ▲ Another word that sounds like this is **week**.

wealth **1.** A great amount of money or valuable things; riches. **2.** A great amount of anything. The class came up with a *wealth* of ideas for the science project. **wealth** (welth) *noun*.

wealth

wear 1. To carry or have on the body. We *wear* warm clothes in the winter. **2.** To have or show. She *wears* her hair long. *Verb.* —**1.** The act of wearing or the state of being worn. This suit has had five years of *wear*. **2.** Clothing. The store sells both men's and women's *wear. Noun.* **wear** (wâr) *verb,* **wore, worn, wearing;** *noun.* ▲ Another word that sounds like this is **ware.**

weary Very tired. The man was **weary** after a hard day of work. *Adjective.* —To make or become weary; tire. The long walk *wearied* the children. *Verb* **wea•ry** (wîr´ē) *adjective,* **wearier, weariest;** *verb,* **wearied, wearying.**

weather The condition of the air or atmosphere at a particular time and place. The *weather* has been cold and rainy. **weath•er** (weth´ər) *noun.*

Wednesday The fourth day of the week. **Wednes•day** (wens´dē *or* wenz´dā) *noun.*

Word History

The word **Wednesday** comes from the Old English word meaning "Woden's day." Woden was the king of the ancient English gods.

---

week A period of seven days. A week is usually thought of as starting with Sunday. **week** (wēk) *noun, plural* **weeks.** ▲ Another word that sounds like this is **weak.**

weekend The period of time from Friday night or Saturday morning until Sunday night or Monday morning. We went to the country for the *weekend.* **week•end** (wēk´end´) *noun, plural* **weekends.**

weird Strange or mysterious; odd. *Weird* sounds came from the scary old house. **weird** (wîrd) *adjective,* **weirder, weirdest.**

welfare 1. The condition of being happy and healthy. Parents are concerned about the *welfare* of their children. **2.** Money or other aid given by the government to people in need. **wel•fare** (wel´fâr´) *Noun.*

we'll Shortened form of "we will" or "we shall." *We'll* see you at the party.

we'll *contraction.*

we're Shortened form of "we are." *We're* going home now. **we're** *contraction.*

weren't Shortened form of "were not." They *weren't* home this afternoon. **weren't** *contraction.*

we've Shortened form of "we have. " *We've* enjoyed seeing you. **we've** *contraction.* ▲ Another word that sounds like this is **weave.**

wharf A structure built along a shore as a landing place for boats and ships; dock. **wharf** (hworf *or* wôrf) *noun.*

what'll Shortened form of "what will." *What'll* happen if I don't dress warmly before going out? **what'll** *contraction.*

what's 1. Shortened form of "what is." *What's* the difference? **2.** Shortened form of "what has." *What's* happened? **what's** *contraction.*

where's 1. Shortened form of "where is." *Where's* he going? **2.** Shortened form of "where has." *Where's* he been? **where's** *contraction.*

whirl 1. To turn or cause to turn quickly in a circle. The breeze *whirled* the bits of paper around in the air. **2.** To move or turn around quickly or suddenly. The guards *whirled* when they heard the noise. **whirl** (hwûrl *or* wûrl) *verb,* **whirled, whirling.**

whittle To cut small bits or pieces from wood or soap with a knife. We *whittled* the wood into interesting shapes. **whit•tle** (hwit´əl *or* wit´əl) *verb,* **whittled, whittling.**

who's 1. Shortened form of "who is." *Who's* the person on the phone? **2.** Shortened form of "who has." *Who's* been eating my food? **who's** (hüz) *contraction.* ▲ Another word that sounds like this is **whose.**

whose 1. Of or belonging to whom or which. *Whose* house is that? **2.** The one or ones belonging to what person or persons.

at; **āpe, fär, câre; end; mē, it, īce; pîerce; hot, ōld: sîng, fôrk; oil; out; up; ūse; rüle; pull; tûrn; chin; sing; shop; thin; this; hw in white; zh in treasure. The symbol ə stands for the unstressed vowel sound in about, taken, pencil, lemon, and circus.**

Spelling Dictionary (side tab)

Whose are those books? **whose** (hüz) *pronoun.* ▲ Another word that sounds like this is **who's**.

wife A married woman. The husbands and *wives* of the teachers are invited to the school party. **wife** (wīf) *noun, plural* **wives.**

wild **1.** Not controlled by people; living or growing naturally. The forest is full of *wild* plants. **2.** Not disciplined or orderly. Those *wild* children often play rough games and hurt themselves. *Adjective.*
—Not under the control of people; naturally. Blueberries grow *wild* in that field. *Adverb* **wild** (wīld) *adjective,* **wilder, wildest;** *adverb.*

wind¹ **1.** Air that is moving over the earth. The *wind* blew my hat off. **2.** The power to breathe; breath. The hard blow knocked the *wind* out of me. *Noun.*
—To cause someone to be out of breath. Running those miles *winded* me. *Verb.* **wind** (wind) *noun, plural* **winds;** *verb,* **winded, winding.**

wind² **1.** To wrap something around on itself or on something else. Please *wind* up this loose string into a ball. **2.** To move or cause to move in one direction or another. The road *winds* through the mountain. **3.** To give a machine power by tightening its spring. Don't forget to *wind* your alarm clock. **wind** (wīnd) *verb,* **wound, winding.**

wolf

window An opening in a wall or roof that lets in air and light. Panes of glass fill the openings of most windows. **win•dow** (win′dō) *noun, plural* **windows.**

windpipe The tube in the body that carries air from the throat to the lungs. For a moment I had a piece of chicken stuck in my *windpipe*. **wind•pipe** (wind′pīp′) *noun.*

winter The season of the year between fall and spring. *Noun.*
—To spend the winter. My parents *winter* in Florida. *Verb.* **win•ter** (win′tər) *noun, plural* **winters;** *verb,* **wintered, wintering.**

wish **1.** A feeling of wanting something; a strong desire. My *wish* to be a singer gets stronger every day. **2.** An expression of what a person wants. Make a *wish* when you blow out your candles. **3.** A thing that a person wants. I wanted a horse, and I got my *wish*. *Noun.*
—**1.** To want something very much; have a wish. I *wish* summer would last longer. **2.** To think of or express a wish. I *wish* you good luck in your new job. *Verb.* **wish** (wish) *noun, plural* **wishes;** *verb,* **wished, wishing.**

within **1.** In or into the inner part or parts of. The troops camped *within* the walls of the fort. **2.** Not beyond the limits or extent of. I promise to return *within* an hour. *Preposition.*
—In or into the inner part or parts of. I heard a noise *within* that sounded like an explosion. *Adverb.* **with•in** (with in′ *or* with in′) *preposition; adverb.*

without **1.** Not having; lacking. We were exhausted after a night *without* sleep. **2.** Not accompanied by. We went to a movie *without* you. **with•out** (with out′ *or* with out′) *preposition.*

wolf A wild animal that looks like a dog. Wolves have thick fur, a pointed muzzle, and a bushy tail. They live and hunt in packs. *Noun.*
—To eat very quickly or hungrily. The children *wolfed* down their lunch so they could go outside and play. **wolf** (wùlf) *noun, plural* **wolves;** *verb,* **wolfed, wolfing.**

woman **1.** An adult female person. **2.** Adult female people as a group. **wo•man** (wùm′ən) *noun, plural* **women.**

wood **1.** The hard material that makes up the branches and trunk of a tree or bush. Wood is cut and prepared for use as building

material and fuel. **2.** An area of trees growing naturally; forest. *noun.*
—Made of or consisting of wood; wooden. We have *wood* furniture on our porch. *Adjective.* **wood** (wùd) *noun, plural* **woods**. ▲Another word that sounds like this is **would.**

wooden Made of wood. I keep my clothes in a *wooden* chest of drawers. **wood•en** (wùd′ən) *adjective.*

woodwork Parts or things that are made out of wood. Windows and frames are parts of the house's *woodwork.* **wood•work** (wùd′wûrk′) *noun.*

wool **1.** The soft, thick, curly hair of sheep and some other animals such as the llama and alpaca. Wool is spun into yarn, which is made into cloth. **2.** Cloth or yarn made of wool. *Noun.*
—Made of wool. I wear a *wool* coat in the winter. *Adjective.* **wool** (wùl) *noun, plural* **wools;** *adjective.*

woolen Made of wool. I have a red *woolen* jacket. **wool•en** (wùl′ən) *adjective.*

world **1.** The earth. I would love to sail around the *world.* **2.** A part of the earth. The United States is in the western *world.* **world** (wûrld) *noun, plural* **worlds.**

worry **1.** To feel or cause to feel uneasy or troubled. The parents *worried* when their children did not call. **2.** To pull or bite at something with the teeth. The puppy *worried* the rug. *Verb.*
—Something that causes an uneasy or troubled feeling. Their biggest *worry* was that they did not have enough money. *Noun.* **wor•ry** (wûr′ē) *verb,* **worried, worrying;** *noun, plural* **worries.**

worst **1.** Most inferior; least good. Panicking when there is danger is the *worst* thing you can do. **2.** Most unfavorable. That's the *worst* news I've heard all week. *Adjective.*
—In the worst way. My throat hurts *worst* in the morning. *Adverb.*
—Something that is worst. None of these photographs is good, but this one is the *worst. Noun.* **worst** (wûrst) *adjective; adverb; noun.*

worth **1.** Good enough for; deserving of. That movie was *worth* seeing. **2.** Having the same value as. This old coin is *worth* thirty dollars. *Preposition.*
—**1.** The quality that makes a person or thing good or useful; excellence. My raincoat proved its *worth* by keeping me completely dry. **2.** The amount of money that something can be exchanged for; value in money. The diamond's *worth* is said to be $50,000. *Noun.* **worth** (wûrth) *preposition; noun.*

would An auxiliary verb that is used in the following ways: **1.** To express something that might have happened if something else had happened first. We *would* be cooler if we had opened the window. **2.** To express something that might happen later. We wondered if the train *would* be on time today. **would** (wùd) *verb.* ▲ Another word that sounds like this is **wood.**

wouldn't Shortened form of "would not." I *wouldn't* do that if I were you. **would•n't** *contraction.*

wreath A circle of leaves or flowers woven together. We hung a holiday *wreath* on the front door. **wreath** (rēth) *noun, plural* **wreaths.**

wren A small songbird with brown feathers, a narrow bill, and a short tail that often sticks upwards. **wren** (ren) *noun, plural* **wrens.**

writer A person who writes stories, poems, or articles; author. **writ•er** (rī′tər) *noun, plural* **writers.**

at; āpe, fär, câre; end; mē, it, ice; pîerce; hot, ōld: sîng, fôrk; oil; out; up; ūse; rüle; pùll; tûrn; chin; sing; shop; thin; this; hw in white; zh in treasure. The symbol ə stands for the unstressed vowel sound in about, taken, pencil, lemon, and circus.

Spelling Dictionary

yarn 1. Fibers that have been twisted into long strands. Yarn is used in knitting or weaving. It is made from cotton, wool, silk, nylon, or other fiber. **2.** A long story; tale. The old sailors liked to tell *yarns* about their sea voyages. **yarn** (yärn) *noun, plural* **yarns**.

yarn

year 1. A period of time made up of the twelve months from January 1 to December 31. A year contains 365 days. There are 366 days in a leap year. **2.** Any period of twelve months. We moved into this house two *years* ago. **year** (yîr) *noun, plural* **years**.

yet 1. At the present time; now. I'm not *yet* old enough to drive a car. **2.** Up to the present time; so far. She has not *yet* broken a rule. *Adverb.*
—Nevertheless; however; but. I thought I knew the way, *yet* I soon got lost. *Conjunction.* **yet** (yet) *adverb; conjunction.*

young 1. In the early part of life or growth. These picture books are for *young* readers. **2.** Having the look or qualities of a young person. My grandmother is quite *young* at heart. *Adjective.*
—Young offspring. The lion was teaching his *young* to roar. *Noun.* **young** (yung) *adjective,* **younger, youngest;** *noun, plural* **young**.

you've Shortened form of "you have." *You've* got to give me a chance. **you've** (ūv or yùv) *contraction.*

Handwriting Models

A B C D E F G H I

J K L M N O P Q R

S T U V W X Y Z

a b c d e f g h i j

k l m n o p q r s

t u v w x y z

Handwriting Models

COVER PHOTO
Stephen Ogilvy

PHOTO CREDITS
3, Pat & Tom Leeson/Photo Researchers, Inc.; **7,** Harvey Lloyd/The Stock Market; **11,** Jean-Marc Loubat/Agence Vandystadt/Photo Researchers, Inc.; **15,** Roy Morsch/The Stock Market; **17,** Peter Gridley/FPG International; **19,** Hermann Eisenbeiss/Photo Researchers, Inc.; **29,** Lawrence Migdale/Photo Researchers, Inc.; **33,** Sandy Clark/The Stock Market; **37,** Rob Triangali Jr./Sportschrome East/West; **39,** Christian Michaels/FPG International; **41,** Ray Atkeson/The Stock Market; **45,** R.J. Erwin/Photo Researchers, Inc.; **47,** Chris Bartlett/FPG International; **55,** Stephen Ogilvy; **59,** Lefever/Grushow/Grant Heilman Photography; **61,** José L. Pelaez/The Stock Market; **63,** Hiller/Monkmeyer Press Photos; **67,** Tom Brakefield/The Stock Market; **71,** Lew Merrim/Monkmeyer Press Photos; **81,** Craig Tuttle/The Stock Market; **85,** Bill Bachmann/Photo Researchers, Inc.; **87,** George Godwin/Monkmeyer Press Photos; **89,** Mimi Forsyth/Monkmeyer Press Photos; **93,** Townsend P. Dickinson/Comstock; **95,** Terje Rakke/The Image Bank; **97,** Robert A. Jureit/The Stock Market; **99,** North Wind Picture Archives; **107,** Lew Merrim/Monkmeyer Press Photos; **111,** Stephen Krasemann/Photo Researchers, Inc.; **113,** George Goodwin/Monkmeyer Press Photos; **115,** Stephen J. Krasemann/Photo Researchers, Inc.; **119,** John Gillmoure/The Stock Market; **123,** Roy Morsch/The Stock Market; **133,** Skye/Monkmeyer Press Photos; **137,** Zefa/The Stock Market; **141,** Tim Davis/Photo Researchers, Inc.; **143,** G.C. Kelley/Photo Researchers, Inc.; **145,** Chuck Savage/The Stock Market; **147,** Barry O'Rourke/The Stock Market; **149,** McGraw-Hill Photo; **215,** Tibor Bognar/The Stock Market; **217,** Jon Feingersh/The Stock Market; **222,** G. Büttner/naturbild/OKAPIA/Photo Researchers, Inc.; **225,** Stephen J. Krasemann/Photo Researchers, Inc.; **227,** Tim Davis/Photo Researchers, Inc.; **229,** Charles Fitch/FPG International; **232,** Leonare Lee Rue/Photo Researchers, Inc.; **235,** North Wind Picture Archives; **237,** Gabe Palmer/The Stock Market; **241,** Hermann Eisenbeiss/Photo Researchers, Inc.; **245,** Nancy Ney/The Stock Market; **248,** Naideau/The Stock Market; **252,** Roy Morsch/The Stock Market; **255,** David Burnett/The Stock Market; **259,** Joe B. Blossom/Photo Researchers, Inc.; **262,** Sanford/Agliolo/The Stock Market; **264,** Garry Gay/The Image Bank.

ART CREDITS
Annie Gusman, Rita Lascaro, Harry Campbell, Dan Potash